Total Quality and Human Resources

A Concise Anglo-Saxon Dictionary

Total Quality and Human Resources

An Executive Guide

Barrie Dale and Cary Cooper

First published 1992
Reprinted 1993

Blackwell Publishers
108 Cowley Road
Oxford OX4 1JF, UK

238 Main Street
Cambridge, Massachusetts 02142, USA

British Library Cataloguing in Publication Data

A CIP catalogue record for this book is available from the British Library.

Library of Congress Cataloging-in-Publication Data

Dale, Barrie (Barrie G.)
    Total quality and human resources : an executive guide / Barrie
Dale, Cary Cooper
        p. cm.
    Includes bibliographical references and index.
    1. Total quality management. I. Cooper, Cary L. II. Title.
    HD62.15.D35 1992
    658.5'62—dc20   91–47909
ISBN 0–631–187162 ✓   CIP

Typeset in 11 on 13 Garamond by
Mathematical Composition Setters Ltd, Salisbury, Wiltshire
Printed in Great Britain by T.J. Press (Padstow), Ltd, Padstow, Cornwall.

This book is printed on acid-free paper

Contents

List of Tables and Figures

Preface

A number of books have been published during the past five or so years on the subject of total quality management (TQM). The majority of them have not been specifically targeted at the chief executive officer (CEO) and senior executive level. There is a good chance therefore that not many of them have reached and/or been read by the CEO and his or her senior management team. It is also the case that many quality management buzzwords are liberally scattered around by TQM experts on the assumption that senior managers are familiar with and understand them. This is not always so.

This book is aimed at the chief executive officer and senior managers. Its purpose is to:

1 provide an insight into the issues involved with the quality improvement process;
2 describe the role of senior managers in TQM and some of their common failings in relation to this role; and
3 examine some of the key issues in the introduction, development and advancement of TQM.

The ten chapters forming the main core of the book focus on these types of theme.

Senior executives, in addition to understanding the concept and principles of TQM, their role in the process, organizational change, motivation, teamwork, etc., also need to understand the fundamentals and uses of quality systems and quality management tools and techniques. This material is also covered in the book, but has been placed in four appendices to facilitate easier reading of the text by senior executive readers:

A Quality Systems
B Quality Management Tools and Techniques: An Overview
C Statistical Process Control (SPC)
D Failure Mode and Effects Analysis (FMEA)

The appendices can be considered as an executive guide to quality systems, tools and techniques and, if so desired, used independently of the main text.

The quality-management techniques of SPC and FMEA are singled out in the appendices for special treatment. The use by an organization of SPC and FMEA is now a contractual requirement of doing business with many major customers. For similar reasons, a large part of appendix A is devoted to providing an overview of the requirements of a quality system based on the BS 5750/ISO 9000 series of standards.

The text is intended to be a practical guide for senior management. The material in this book is based to a large extent on involvement with CEOs and senior managers during the course of the TQM research, operation of a TQM multi-company teaching programme, and TQM training and advisory work undertaken during the last eleven or so years by the UMIST Quality Management Centre. This is supplemented by research carried out by Professor Cary Cooper and his colleagues in the field of industrial organizational psychology.

We believe that the collaboration of specialists in TQM and industrial organizational psychology gives the book an added dimension, and provides insights into TQM and the quality improvement process not covered by the more traditional texts on the subject of TQM.

There is considerable interest from industry, commerce and the public sector in the subject of TQM and the process of quality improvement. While the book is targeted at senior management, we are convinced that the text will have a much wider audience and find a distinctive place in the market. In particular, MBA and M.Sc. students, and those studying for Postgraduate Diplomas in TQM and other professional qualifications which involve considerations of quality management should find the book of particular interest as will the increasing number of academics in universities, business schools, polytechnics and colleges of further and higher education with research and/or teaching interests in TQM.

Barrie Dale,
Quality Management Centre,
Manchester School of Management,
UMIST

Cary Cooper
Psychology Research Centre,
Manchester School of Management,
UMIST

Acknowledgements

First, in preparing the material for *Total Quality and Human Resources: An Executive Guide* we acknowledge the contribution made to some of the chapters and in particular, Appendix B and Appendix C by our colleague Peter Shaw. The original aim was that Peter would be a joint author of the book, but during the drafting he became ill and could not continue. We wish him a speedy and successful recovery to full health. We would also like to thank Charles Cox and Peter Makin for their psychological insights at different points in the book.

Second, we wish to thank those executives who have provided examples and experiences from their organizations.

Third, much of the text has been commented on by CEOs, senior and middle managers, and technical and quality specialists. They are too numerous to mention individually, but their letters and comments are on our file. We thank you for giving us useful insights into TQM and helping to identify the key issues for executives.

List of Abbreviations

AQL	acceptable quality level
ASQC	American Society for Quality Control
BS	British Standard
BSI	British Standards Institution
CEN	European Committee for Standardization
CENELEC	European Committee for Electrotechnical Standardization
CEO	chief executive officer
Cpk	process capability index
CQAD	corporate quality assurance department
DHU	defects per hundred units
DTI	Department of Trade and Industry
EFQM	European Foundation For Quality Management
FMEA	failure mode and effects analysis
FMECA	failure mode effect and criticality analysis
FTA	fault tree analysis
ISO	International Organization for Standardization
JUSE	Union of Japanese Scientists and Engineers
MOD	Ministry of Defence
NACCB	National Accreditation Council for Certification Bodies
NEDC	National Economic Development Council
NEDO	National Economic Development Office
OD	organizational development
PDCA	plan–do–check–action
PDPC	process decision program chart
PIMS	Profit Impact of Market Strategy

PPB	parts per billion
PPM	parts per million
QC	quality circle
QCD	quality, cost and delivery
R & D	research and development
RPN	risk priority number
RPQ	relative perceived quality
SPC	statistical process control
STA	success tree analysis
TPM	total productive maintenance
TQC	total quality control
TQE	total quality excellence
TQM	total quality management
UMIST	University of Manchester Institute of Science and Technology

1

Total Quality Management: An Overview

This chapter provides for the chief executive officer (CEO) and other executives a critique on some of the popular definitions of quality, the reasons product and service quality is a key business issue, and the evolution, key elements and benefits of total quality management (TQM).

What is quality?

'Quality' is a familiar word to us all; however, it has a variety of uses and meanings. Some may claim it is over-used; there is little doubt that we all use it much more than was the case a few years ago. For example, when a case is being made for extra funding and resources, preventing a reduction in funding or keeping a unit in operation, etc., just count the number of times 'quality' is used in the ensuing argument.

Most people say they know what is meant by quality, typically claiming 'I know it when I see it' (i.e. quality by feel, taste and/or smell). This simple statement, and the common interpretations of quality, mask the need to define product and service quality in an operational manner. In fact, quality as a concept is quite difficult for many people to grasp and understand, and there is much confusion.

In a linguistic sense, quality originates from the Latin word *qualis*, which means 'such as the thing really is'. In today's business world there is no single accepted definition of quality. However, irrespective of the context in which it is used, it is usually meant to distinguish one organization, event, product, service, process, person, result, action, communication, etc., from another. For the word to have the desired effect as intended by the user, and to prevent any form of misunderstanding in the communication, the following points need to be considered:

- The person using the word must have a clear understanding of its meaning.
- Those to whom the communication is directed should have a similar understanding.
- When quality is discussed within an organization, to prevent confusion and ensure that everyone in each department is focused on the same objectives there should be an organizational definition of quality.

Quality defined

There are a number of ways or senses in which quality may be defined, some being broader than others.

Qualitative

When used in this way, it is usually in a *non-technical situation*; ISO 8402[1] refers to it as 'comparative sense' or 'degree of excellence'. For example:

- in advertising slogans to assist in building an image: Esso – Quality at work; Hayfield Textiles – Committed to Quality; Kenco – Superior Quality; and many others;
- by television commentators (a quality player, goal, try);
- by directors and managers (quality performance, quality of communications); and
- by people in general (top quality, high quality, original quality, loss of quality, foreign quality, and jeopardize quality).

It is frequently found in such cases that the context in which the word is used is highly subjective and, in its strictest sense, it is often misused. For example, the authors know of a shop whose name is Quality Seconds. What *is* a 'quality second'?

Quantitative

ISO 8402 defines this 'as used in manufacturing, product-release and for technical evaluations, sometimes referred to as "quality level"'.

The traditional quantitative term which is still used in some business environments is acceptable quality level (AQL): When product and/or production quality is, paradoxically, defined in terms of non-conforming parts per hundred (i.e. some defined degree of imperfection).

AQLs are used by some companies in the mistaken belief that trying to eliminate all defects is too costly. However, setting AQLs works against a 'right first time' mentality in the workforce. It appears to condone the production of non-conforming parts and delivery of imperfect services, suggesting that errors are acceptable to the organization. It is tantamount to planning for failure. Take, for example, a final product made up of 3,000 parts: if the standard set is a 1 per cent AQL, the product is planned to contain thirty non-conforming parts – in reality there are likely to be many more due to the vagaries of the sampling used in the plan or scheme whereby acceptance or rejection of the batch of product is decided. This is clearly an unacceptable situation in today's business environment and represents a non-survival performance.

The authors cannot recommend the use of AQLs, and they have no part to play in TQM and a process of continuous quality improvement.

World-class companies assess their quality performance and that of suppliers not in parts per hundred but in parts per million (PPM) and sometimes in parts per billion (PPB). It is not practical to measure performance at this sort of level at the producing company. The usual method is to enter into an agreement with the customer to feed back all line rejects and then, using the consumption and delivery rates, to work out the PPM performance.

Uniformity of the product characteristics or delivery of a service around a nominal or target value

Consider a manufacturing situation. If a product's dimensions are within the design specification or tolerance limits we tend to say it is acceptable; conversely, if outside the specification we indicate that it is not (see figure 1.1). The difference between just inside and just outside the specification is marginal. It may also be questioned whether this step between pass and fail has any scientific basis and validity. The absurdity of this situation is put into perspective when considering how traditional

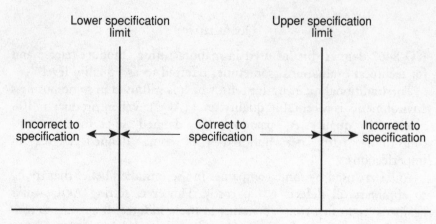

Figure 1.1 The inside/outside specification dilemma

co-ordinate specification limits (known as the plus and minus system) are established in the first place.

Designers often establish specification limits without sufficient knowledge of the processes by which the product or service is to be produced, and the capability of the producing processes to reproduce the design. Often designers cannot agree among themselves about the tolerances and it is not uncommon to find outdated reasoning being used. They also tend to establish tight specifications to provide safeguards and protect themselves, and take the view that production/operations personnel will find the tolerances too tight and the parts difficult to make, and will ask to have them relaxed. The situation is compounded by the fact that most designers care little about what happens to the parts once they have been designed. In too many situations there is inadequate communication between design and manufacturing (the use of simultaneous or concurrent engineering will help to eradicate this problem). In such cases, production personnel will tend to treat any specification limits with scepticism and adopt the attitude: the product works, the customers accept it; why worry?

The problem with working to the specification limits is that it frequently leads to tolerance stack-up, and parts not fitting together correctly. This is especially so when one product which is just inside the lower specification limit is assembled to one just inside the upper limit. If the process is controlled such that the products are produced around the nominal or target dimension (see figure 1.2), this problem does not occur and the fit and smooth operation of the product are enhanced.

The idea of reducing the variation of product characteristics and

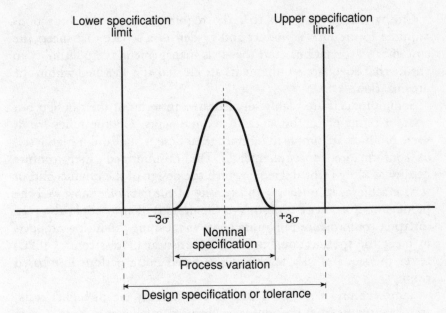

Figure 1.2 Design tolerance and process variation relationship

process parameters so that they are centred around a target value can be attributed to Taguchi.[2] He writes: 'The quality of a product is the (minimum) loss imparted by the product to the society from the time the product is shipped.' This is defined by a quadratic loss curve. Among the losses he includes consumers' dissatisfaction, warranty costs, loss of reputation and, ultimately, loss of market share.

The relationship of design specification and variation of the manufacturing and/or producing process can be quantified by a capability index – process potential – (Cp), as follows:

$$Cp = \frac{\text{Total specification width}}{\text{Process variation width}}$$

Conformance to agreed and fully understood requirements

This definition is attributed to Crosby.[3] He believes that quality is not comparative, and there is no such thing as high quality or low quality, or quality in terms of goodness, feel, excellence, luxury, etc. A product or service either conforms to requirements or it does not. In other words, quality is an attribute (a characteristic which, by comparison to a standard or reference point, is judged to be correct or incorrect) not a variable (a characteristic which is measurable).

Crosby makes the point that the requirements are all the actions required to produce a product and/or deliver a service that meets the customer's expectations, and that it is management's responsibility to ensure that adequate requirements are created and specified within the organization.

Some products are highly sophisticated in terms of their design but poor in terms of conformance to requirements. On the other hand, some products are simple in terms of their design but exhibit high levels of conformance to requirements. The misinformed often confuse quality of *design* (the degree to which the design of the product and/or service achieves its purpose) and quality of *conformance* (how well the product and/or service conforms to the design). Some people also misinterpret conformance to requirements as meaning producing products to meet the specification limits – in statistical process control (SPC) terms this equates to a tolerance-based and not a performance-based concept.

Some executives still hold that 'better' quality means higher costs; this view results from the confusion between quality and grade. Grade represents the addition of features and characteristics to satisfy the additional needs of customers, and this clearly increases costs, but grade is different from quality.

The definition of conformance to requirements is useful in facilitating the internal customer–supplier relationship discussed later in the book.

Fitness for purpose/use

This is a standard definition of quality used by Juran[4] and adopted and described in ISO 8402,[1] as 'that which relates to the evaluation of a product or service to its ability to satisfy a given need'. Juran classifies fitness for purpose/use into the categories of quality of design, quality of conformance, abilities and field service. Focusing on fitness for use helps to prevent the overspecification of products. Overspecification can add greatly to costs and tends to militate against a right-first-time performance. Fitness for use has obviously to be judged by the purchaser, customer or user of the product and/or service.

Satisfying customers' expectations and understanding their needs and future requirements

While the definitions of 'conformance to requirements' and 'fitness for purpose' have their starting points with satisfying the customer, we believe the definition of quality which is now examined goes much further than this.

This definition of quality – the attributes of a product and/or service which, as perceived by the customer, make the product/service attractive to them and gives them satisfaction – is perhaps the simplest of the definitions examined. It focuses on adding value to the product/service.

Satisfying customer expectations, and understanding and anticipating their needs, are the crux of TQM, which concerns itself with effective and efficient management, with having totally satisfied customers who come back for more of the same product/service. This is perhaps the only measure of organizational success. In most situations customers have a choice, they need not place future orders with a supplier who does not perform as they expect. They will certainly not jeopardize their own business interests out of loyalty to a supplier whose products and service fail to perform properly. Thus the aim of superior-performing companies is to become their customers' *supplier of choice*.

The process of continuous improvement is all about customer orientation and many organizational missions are based entirely on satisfying customer perceptions. The world-class organizations go beyond satisfying their customers, and emphasize the need to delight customers by giving them more than the contract requires; they also talk of winning and 'cuddling' customers. The wisdom of this is clear when we think of situations in which we have received more than expected from a supplier (an extra cup of coffee on an aircraft, say, or a sales assistant going out of his or her way to be courteous, helpful and provide detailed information) and the warm feeling this engenders.

This class of organization also places considerable effort in anticipating the future expectations of its customers and, by working with them in long-term relationships, helping them to define their future needs and expectations. A number of organizations have corporate quality definitions which focus on the customer. For example, Ford of Europe:

> Quality is defined by the customer. The customer wants products and services that throughout their life meet his or her needs and expectations at a cost that represents value.

These superior-performing organizations listen closely to their customers and 'real' users of the product/service, in order to gain a clearer perspective of customer experiences. Their aim is to *build quality upstream*, when a new product or service is still at the idea/concept stage or in the process from planning to design.

A mechanism for facilitating a continuous two-way flow of information between the organization and its customers is essential to the process of company-wide and never-ending quality improvement. A variety of means are available to companies for them to assess issues such as:

- how well they are meeting customers' expectations;
- the customers' chief causes of concern;
- the main complaints; and
- suggestions customers might have for improvements

The trend is to increase the level of contact with customers. Methods of achieving this, used more by public sector and service organizations than in manufacturing, include customer workshops, panels and clinics, focus groups, customer interviews, market research, questionnaire surveys, 'trailing' the service/product, and using 'test' consumers and mystery shoppers.

Organizations need to identify elements and characteristics of their product/service which the customer will find attractive, and to translate customers' quality and other requirements into *internal* needs, ensuring that these then permeate all levels in the organizational hierarchy. Clarifying the quality elements of the product/service required by customers, and those which they find attractive and charming, enables a company to determine the key quality characteristics, and this is obviously central to the issue of total customer satisfaction. Techniques such as quality function deployment (QFD), departmental purpose analysis (DPA) and failure mode and effects analysis (FMEA) (see appendices B and D) are important aids in making this translation.

Customer needs and requirements are always changing, and organizations must live up to their customers' expectations. Executives must never forget that customers are *never* satisfied even though they – and the supplying organization – may think they are.

Never having to say sorry to a customer

When discussing customer satisfaction, John Whybrow (Technical Director, Philips) often quotes the words of a line operator at Philips Components, Blackburn – her definition of quality is 'never having to say sorry to a customer'. This view reflects the fact that it is highly desirable for an individual's personal esteem and pride to be associated with a product, service and organization with which the customer is totally satisfied.

Are your staff always having to apologize to customers? If so, perhaps you have an unhealthy organization.

Why is quality important?

Quality is regarded by most producers, customers and consumers as more important than ever in their manufacturing, service and purchasing strategies. To understand why, we need only recall the unsatisfactory examples of product/quality service we have experienced, how we felt about them and the actions we took, and the people we told about the experience and the outcome.

The following two sections cite three examples of survey data which have focused on the perceived importance of product and service quality.

Public perceptions of product and service quality

In 1988 the American Society for Quality Control (ASQC) commissioned Gallup to survey public perceptions on a variety of quality-related issues. The survey was the fourth in a series which began in 1985; the 1985 and 1988 surveys focused on consumers and the 1986 and 1987 studies surveyed attitudes of company executives. The 1988 study involved telephone interviews with 1,050 adults in the United States during the summer of 1988. A selection of results, as reported by Ryan[5] and Hutchens,[6] is outlined below:

1 The following is a ranking of factors people consider important when they purchase a product:
   (a) performance;
   (b) durability;
   (c) ease of repair, service availability, warranty and ease of use (these four factors were ranked about equal);
   (d) price;
   (e) appearance;
   (f) brand name.
2 People will pay a premium for what they perceive to be higher quality.
3 Consumers are willing to pay substantially more for better intrinsic quality in products.
4 The factors that make for 'higher' quality in services are courtesy,

promptness, a basic sense that one's needs are being satisfied, and attitude of the service provider.

5 When consumers do experience a problem with the product, they appear reluctant to take positive action with the manufacturer. The 1987 survey revealed that executives regard customers' complaints, suggestions and enquiries as key indicators of product and service quality; this feedback gap clearly needs to be bridged.

Views of chief executive officers

The European Foundation For Quality Management (EFQM) contracted McKinsey and Company to survey the CEOs of the top 500 Western European corporations in relation to quality performance and the management of quality; 150 CEOs responded to the survey. The following are some of the main findings as reported by McKinsey.[7]

- Over 90% of CEOs consider quality performance to be 'critical' for their corporation.
- 60% of CEOs said that quality performance had become a lot more important than before (late 1970s).
- The four main reasons why quality is important are:
  - primary buying argument for the ultimate customer
  - major means of reducing costs
  - major means for improving flexibility/responsiveness
  - major means for reducing throughput time
- The feasible improvement in gross margin on sales through improved quality performance was rated at an average of 1.7%.
- More than 85% of leading CEOs in Europe consider the management of quality to be one of the top priorities for their corporations.

Lascelles and Dale,[8] reporting on a survey they carried out of seventy-four UK CEOs, say that 'Almost all the respondents believe that product and service quality is an important factor in international competitiveness. More than half have come to this conclusion within the past four years.'

The importance of quality: some specific illustrations

Quality is not negotiable

An order, contract or customer which is lost on the grounds of non-conforming product and/or service quality is much harder to regain than one lost on price or even delivery grounds; the customer could be lost for ever – in simple terms the organization has been outsold.

If we doubt the truth of this statement we need only consider the number of organizations which have gone out of business or lost a significant share of a market, and consult the reported reasons for this. Quality is one of the factors which is not negotiable. In today's business world, the penalties for unsatisfactory product quality and poor service are likely to be punitive.

Quality is all-pervasive

There are a number of what are termed single-focus competitive business initiatives and strategies which have been used by organizations for many years. However, the improvements made by companies, reduction in monopolies, government legislation, deregulation, changes in market share, mergers, takeovers, collaborative joint ventures, etc., have resulted in less distinction between companies than there was some years ago. A commitment to a continuous process of company-wide quality improvement is now being recognized by many organizations as the main means by which they can achieve and maintain an edge over their competitors.

TQM is a much broader concept than the initiatives which have gone before, encompassing not only product, service and process quality improvements but those relating to costs and productivity, and people involvement and development. It is also a relatively low-risk strategy, and has the added advantage that it is totally focused on satisfying customer needs. No matter how good an organization's innovation, technology, marketing efforts, financial and pricing policies, if the product and service quality do not meet customers expectations it will lose market share.

An increasing number of CEOs now firmly believe that if quality is right everything else will follow, and TQM is the only business strategy by which they can achieve this. This is why TQM is top of the agenda at many board meetings. We know of at least one case where the CEO leaves the board meeting once the quality item has been discussed. This conveys clearly to senior management what the CEO considers to be important. For a quick indication of how your top management view the importance of quality, analyse where the quality item features on the board agenda in your company.

'How long will TQM last?' 'TQM has passed its peak.' 'What is the next trend?' Such comments are already heard, but the cynics will be disappointed. Many executives and organizations have committed themselves to TQM, and organizational cultural changes are taking place that will not be easy to reverse. Executives now have a first-hand direct comparison of the strategy of TQM and those strategies which have gone before, and there is the considerable wisdom, experience and success of the Japanese companies over the last thirty years from which to draw.

Quality increases productivity

Some CEOs and senior managers believe that cost, productivity and quality improvements are alternative objectives. These executives often say that their company does not have the time to ensure that product/service quality is right the first time. They argue that to concentrate on planning for quality will mean losing valuable production and operating time, and as a consequence output is lost and costs will rise. Executives should, however, remember Murphy's Law: *There is never time to do it right, but always time to do it once more*. Management and staff will make the time to rework the product/service a second or even a third time, and spend considerable time and organizational resources on corrective action and placating disappointed customers. *This* is what increases costs.

Another argument is that it is more cost effective to make more product even though some of it is non-conforming than to aim for a defect-free product. Sooner or later, however, this will result in over-production and having to put into inter-process and finished stores those parts which are in excess of customers' requirements. The assumption that the surplus can be reprocessed and/or sold at some future date may be correct, but even so the holding cost is likely to be considerable. In such situations, it is clear that much of a company's activities are devoted to redoing things which have gone wrong. We will leave it to readers to judge the wisdom of this approach.

Improving quality will improve productivity and reduce costs, and in turn lead to more satisfied customers and increased profitability (see Deming).[9]

Quality leads to better performance in the market place

The Strategic Planning Institute in Cambridge, Massachusetts, which conducts the Profit Impact of Market Strategy (PIMS), has a database containing over 3,000 records of detailed business performance, which allows powerful analysis of the parameters influencing business performance. A key PIMS concept is that of relative perceived quality (RPQ): the product and service offering as perceived by the customer. It has been established that the factors most affecting return on investment are RPQ and relative market share, and that companies with large market shares are those whose quality is relatively high, whereas companies with small market shares are those whose quality is relatively low (see Buzzell and Gale).[10]

Quality means improved business performance

Kano et al.[11] carried out an examination of twenty-six companies which won the Deming Application Prize between 1961 and 1980. They found that the financial performance of these companies in terms of earnings rate, productivity, growth rate, liquidity and net worth was above the average for their industries.

The cost of non-quality is high

Based on a variety of companies, industries and situations, the cost of quality (or to be more precise the cost of not getting it right the first time) ranges from 5 to 25 per cent of an organization's annual sales turnover. An organization need only compare its profit to sales turnover ratio to its quality costs to sales turnover ratio to gain an immediate indication of the importance of product and service quality to corporate profitability. (Chapter 2 is devoted to the subject of quality costing.)

Product liability

The 1987 Consumer Protection Act and the 1988 legislation on strict product liability have resulted in CEOs and senior managers becoming more aware of the importance of having a recognized quality system which meets the requirements of the BS 5750[12]/ISO 9000 series (registration to this system is seen by many executives as some defence against product liability claims) or those of a major purchaser, for example the Ford Motor Q-101 Quality System Standard.[13] In addition, it is encouraging managers to:

- be in a position to trace batches of work which have been produced some time in the past;
- keep detailed records of actions taken; and
- engage in advanced quality planning using techniques such as FMEA to pinpoint, early on in the planning of the design and operating processes, potential areas of failure.

The customer is king

In today's markets, customer requirements are becoming increasingly more rigorous and their expectations of the product/service in terms of its conformance, reliability, durability, interchangeability, performance, features, appearance, serviceability, environment- and user-friendliness, safety, etc., are also increasing. At the same time, it is likely that the existing competition will be improving and new and lower cost competitors may emerge in the market place; consequently, the process of quality improvement needs to be continuous and involve everyone in the company. Organizations claiming that they have achieved TQM will be overtaken by the competition. Once quality improvement has been halted, under the mistaken belief that TQM has been achieved, it is much harder to restart and gain the initiative on the competition (see figure 1.3). This is why TQM should always be referred to as a process, *not* a programme.

Quality is a way of life

Quality is a way of organizational and everyday life; a way of doing business, living and conducting one's personal affairs. Whatever each of us does, in whatever situation, the task(s) must be undertaken in a quality-conscious way. Quality is driven by our own internal mechanisms, our personal beliefs.

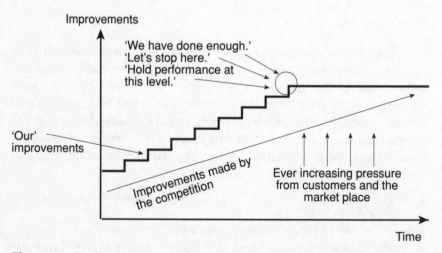

Figure 1.3 Quality improvement is a continuous process

The evolution of total quality management

Organizations go through a number of phases or stages in their process of quality improvement; quality improvement is the enabling process which facilitates progress along the TQM journey. Figure 1.4 (developed from Dale and Plunkett)[14] shows one such representation of this development through the phases of inspection, quality control and quality assurance. Quality control embraces inspection, quality assurance embraces quality control and, likewise, TQM embraces quality assurance – the Russian doll analogy.

Detection and firefighting environment

Organizations whose approach to product and service quality is based on inspection are operating in a detection-type environment (i.e. finding and fixing mistakes); at one time this was thought to be the only way to ensure quality. The same is also true of those organizations using a quality control approach. In this case, however, there will have been some development from the basic inspection activity in terms of advancement of methods and systems, and the quality management tools and techniques employed (see figure 1.4).

In a detection or firefighting environment, the emphasis is on the product and the downstream processes. Considerable effort is expended on inspecting, checking, screening and testing the product/service after production, and providing reactive 'quick fixes' in a bid to ensure that only conforming product are delivered to the customer. There is a lack of creative and systematic work activities, and planning and inspection are the primary means of control, thereby encouraging a production versus inspection situation – the question must be asked whether the policing of work by inspectors hurts an individual's quality pride. The emphasis is on 'today's events', with little attempt to learn from the lessons of the current problem or crisis.

With this approach, non-conforming products are culled, sorted and graded, and decisions made on rework, repair, downgrading, scrap or disposal. It is not unusual in a detection system to find products going through this cycle more than once. While a detection-type system may prevent non-conforming products and services being shipped and delivered to the customer, it does not stop them being made. Indeed, it may be questioned whether such a system does in fact cull out the offending products and services.

Further, a non-conforming product must be made before the process

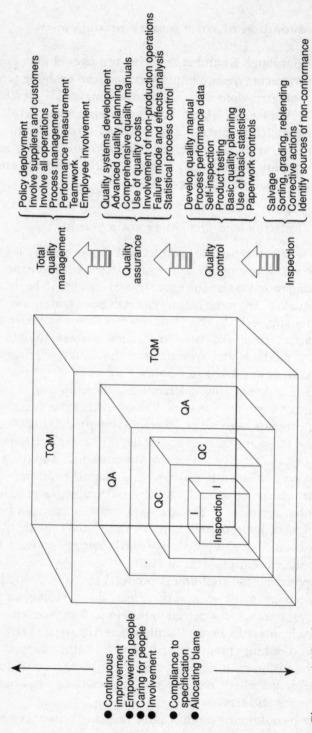

Policy deployment
Involve suppliers and customers
Involve all operations
Process management
Performance measurement
Teamwork
Employee involvement

Quality systems development
Advanced quality planning
Comprehensive quality manuals
Use of quality costs
Involvement of non-production operations
Failure mode and effects analysis
Statistical process control

Develop quality manual
Process performance data
Self-inspection
Product testing
Basic quality planning
Use of basic statistics
Paperwork controls

Salvage
Sorting, grading, reblending
Corrective actions
Identify sources of non-conformance

Total quality management

Quality assurance

Quality control

Inspection

● Continuous improvement
● Empowering people
● Caring for people
● Involvement
● Compliance to specification
● Allocating blame

Figure 1.4 The four levels in the evolution of total quality management

Source: Developed from Dale, B. G. and Plunkett, J. J. (1990) *Managing Quality*, Philip Allan, Hertfordshire.

can be adjusted and this is inherently inefficient in that it creates waste in all its various forms. The scrap, rework or whatever involves extra time and costs over and above budget, which ultimately results in a loss of profit. Figure 1.5, taken from the Ford Motor Company SPC course notes,[15] is a schematic illustration of a detection-type system.

It should also not be forgotten that an environment in which the emphasis is on making good rather than preventing the non-conformance is not ideal for engendering team spirit, co-operation and a good climate for work. The focus tends to be on switching the blame to others, making oneself 'fireproof', not being prepared to accept responsibility, and taking disciplinary action against those who make mistakes. This behaviour and attitude generally emanate from middle management and quickly spread downwards through the hierarchy. The detection-type approach also encourages the view some hold that achieving quality is the responsibility solely of the quality control or quality assurance department.

Prevention-based systems

Finding and solving problems after the event is not an effective way of eliminating their root causes. A lasting and continuous improvement in

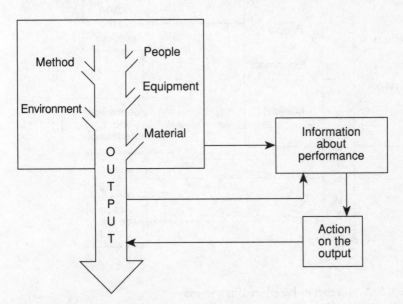

Figure 1.5 A detection-based quality system
Source: Ford Motor Company (1985) *Three Day SPC Course Notes*, Ford, Brentwood.

quality can be achieved only by directing organizational efforts towards preventing problems occurring at source. This concept leads to the next stage of development: quality assurance.

Quality assurance is a prevention-based system which improves product and service quality, and increases productivity by placing the emphasis on product and process design and process control. By concentrating on source activities, it prevents the emergence of non-conforming products or services. This is a more creative approach than detection: there is a clear change of emphasis from the downstream to the upstream processes (see figure 1.6).

Quality is created in the design stage (product and processes) and not in the control stage; the majority of quality-related problems are caused by poor or unsuitable designs. In the prevention approach, there is a recognition of the process as defined by its input of people, machines,

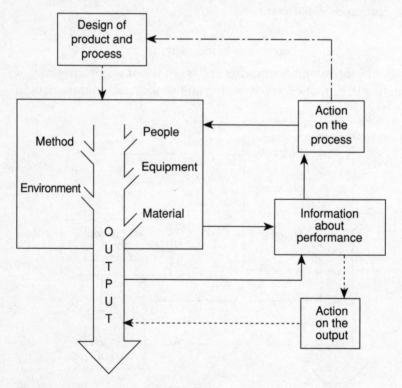

Figure 1.6 · A prevention-based quality system
Source: Ford Motor Company (1985) *Three Day SPC Course Notes*, Ford, Brentwood.

materials, method, management and environment. As figure 1.4 indicates, in the quality assurance phase more emphasis is placed on advanced quality planning, improving the design of the product, process and services, improving control over the process, and involving and motivating people.

From detection to prevention

Changing from detection to prevention requires not just the use of a set of quality management tools and techniques but the development of a new operating philosophy and approach, which requires a change in management style. Quality planning and improvement truly begin when top management includes prevention (as opposed to detection) in the organizational policy and objectives, and starts to integrate the improvement efforts of various departments.

Total quality management

What is total quality management (TQM)? Put simply, it involves everyone in an organization and associated business processes co-operating to furnish products and services that meet their customers' needs and expectations. That said, there are many interpretations of TQM, but a number of common principles run through them:

- everyone in the organization is involved in continually improving the processes under his or her control and takes responsibility for his or her own quality assurance;
- each person is committed to satisfying his or her customers (internal or external);
- teamwork is practised in a number of forms;
- there is a commitment to the development of employees through involvement;
- participation by everyone in the business is positively encouraged and practised;
- a formal programme of education and training is in place and this is viewed as an investment in developing people's ability and knowledge and helping them realize their potential;
- suppliers and customers are integrated into the improvement process;
- honesty, sincerity and care are an integral part of daily business life; and
- simplicity in processes, systems, procedures and work instructions is pursued.

The key elements of total quality management

The following brief outline of the key elements of TQM is discussed in more detail in later chapters.

Commitment and leadership of the chief executive officer

Without the total commitment of the CEO and his or her immediate executives and other senior managers, nothing much will happen and anything that does will not be permanent. They must take personal charge and exercise forceful and personal leadership.

Culture change

An organizational culture which is conducive to continuous quality improvement with everyone participating must be created and quality assurance needs to be integrated into all the processes and functions of an organization. This requires changing people's behaviour, attitudes and working practices in a number of ways. All employees must, for example:

- accept that there is no ideal state, and never take the view that their level of process, performance and service is as good as it possibly could be;
- inspect their own work;
- not pass on defects to the next process;
- recognize the internal customer relationship (everyone for whom you perform a task or service is a customer); and
- view mistakes as an improvement opportunity – in the words of the Japanese: every mistake is a pearl to be cherished.

Considerable thought needs to be given to facilitating and managing culture change. Changing people's behaviour and attitudes is one of the most difficult tasks facing management, who must develop their powers and skills of motivation and persuasion.

Planning and organization

Many facets of the quality improvement process feature planning and organization:

- building product and service quality into designs and processes;
- developing prevention-based activities;

- putting into place quality assurance procedures that facilitate closed-loop corrective action;
- planning the approach to be taken to the use of quality systems, procedures and quality management tools and techniques;
- developing the organization and infrastructure and allocating the necessary resources to support the improvement activities;
- standardization, systematization and simplification of work instructions, procedures and systems.

Education and training

Employees need to be provided with the right level of education and training to ensure that their general awareness of quality management concepts, skills and attitudes is appropriate and suited to the continuous improvement philosophy. Education and training also provide a common language throughout the business. Training needs to be planned and provided on a timely and regular basis to enable people to solve increasingly complex problems. Without it changes in behaviour and attitude will not take place. The training must also focus on helping managers to identify improvements available in their areas of responsibility.

It must also be recognized that not all employees will have the necessary educational levels. The structure of the training may incorporate some updating of basic educational skills in numeracy and literacy, but it must promote continuing education and self-development. In this way, the latent potential of many employees will be released and the best use made of each individual's ability.

Involvement

All available means, from suggestion schemes to various forms of teamwork, must be considered for achieving broad employee interest, participation and contribution in the process of quality improvement; management must be prepared to share some of their powers and responsibilities. This also involves seeking and listening carefully to the views of employees and acting upon their suggestions. Part of the approach to TQM is to ensure that everyone has a clear understanding of what is required of him or her and of each job's relevance to the business as a whole. The more people understand the business, the greater the role they can play in the quality improvement process. People must be encouraged to manage and improve the processes within their sphere of responsibility.

Recognition

Positive performance and achievement must be recognized, and success rewarded. People must see the results of their activities and be constantly encouraged through active communication. For TQM to be successful it is essential that management must communicate as never before.

Measurement

Progress must be continually measured against a series of key results indicators, internal and external. From these measurements, action plans must be developed to meet objectives.

What are the benefits of total quality management?

To close this introductory chapter the benefits of TQM, as volunteered in different ways by three CEOs from diverse business situations and with differing periods of TQM experience, are summarized.

Bob Dixcy, Managing Director of Hilti (Gt Britain) Ltd, a sales and marketing organization selling a range of fastening systems into the construction industry:

- Hilti has recognized that human resource is one of its most important assets, by integrating TQM into the company's one-year operational plan and three-year strategic plan. The company continually capitalizes on the contribution its employees can make. This involvement of employees in the process is having a positive effect in sustaining dynamism in the company's growth.
- TQM demanded that the company improve its methods of internal communication to inform and motivate its human resource. This has been achieved by the development of an annual internal marketing plan for TQM. This plan includes a company-wide monthly team briefing activity, monthly meetings between top management, quality circles and project teams, quarterly journal and an annual quality conference.
- One of the keys to the success of TQM is the involvement of middle managers, who can be an impervious layer. Senior managers understand because they are involved in the planning of the process, employees lower down the organizational hierarchy can quickly appreciate that TQM offers them an opportunity to demonstrate that

they are intelligent thinking human beings. Middle managers may initially see TQM as more work bolted on to existing tasks. Leadership and problem-solving training linked to involvement in quality cost analysis have helped to break down these various barriers.

- Problem-solving training at all levels has reduced the previous tendency of individuals to 'quick fix' problems, which invariably meant treating effects and not the causes of problems. This has also resulted in causes being identified quickly both at an individual and group level. The time saved is available to add more value to the company's business.
- The introduction of quality circles into departments like Customer Services, Telemarketing, Office Services, Purchase Ledger and Warehouse demonstrated very quickly that personnel at all levels can make a very positive contribution to Hilti's business; this was a massive untapped resource which previously had no means of expressing itself. Some of the more sceptical managers also discovered they did not have a monopoly on good ideas.
- Conducting a quality cost analysis has helped to identify where waste is occurring, and quantified the monetary loss. Clear opportunities for improvement have been identified and addressed by individuals, project teams or quality circles, depending on the level of complexity of the opportunity.

Stephen Ward, Managing Director of John Cotton Ltd, a manufacturer of interior trims, roof linings, door panels, etc., for the automotive industry:

TQM is the catalyst which has helped turn the company around in terms of profitability and customer perceptions. It is the bedrock on which operating activities are based and has helped to generate company growth. The following are some specific points:

- Internal rejection rate has been reduced from 9 to 2 per cent over a two-year period.
- Customer complaints have remained at zero over many months during 1990 and 1991.
- Profit has increased by 50 per cent in terms of the percentage of profit to sales.
- The company has grown by 50 per cent in terms of sales and, as a direct result of TQM, has landed major contracts which will increase the business by an additional 50 per cent over the next few years.
- There is a much greater involvement and participation of employees in the business.

- TQM has provided a common language of communication throughout all levels of the organizational hierarchy.
- People have an increased pride in the organization and its product.
- The company's TQM achievements have been recognized by the following prestigious quality awards: Jaguar Cars Customers Award (1989), Rover Stirling Award (1990) and Ford Motor Company Q1 Quality Award (1991).

Ian Priestnell, Managing Director of Grace Dearborn Ltd, a supplier of speciality service chemicals for the industrial water treatment, pulp and paper, food and beverage, fermentation and oil process chemicals markets:

- Enhanced job 'ownership' by employees.
- Increased employee awareness of the importance of their function to the overall company performance.
- Willingness (indeed eagerness) of individuals and groups of employees proactively to identify quality improvement and waste elimination opportunities.
- Enhanced employee commitment to achieving projected benefits from quality improvement projects.
- Clear identification of internal 'customers and suppliers', which has led to improved mutual respect between departments.
- Growing belief that management will listen to, and value, ideas from all levels, from top to bottom, of the organization.
- Internal and external projection of 'Pride in our Quality'.

It can be seen from the views expressed that the results of TQM and continuous quality improvement are not measured in monetary gains alone, but also in terms of the organizational culture, environment and morale, teamwork and people development and participation.

Executive summary

- The word quality has many different meanings.
- Customer orientation is central to the quality definition.
- An organizational definition of quality will help to prevent misunderstanding and avoid different interpretations being made by people and the various functions within a business.
- An organization which has not adopted TQM as its number one business strategy is swimming against the tide.

- Inspection, quality control and quality assurance are the main phases through which organizations pass in the progress towards TQM.
- The focus should be on prevention rather than detection-type activities.
- TQM is not a programme, it is a process which is continuous and involves everyone.
- A process of continuous quality improvement is the enabling mechanism by which an organization can make progress towards TQM.
- TQM involves the co-operation of everyone in an organization and associated business processes to furnish products and services which meet the needs and expectations of customers.
- A number of principles are involved in TQM, including:
  - each individual takes responsibility for the quality assurance of his or her own processes;
  - everyone in the organization is involved in improving on a continuous basis the processes under his or her control;
  - all personnel recognize that anyone for whom they perform a task is a customer and they are totally committed to satisfying their needs;
  - teamwork is practised;
  - every individual's skills and abilities are fully utilized;
  - participation and development of employees in the business are positively encouraged;
  - training and education are considered an investment;
  - supplier and customers are integrated into the improvement process;
  - honesty, sincerity and care are an integral part of the organization.
- The key elements of TQM are:
  - commitment and leadership of the CEO;
  - culture change;
  - planning and organization;
  - education and training;
  - involvement;
  - recognition;
  - measurement.
- The benefits of TQM cannot be measured just in monetary terms.

Notes

1 ISO 8402 (1986) *Quality Vocabulary*, International Organization For Standardization, Geneza, Switzerland.
2 Taguchi, G. (1986) *Introduction to Quality Engineering*, Asian Productivity Organization, Dearborn, Michigan.
3 Crosby, P. B. (1979) *Quality is Free*, McGraw-Hill, New York.
4 Juran, J. M. (1988) *Quality Control Handbook*, McGraw-Hill, New York.

5 Ryan, J. (1988) 'Consumers see little change in product quality', *Quality Progress*, December, pp. 16–20.

6 Hutchens, S. (1989) 'What customers want: results of ASQC/Gallup survey', *Quality Progress*, February, pp. 33–6.

7 McKinsey and Company (1989) *Management of Quality: The Single Most Important Challenge for Europe*, European Quality Management Forum, 19 October, Montreux, Switzerland.

8 Lascelles, D. M. and Dale, B. G. (1990) 'Quality management: the chief executive's perception and role', *European Management Journal*, vol. 8, no. 1, pp. 67–75.

9 Deming, W. E. (1982) *Quality Productivity and Competitive Position*, MIT Press, Cambridge, Massachusetts.

10 Buzzell, R. D. and Gale, B. T. (1987) *The Profit Impact of Marketing Strategy Principles: Linking Strategy to Performance*, Free Press, New York.

11 Kano, N., Tanaka, H. and Yamaga, Y. (1983) *The TQC Activity of Deming Prize Recipients and its Economic Impact*, Union of Japanese Scientists and Engineers, Tokyo.

12 BS 5750 (1987) *Quality Systems*, British Standards Institution, London.

13 Ford Motor Company (1990) *Worldwide Quality System Standard Q-101*, Ford, Plymouth, Michigan.

14 Dale, B. G. and Plunkett, J. J. (1990) *Managing Quality*, Philip Allan, Hertfordshire.

15 Ford Motor Company (1985) *Three Day SPC Course Notes*, Ford Motor Company, Brentwood, Essex.

2

What Senior Executives Need to Know about Quality Costing

The Role of Quality Costing in Total Quality Management

What Are Quality Costs?

Why Are Quality Costs Important?

Why Measure Quality Costs?

Uses of Quality Costs

Pointers for Setting Up a Quality Costing System

Executive Summary

The purpose of this chapter is to provide senior executives with an overview of the subject of quality costing and the wherewithal to understand what is involved in a quality costing exercise, and how the data may be used to assist with the quality improvement process.

The role of quality costing in total quality management

Total quality management as a key organizational business parameter and strategy is here to stay, and needs to be treated by executives as such. However, most CEOs and senior executives want tangible proof of the need for quality improvement and for top-level leadership in the process – they need to be convinced. One of the means of providing this proof and a factor in promoting a process of continuous and company-wide quality improvement is the collection, reporting and use of quality-related cost information. It helps to quantify the benefits of quality improvement in commercial terms.

Continuous quality improvement requires patience, tolerance, tenacity and considerable commitment from every level in the organization, in particular the CEO, board of directors and senior management. It requires considerable effort to sustain this process and will often involve justifying to a parent company, board, and shareholders, that the investment in improvement is cost effective.

Some quality management protagonists argue that there should be no need to justify investment in quality improvement activities. We disagree. Western organizations and their managements are judged over relatively short time periods; indeed, one of the main criticisms made of executives is that they place too much emphasis on short-term objectives. Committing huge amounts of expenditure in quality improvement activities without some measure of cost effectiveness can be considered a blind act of faith and is contrary to the way in which Western businesses operate.

In Japanese organizations the situation is quite different. Investment in improvement initiatives over a long period without thought of immediate benefits appears to be accepted without question by executives, senior managers, shareholders and financial institutions. The Japanese have considerable tangible evidence, over the last thirty years or so, of the wisdom of pursuing this long-range management view.

In addition to product and service quality, organizations need to be competitive on cost and delivery, a considerable number of organizations need to achieve substantial cost reductions if they are to survive in today's market place. Many organizations are vulnerable to any breakthrough by their competitors in relation to quality improvement and technology. In many instances, quality-related costs are a major potential source of the necessary savings that maintain competitive edge, and are one of several tools and techniques which can assist companies with improving product and service quality.

Quality costing may be more useful for organizations taking the first steps towards TQM than it is for those who have considerably more operating experience of TQM and with first-hand experience of the benefits of becoming a total quality organization. However, even in these organizations, it is still considered by many to be a key internal quality performance measure.

While there is clearly a good case for quality costing, it is not a panacea for all quality problems.

Justifying the investment

A knowledge of quality costs helps executives justify the investment in quality improvement and assists them in monitoring the effectiveness of the efforts made. Quality costing expresses an organization's quality performance in the language of the senior management team, shareholders and financial institutions: money. Senior management are often unmoved by quality assurance data as such but are spurred into action when the same data are presented in monetary terms. Operators and line supervisors are also found to react positively when non-conformance data are presented in this way, in addition to the normally expressed measure of numbers and percentages. This generally occurs when they have the opportunity to compare the costs of departmental non-conformance to their salaries; a matter of particular relevance in cases such as a salary increase below the rate of inflation, no salary increase or a salary reduction.

Quality costing is not easy. There may be internal opposition to the concept and obscurity of the data, but those executives, managers and organizations who have persevered have found the exercise very rewarding; indeed, some see it as vital if they are to remain profitable in an increasingly tough, competitive market place. Those organizations which have undertaken quality costing have benefited from the experience and the findings.

Many organizations are surprised when they learn of the potential savings, and soon want to develop their quality-related costing systems to gain greater benefits and improve cost control. However, the fact that improvements in quality performance do not necessarily produce pro rata changes in quality-related costs should not be overlooked by the CEO. It is not enough to have the necessary mechanisms in place for collecting quality-related costs, it is also necessary for the CEO and his or her senior management to have the will to carry it out and use the results.

Executives' views

The following are some comments made by executives in the Department of Trade and Industry booklet *The Case For Costing Quality*.[1]

It is important that we invest more at the front end of our programmes in design and development, if we are to reduce the high failure costs. The need for programmes designed for ease of manufacturing at the earliest possible stage is essential if profitable trouble-free production is to be achieved. This does not require an increase in project cost overall, but a re-allocation of costs. (Norman Wallwork, Quality Director, British Aerospace (Dynamics) Ltd.)

Quality costs allow us to identify the soft targets to which we can apply our improvement efforts. (John Asher, Managing Director, Crown Industrial Products.)

Four years ago we could still use quality as a selling feature for our product, now that's all changed. If you are still a supplier to the automotive industry today, you will have achieved a high level of quality that is the accepted norm in the industry. Those companies who have failed to improve their quality are no longer suppliers. Customers expect to share in the benefits of our continuous quality improvement efforts through agreed cost reduction programmes and extended warranty agreements. Without tracking quality costs we could seriously impair our bottom line profitability and not know the reason why. (Tony Harman, Managing Director, Garrett Automotive.)

With the prospect of increased competition as a result of activities surrounding 1992, it is important for us to continually improve our operational methods. The formal measurement of quality costs is central to that process, and has the added benefit of showing us how we can tackle certain areas of costs. (John Barbour, Managing Director, John Russell (Grangemouth) Ltd.)

Quality must be one of the cornerstones for a growing company, otherwise spectacular growth can be followed by an equally rapid descent and quality costs are one of the measures by which this can be monitored. (Ian Elliot, Managing Director, Pirelli Focom.)

What are quality costs?

When considering the nitty-gritty of quality costs, there can be considerable controversy about which activities and costs are quality-related. There is by no means a uniform view of what is meant by a quality cost and what should be included under the quality cost umbrella. Definitions are a key feature in quality costing: without clear definitions, there can be no common understanding or meaningful communication on quality costs. Unfortunately, however, there is no general agreement on a single broad definition of quality costs, and there are many grey areas where good production/operations procedures and practices overlap with quality-related activities.

Ideas of what constitutes quality costs have been changing rapidly in recent years. Only a few years ago the costs of quality were perceived as the cost of running the quality assurance department, plus scrap and warranty costs; now it is widely accepted that they are the *total* costs incurred in the design, implementation, operation and maintenance of an organization's quality system, the cost of organizational resources committed to the process of continuous quality improvement, and the costs of system, product and service failures.

Quality systems may range from simple inspection to systems surpassing the requirements of the BS 5750/ISO 9000 series[2] or any other recognized quality system standard (e.g. the Ford Q-101 Quality System Standard).[3] System failures can result in obsolete stocks, lost items, production or operational delays, additional work, scrap, rectification work, late deliveries, additional transport costs, poor service, and nonconforming products. Product and/or service failures result in warranty, guarantee and product liability claims, product replacement, complaint administration and investigation, product recall, additional customer service costs and loss of customer goodwill.

Thus, quality-related costs are not, as is sometimes thought, just the cost of quality assurance, inspection, monitoring, testing, and scrap materials, components, products and services which do not conform to requirements. They arise from a range of activities and involve virtually every department in an organization, all of which impinge on the quality of the product or service. Nor are they wholly determined or controlled from within the organization: suppliers, subcontractors, stockists, agents, dealers, customers and consumers can all influence the incidence and level of quality-related costs.

Why are quality costs important?

In 1978 quality costs were estimated to be £10,000 million, equal to 10 per cent of the UK's gross national product. There is no reason to suppose that they are any less now. The findings of a NEDO task force on quality and standards, published in 1985,[4] claim that some 10 to 20 per cent of an organization's total sales value is accounted for by quality-related costs and, based on the 10 per cent figure, it is estimated that UK manufacturing industry could save up to £6 billion each year by reducing such costs. The available information indicates that quality-related costs commonly range from 5 to 25 per cent of a company's annual sales turnover. The level depends on the type of business, the view it takes of what is or is not a quality-related cost, the approach to TQM and the extent to which continuous and company-wide quality improvement is practised in the organization.

Examples of quality costs taken from *The Case for Costing Quality*[5] include:

- British Aerospace Dynamics: 11 per cent of the total cost of production;
- in British Aerospace Technical Workshops, staff time spent on quality-related activities is: failure, 22.9 per cent; prevention, 19.4 per cent; appraisal, 6.8 per cent.
- Courtaulds Jersey: reduced from 12.1 to 7.6 per cent of annual sales turnover over a period of four years;
- Standfast Dyers and Printers: reduced from 20 to 7 per cent of annual sales value over a period of four years;
- Grace Dearborn: 20 per cent of annual sales turnover;
- NatWest Bank: 25 per cent of operating costs is absorbed in the difference between the cost actually incurred in accomplishing a task and the cost that should be incurred if a 'right first time' approach is successfully adopted;
- Philip Components Blackburn: plant-wide quality costs reduced by 60 per cent over a period of six years.

Ninety-five per cent of quality costs is usually expended on appraisal and failure-type activities. These expenditures add little to the value of the product or service, and the failure costs, at least, may be regarded as avoidable. Reducing failure cost by eliminating causes of non-conformance can also lead to substantial reductions in appraisal costs. The research evidence of Dale and Plunkett[6] suggests that quality-related costs may be reduced to a third of their existing level, within three to five years, by commitment to a process of continuous and company-wide quality improvement.

Unnecessary and avoidable costs make goods and services more expensive. This in turn affects competitiveness and, ultimately, wages, salaries and standards of living.

Finally, despite the fact that the costs are large, and that a substantial proportion of them is avoidable, it is apparent from the UMIST research that the costs and economics of many quality-related activities, including investment in prevention and appraisal activities, are not known by companies. Such a state of affairs is indefensible in any well-run business.

Why measure quality costs?

The measurement of costs allows quality-related activities to be expressed in monetary terms. This in turn, allows quality to be treated as a business parameter like, for example, marketing, research and development, and production/operations. Drawing quality costs into the business arena helps to emphasize the importance of product and service quality to corporate health. They will help to influence employees' behaviour, attitudes and values at all levels in the organization towards TQM and continuous quality improvement. In many organizations some employees will need to be convinced that their senior management are serious about TQM. Typical comments are: 'We have heard all this before', 'TQM is the latest management fad and it will not last.' Quality costing is a way of highlighting to all employees the importance of product and service quality to business profitability.

Quality cost measurement focuses attention on areas of high expenditure and identifies potential cost-reduction opportunities. It allows measurement of performance and provides a basis for comparison between products, services, processes and departments. Measurement of quality-related costs also reveals quirks and anomalies in cost allocation and standards, which may remain undetected by the more commonly used production/operation and labour-based analyses; quality costing has even uncovered cases of fraudulent practice. Measurement can also obviate the dumping of embarrassing after-sales costs under quality-related headings.

Finally, and perhaps most important, measurement is the first step towards control.

Uses of quality costs

Collecting quality costs is pointless if the data are not to be used. Usefulness is the only justification for their collection, and clearly this is one of the most important criteria in setting up a cost collection system. Most executives are looking to quality cost data to show things that their other quality-related information and reports do not reveal. The uses of quality costs are numerous and diverse; this section considers the main ones.

Quality costs display the importance of quality-related activities in meaningful terms, and help to shock people into action. They can also be used to educate staff in the concept and principles of TQM and explain why the organization is embarking on it.

Knowledge of quality-related costs enables business decisions about quality to be made objectively. It permits the use of sensitivity analyses, discounted cash flow and other accounting techniques for the evaluation of expenditure projects, as in any other area of the business. In this way it helps companies to decide *how*, *when* and *where* to invest in preventive activities and/or equipment.

Costs may be used to monitor performance, to identify products, processes and departments for investigation, to set cost-reduction targets, and to measure progress towards targets. They may be used to evaluate the cost benefit of individual quality activities, such as accreditation statistical process control (SPC) and supplier development, or to compare performances between departments, works or divisions. Quality costs are tools for initiating improvement projects, and levers for uncovering quality problems and areas of chronic waste.

Costs are the bases for budgeting and eventual cost control. They also enable valid comparisons to be made with other costs via the usual measurement bases (such as sales turnover, units of saleable product, or standard hours).

Quality costs help to provide information for quotations for products or contracts having onerous quality conditions.

Finally, costs keep quality aspects of the business under the spotlight – but only if featured in the regular management accounts and reporting systems.

Pointers for setting up a quality costing system

1   It is unlikely that an organization's management accounts will contain the necessary information in the right form. Hence it is essential to involve accountants in the cost collection exercise from the outset.

2   There is no point in collecting quality-related costs just to see what they may reveal. Many executives have successfully resisted pressure to co-operate in the collection of quality costs on the grounds that they would not reveal any problems of which they were not already aware from the existing quality management information system. The purpose of quality costing should be clarified at the start of the project as this may influence the strategy of the exercise and will help to avoid difficulties later. If, for example, the main objective of the exercise is to identify high-cost problem areas, approximate costs will suffice. If, on the other hand, the purpose is to set a percentage cost-reduction target on the organization's total quality-related costs, it will be necessary to identify and measure all the contributing cost elements in order to be sure that costs are reduced and not simply transferred elsewhere. Thus, the matter is important not only from a philosophical point of view but from purely practical considerations as well.

3   It will also be necessary to decide how to deal with overheads, since many quality-related costs are normally included as part of the overhead, while others are treated as direct costs and attract a proportion of overheads. Failure to clarify this can lead to a gross distortion of the picture derived from the quality-related cost analysis. It is also easy to fall into the trap of double counting. For these and other reasons quality-related costs should be made the subject of a memorandum account. However, the costs should not include recovery of overheads in calculating costs of personnel. These are areas where the accountant's advice and assistance can be invaluable.

4   Another area of difficulty is deciding whether some activities, usually of a setting-up, testing or running-in type, are quality activities or an integral and essential part of the production/operations activity. These costs are often substantial and can alter quite markedly the relative proportions of quality-related costs categories. There are also factors which serve to ensure the basic utility of the product/service, guard against errors, and protect and preserve product and service quality. Examples are the use of design codes, preparation of engineering, technical and administrative systems and procedures, capital premiums on machinery and equipment, document and drawing controls, and handling and storage practices. Whether such factors give rise to costs which may be regarded as being quality-related is a matter for judgement in individual cases. These problems need to be discussed with purchasing, engineering, production/operations, and accountancy personnel, as appropriate, in order to resolve them. Deciding which activities should be included under the quality-related cost umbrella is by no means straightforward: note the point made earlier about definitions.

Over-ambition or over-zealousness may prompt the quality specialist and management consultants to try to maximize the impact of quality costs on the CEO and board of directors. They tend to stretch their definitions to include costs which have only the most tenuous relationship with product and service quality, to try to create a financial impact. Unfortunately, this can backfire if the costs later prove not to be influenced by quality-management initiatives.

The comparability of sets of data depends on the definitions of the cost categories and elements used in compiling them. This makes collation and comparisons of data from different sources difficult. Consequently, the value of much of the published quantitative data on quality-related costs must be questionable because of the absence of precise definitions and lack of qualification. Senior managers must resist the temptation to compare their quality costs with those of other organizations.

5 One of the maxims of quality cost collection seems to be that *costs need to be large to hold people's attention* – senior executives in particular. Magnitude is often regarded as synonymous with importance, though it is magnitude coupled with relevance and potential for reduction which determines the real importance of costs. Clearly, it may be much more advantageous to pursue a small percentage reduction in a large cost than a large reduction in a small cost, depending on the ease of achievement. This creates a dilemma for cost collectors because large costs are often insensitive to changes, but they cannot omit large costs and concentrate only on smaller ones which may be readily seen to change. Hence cost groupings need to be chosen carefully so that the cost reductions achieved are displayed in such a way that both the relative achievement and absolute position are clearly shown. Another dilemma arises from the fact that one-off estimates of quality costs tend not to change and some people take the view that there is no point in collecting costs which do not change. The only solution is to measure directly, or through surrogates, those costs it is thought worth collecting.

6 A checklist of quality cost elements can provide a useful starting point for the cost collection exercise. However, there is no substitute for a thorough analysis of all an organization's activities and some key elements may be missed if only this method is used. BS 6143: Part 2[7] provides such a list of elements under the cost categories of prevention, appraisal, internal failure, and external failure. Some organizations have identified cost elements by scanning the quality costing literature; others, from analysis of their processes, have identified the costs of non-conformance incurred from not getting operations right the first time. In non-manufacturing situations the process cost model outlined in BS 6143: Part 1[8] can prove a useful aid in identifying quality costs.

7 In the absence of an established quality-related cost reporting system, the exercise should commence by investigating failure costs, namely:

- those attributable to suppliers and or subcontractors;
- in-house mistakes, scrap, rework and rectification costs;
- downgraded products or seconds;
- free repairs or replacements for products or services which are defective as delivered and/or fitted;
- warranty and guarantee costs and field failures;
- litigation costs.

This should be followed by inquiring into the costs of inspection, checks, audits, false starts, disruption to routine production and operations activities, and quality-related inefficiencies built into standard costs. The way in which quality-related costs are computed should be recorded so that the validity of comparisons made across departments, products, processes, services or time may be checked.

8 When cost information is available it should be analysed and costs attributed to department, business unit, defect type, product, cause, supplier, etc. The responsibility for costs should be identified with functions and people. Problems and cost-reduction projects need to be ranked by size and importance. The collection, analysis and reporting of quality-related costs should be integrated into the organization's accounting system with the aim of keeping paperwork to a minimum.

9 The reporting of quality costs should be such that the costs make an impact and the data are used to their full potential. In most organizations the standard of quality cost reporting is poor. Consideration needs to be given to issues such as:

- a standardized reporting format;
- clarity, simplicity and brevity of reporting;
- the quality cost data being well presented;
- the data being complete;
- the decisions to be taken by the CEO and senior management team based on the reported data being clear;
- if quality costs are to be reported to different levels of the organizational hierarchy, the needs of those receiving the data should be considered. Typical of the questions to be kept in mind are: What are we trying to communicate? and What will they understand from the data?

The summarized data – especially the failure costs – should be supported by detailed information. Attention should also be given to the use of histograms and pie charts with standard ranges and scales. This ensures that the relative magnitude of cost elements plotted on separate charts is kept in perspective, thus simplifying comparisons and judgements. Quality costs should always be separated from other aspects of product and service quality and presented in the context of other costs. Executives should not be required to disentangle and analyse quality cost data in order to decide what to do but, rather, whether to act, which course of action to pursue, and to ensure provision of necessary resources.

10 Successful quality costing systems, as an everyday feature of an organization's management activities, can take up to five years to attain

the credibility and usefulness that should be expected of data featured in a management information system.

Executive summary

The collection and use of quality-related costs are crucial factors in a process of continuous and company-wide quality improvement. The task is not an easy one. There may be internal opposition and obscuration of the data, but those who have persevered and succeeded have found the exercise most rewarding. Many executives are surprised when they learn of the potential savings and soon want to develop their quality-related costing systems to gain greater benefits and cost control. It has also been found helpful in ensuring that CEOs and senior management persevere with TQM.

A few dos and don'ts to help executives to avoid some of the difficulties and traps typically encountered in a quality cost collection exercise are summarized below.

Do

- Get the purpose and the strategy clear at the start.
- Report only costs produced or endorsed by the accounts department.
- Take data and costs from standard data wherever possible.
- Seek independent corroboration of any doubtful data.
- Doubt the validity of people's claims that quality costs are in excess of 25 per cent of annual sales turnover.
- Avoid becoming bogged down with trying to understand all the underlying details.
- Start with failure costs.
- Consider appraisal costs as a target for cost reduction.
- Consider ease of collection and start with the easiest cost elements.
- Ensure that any first-off quality costing is soundly based.
- Refine large costs rather than attempt to quantify small unknown costs.
- Concentrate on costs that do or can change with quality improvement activities.
- Remember that rigid systems make for easier quality cost collection.
- Analyse and report costs clearly in a business context.
- Relate quality costs to profit.
- Avoid a multiplicity of quality costing reports.
- Consider displaying at appropriate places within the organization, as part of a visual management system, the main elements of failure cost.

- Consider reporting warranty and guarantee payments as a separate quality cost category.
- Treat 'economic cost of quality' models with suspicion; their validity is disputed.

Don't

- Forget that there are many complexities and difficulties in the measurement and collection of quality-related costs.
- Expect managers to go it alone – accounting, engineering and technical help needs to be sought as appropriate.
- Expect accountants to take the initiative.
- Expect accountants to arbitrate on what is or is not quality-related; accountants dread dealing with grey areas.
- Believe that standard accounting systems will yield the information needed; some conventional accounting systems are inept at dealing with quality-related costing.
- Forget that to identify costs which are quality-related the cost collector has, more often than not, to adopt a Sherlock Holmes-type approach in sifting through the data.
- Underestimate the difficulties with definitions of quality costs.
- Be too ambitious – start small.
- Expect too much from the first attempt, which is likely to underestimate the costs.
- Lose sight of the fact that it is primarily a cost collection exercise.
- Agonize over relatively trifling costs; keep the cost elements and/or categories in perspective.
- Make guesses, even informed ones
- Make comparisons unless you can guarantee comparability.
- Assume straightforward operations will necessarily be easy to cost.
- Overlook the fact that transactions between companies and their customers and suppliers are often as difficult to cost as in-house activities.
- Forget that prevention is the most difficult category to cost.
- Deduct from quality costs income from scrap.
- Forget that costs derived from estimates of time or from special intensive studies are often not revised.
- Concentrate exclusively on what is already known.
- Overlook the fact that concessions, modifications, and design, document and engineering changes are a major source of quality-related costs which often do not receive the attention they merit.
- Be constrained by the traditional prevention–appraisal–failure categorization of quality costs; there are other categorizations which are closer to standard business practices.

Notes

1 Dale, B. G. and Plunkett, J. J. (1990) *The Case for Costing Quality*, Department of Trade and Industry, London.
2 BS 5750 (1987) *Quality Systems*, British Standards Institution, London.
3 Ford Motor Company (1990) *World Wide Quality System Standard Q-101*, Ford, Plymouth, Michigan.
4 National Economic Development Council (1985) *Quality and Value for Money*, NEDO, London.
5 Dale and Plunkett, *The Case for Costing Quality*.
6 Dale, B. G. and Plunkett, J. J. (1991) *Quality Costing*, Chapman and Hall, London.
7 BS 6143 (1990) *Guide to the Economics of Quality: Part 2 Prevention, Appraisal and Failure Model*, British Standards Institution, London.
8 BS 6143 (1992) *Guide to the Economics of Quality: Part 1 Process Cost Model*, British Standards Institution, London.

The works in notes 1 and 6 have been used in preparation of this chapter. In particular, Barrie Dale is indebted to his friend and colleague the late Jim Plunkett for allowing some of his research findings to be used.

3

The Role of Senior Management in Total Quality Management

Why Senior Executives Should Be Involved in TQM

What Senior Executives Need to Know about TQM

What Senior Executives Need to Do about TQM

Executive Summary

In opening this chapter we make the point that TQM concerns good management behaviour and practice. The principles involved in TQM are similar to those involved with, for example, human resources, equal opportunities and environmental management. No executive who wishes to improve his or her management skills and abilities can afford not to understand more about the subject and become personally involved with its introduction and development.

The chapter outlines the main reasons the CEO and senior managers should become personally involved in TQM, and examines what they need to know about TQM and what positive action they should take.

Why senior executives should be involved in TQM

Strategic weapon

Product and service quality provides a significant business opportunity and is a key business strategy. Indeed, many executives now claim it is their number one strategy in influencing competitive performance and success.

TQM is a strategic decision and one which can be taken only by the

CEO and senior management. Developing and deploying organizational vision, mission, philosophy, strategies, objectives and plans are also the province of senior management – which is why they must become personally involved in TQM and the quality improvement process, and demonstrate visible commitment to it by leading th·s new way of thinking. The necessary total corporate commitment to improve every aspect of the business requires a significant investment of their time. Executives can *always* find time for the things they really want to do.

The responsibility for product and service quality rests with the CEO and senior management. TQM requires the CEO's commitment, confidence and conviction to false starts. Everyone in the organization has a role to play in quality improvement but their efforts are likely to be disjointed and spasmodic if the CEO has not made the organizational requirements for product and service quality crystal clear. If the CEO does not become involved, the quality improvement process may stagnate and disillusionment set in; the corporate health of the organization will then suffer. Quality is too important an issue to delegate to technical and quality specialists, it is an integral part of the management of an organization and its business processes.

There is a strong relationship between an organization's business achievements and the CEO's understanding of the TQM philosophy and commitment to continuous and company-wide quality improvement. In superior-performing companies, TQM is a way of life, and people within the organization are obsessed with quality; only the CEO can ensure that this becomes a reality. As chapter 2 has demonstrated, the cost of non-conformance, or mismanaging quality, is likely to be 5 to 25 per cent of annual sales turnover. If these figures are compared to profit as a percentage of sales turnover, the key questions are: Can the CEO afford *not* to get involved in TQM? and How much will it cost the organization *not* to put in place a process of quality improvement which is both continuous and company-wide?

McKinsey and Company's[1] survey of the CEOs of the top 500 European corporations (see chapter 1 for details) found the following in relation to the key requirements for success in TQM:

- top management attention   95 per cent agreement;
- people development   85 per cent agreement;
- corporate team spirit   82 per cent agreement;
- quality performance information   73 per cent agreement;
- top management capability building   70 per cent agreement;
- sense of urgency   60 per cent agreement.

Lascelles and Dale[2] reporting on their research also make the point that 'the CEO is the primary internal change agent for quality improvement, and in this capacity he/she has two key roles: shaping organisational values, and establishing a managerial infrastructure to actually bring about change'.

Credibility within the organization

Commitment by the CEO and senior management to TQM and the process of quality improvement is vital to gain credibility within the organization for the concept, assure continuity and establish longevity. The CEO, supported by senior management, is the only person who can make product and service quality the top organizational priority and the first item on the management agenda. Ultimately, he or she is responsible for the organizational culture, behaviour, values, climate and style of management in which TQM will either flourish or wither. The need is to create and promote a culture in which, for example:

- people can work together as a team;
- teams work with teams;
- mistakes are freely admitted without recriminations;
- people are involved in the business through decision-making;
- ideas are actively sought from everyone;
- development of people is a priority;
- permanent solutions are found to problems;
- departmental boundaries between functions are non-existent.

Only the CEO can persuade and encourage everyone in the organization to change their behaviour and attitude to accept that mistakes, when admitted, are an improvement opportunity; improve on a continuous basis the processes under their control; and direct their attention to identifying, satisfying, and delighting and winning over customers, whether internal or external. It should also be mentioned that the 'stick and carrot' approach to getting people to do things has, in recent years, become increasingly less effective.

Anyone for whom you perform a task is a customer (see figure 3.1), and if everyone in the organization is committed to satisfying his or her *internal* customers, there is much greater chance of external customers being satisfied with the final product/service. With this approach, a supplier identifies his or her customers and determines their requirements. In some cases the supplying process may have to be developed to meet such requirements. The supplier then undertakes the task and carries

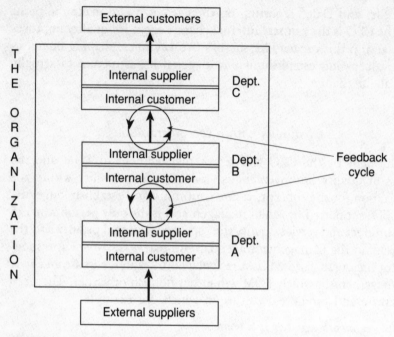

Figure 3.1 The customer/supplier network

out self-inspection and control before the work is passed to the internal customer. Taking responsibility for following processes is part of this approach.

Change is not something that any department or individual takes to easily, and administering changes in organizational practices has to be considered with care (this is discussed in chapter 6). Senior managers should also bear in mind that a minority will be entirely negative toward the concept and principles of TQM. They can have the greatest impact on such individuals, but if the latter are not prepared to change their behaviour and attitudes, harsh decisions will be required.

Not a fad or fancy

In the majority of Western organizations the latest fads and 'flavours of the month' come and go. Senior managers have tended to say a great deal about a topic or issue, but fail to demonstrate any visible commitment to it. A common view is that TQM is just the latest fad. It is only the CEO and his or her senior managers who can break down this cynicism, influence the indifference and persuade people that the organization is serious about TQM. Indeed, it is they who must communicate in person to their staff why the organization is introducing TQM. The CEO and senior managers must demonstrate that they really care about product and service quality; this can be done by, for example:

- identifying the major quality issues facing the organization and becoming personally involved in investigating them, ideally as a leader, member or foster parent (sponsor) to a quality improvement team, problem elimination team or the like;
- setting up and chairing a TQM steering committee or quality council;
- being involved in quality planning, audit and improvement meetings and housekeeping;
- instigating and carrying out regular audits and diagnoses of the state of the art of TQM and quality improvement.
- dealing with customer complaints and visiting customers and suppliers;
- leading customer workshops and panels;
- regularly visiting all areas and functions of the business, and discussing quality improvement issues; and
- communicate as never before on TQM and quality improvement issues.

TQM hero

CEOs lead and teach by example and, consequently, everyone in the organization begins to share the same value system and develop a sense of company loyalty. It is also helpful if they have a charismatic leadership style, and make a deliberate attempt to create some organizational folklore relating to the lengths they have gone to in terms of commitment to TQM, satisfying customers, ensuring a right-first-time performance, etc. In other words, they need to become a TQM hero and a legend in their own right. A major caveat must, however, be stated: it is imperative that people within the organizational hierarchy do not regard the CEO as the customer. He or she may well be an internal customer, but subordinates can easily come to regard satisfying the boss as their quality objective.

Crisis of confidence

Executives need to understand and accept that the improvement process is a roller-coaster of troughs and peaks (see figure 3.2). At certain points the situation will arise that despite a considerable amount of organizational resources being devoted to quality improvement, little progress

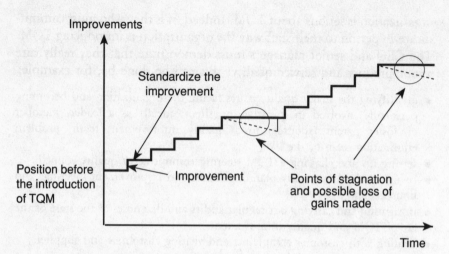

Figure 3.2 The quality-improvement process cycle

appears to be made. This is a fact of organizational life and is independent of whether or not the CEO is fully involved in TQM.

In the first five or so years of launching quality improvement, and when the process is in one of these low points, it is not uncommon for some managers and functional specialists to claim that TQM is not working and to start to question why it has been undertaken, and whether there are any real improvements or benefits. Consequently, they may wish to concentrate on what *they claim* are other, more pressing matters. It should never be forgotten that all levels of the organization hierarchy will always want to be associated with success. If the CEO is personally involved in TQM, people are much less likely to express this type of view. The CEO and senior managers have a key role to play in helping to overcome this crisis of confidence in TQM.

In most Western organizations a few key people are vital to the development and advancement of the quality improvement process, and if such a person leaves there will often be a major gap in the management team. To minimize the effects of such changes, the CEO must play a leading role in developing new managers' and technical/business specialists' understanding of TQM and spreading belief in it. When key people leave and the process continues without interruption, it is an indication that an organizational culture conducive to TQM is firmly established.

Holding gains made

The UMIST research indicates that most organizations are not experienced in holding the gains made in TQM. In addition to leadership and organizational changes, factors such as takeovers, mergers, industrial relations problems, short-time working, redundancies, cost cutting, streamlining, no salary increases, etc., can call have an adverse effect on the gains made. The CEO and senior managers will be expected to provide continuity and leadership in such circumstances. For example, whenever there is a shortfall in the order book Western organizations tend to lay staff off and operate a policy of short-time working. This is a short-sighted response; in most companies labour costs are less than a quarter of materials costs. When there is such a downturn, a CEO who is totally committed to TQM would involve staff in housekeeping, improvement activities, additional training, visiting customers, etc. In addition to the practical benefits arising from activities of this kind, they would help to build loyalty among the workforce and provide clear signals of what the CEO and senior managers consider to be important.

Middle management resistance

It is highly likely that there will be more middle management resistance to TQM than from staff and operatives. The CEO and senior management can break down such resistance by explaining their own role uncertainties in relation to TQM, the mistakes they made, and how they overcame the stumbling blocks and the crisis of confidence. They must demonstrate and communicate the TQM message to their subordinates. It is important that top and middle management have unified thinking on TQM.

What senior executives need to know about TQM

No quick and easy solutions

Senior executives must realize from the outset that TQM is a long-term and not a short-term business strategy; it is an arduous process. There are no quick and easy solutions, no quality-management tools, techniques or systems to provide all the answers, and no ready-made packages which can be plugged in and will guarantee success. TQM is a long-term culture change, taking at least ten years to put the basics into place. It is, however, worth stressing that bottom-line benefits will be achievable in the short term. Japanese manufacturing companies typically work on sixteen-year divided into four-year cycles: introduction, promotion into non-manufacturing areas, development/expansion, and fostering, advancement and maintenance. Executives must both practise and communicate the need for patience, tolerance and tenacity.

No best way

Notwithstanding the claims made in some quarters, executives must recognize that there is no one or best way of beginning a process of quality improvement and fostering TQM. Although some common strands and principles apply in all organizations, each one is different in terms of people, culture, history and customs, prejudices, structure, and products, technology and processes. What works successfully in one organization or situation will not necessarily work in another. This is why executives need to be wary of people selling 'TQM packages'.

The way TQM is introduced matters little; what *is* important is that senior managers demonstrate long-term commitment and leadership to the process of quality improvement and that this process is cost effective.

People are more important than systems

While quality systems and procedures and quality-management tools and techniques are important features of TQM, the concept depends largely upon people; TQM is a culture, not a system. In general, TQM is people-orientated rather than based on systems and techniques, and it is they who make TQM a reality and a success. TQM cannot be implemented – it must be practised, lived and nurtured. This is why it is so important to ensure that organizational culture and values are conducive to TQM.

Avoid false trails

Senior managers need to devote time to develop their own personal understanding of the subject: to read books, attend conferences and courses, visit the best TQM practitioners and talk to as many people as possible. The assessment criteria of national quality award schemes such as the Malcolm Baldrige National Quality Award, the Deming Application Prize for overseas companies and the European Quality

Company Award are relevant to developing this overall understanding. Quality improvement ideas should be constantly circulating in the senior managers' minds.

In this way they will avoid the false trails laid down by their own staff and outside influences. Flaws in thinking are often a result of a lack of understanding of the subject. For example, a common mistake is that a particular quality management tool or method is a cure-all.

Diagnose your own organization

This understanding of TQM will also assist the CEO in deciding, together with senior managers and other key staff, how to begin the quality improvement process. This is not an easy issue. Most organizations will already have undertaken a number of quality improvement initiatives, and a key issue is how to bring these together. A number of elements of TQM are nebulous and senior managers often experience some difficulty in seeing how they might operate in their organization. It is important that these elements are combined with readily understood aspects such as quality systems and practices, teamwork, and tools and techniques. As part of the starting process the CEO and senior managers must diagnose the organization's strengths and weaknesses in relation to the management of quality. This typically takes the form of an internal assessment of employees' views and perceptions, a systems audit, a cost of quality analysis and obtaining the views of customers (including those accounts who have been lost) about the organization's performance in terms of products and services, people, administration, innovation, strengths and weaknesses, and the like. This type of internal and external assessment of perspectives should be carried out regularly to gauge the progress being made towards TQM.

Getting started

The process can be started in a number of ways.

1 Adopt the teachings of one of the internationally respected experts on TQM, e.g. Crosby,[3] Deming,[4] Feigenbaum[5] or Juran.[6] In UMIST's experience organizations may start in this way, but as the process develops they tend to draw on the work of others, notwithstanding that each of them – and their supporters – claim that the different approaches and methodology are mutually exclusive.

2 Award a contract to one of the major management consultancies.

3 Apply one or two of the quality management tools and techniques. It is a

contractual requirement of many major customers that their suppliers use techniques such as SPC and FMEA (see appendices C and D). This is clearly a useful, albeit forced, starting point.

4 Develop the quality system to meet the requirements of the BS 5750/ISO 9000 series[7] or that of a major purchasing organization such as Ford's Q-101 Quality System Standard[8] (more and more organizations now insist on their suppliers obtaining third-party accreditation to the BS/ISO series).

5 Employ a do-it-yourself approach: by distilling the best ideas from the received wisdom on TQM develop an organizational vision, objectives, strategies and a route map for TQM. This approach will often combine the best from the other four methods, and is the one we recommend.

Senior managers should be aware of a number of matters in the context of beginning and developing a process of quality improvement. These are considered in the following sections.

Meeting the requirements of BS 5750/ISO 9001 should be considered the bare minimum

The organization should be encouraged to surpass the BS/ISO requirements. These tend to be a static representation of an organization's quality system at one point in time, and do not adequately encourage year-to-year improvements. The management review and corrective action procedure can be used to develop this continuous improvement spirit, but only if the action is focused on long-term improvement. It is unfortunate that a number of organizations and their managements regard BS 5750/ISO 9000 system series registration as the pinnacle of their achievements – and go to amazing lengths to publicize this.

There is much more to TQM than achieving the twenty set requirements in the ISO 9001 standard. Indeed, possession of registration often results in a sense of complacency. It should also be noted that there are almost certain to be lapses in the system. In real terms, all that registration establishes is that an organization's quality system has procedures, controls and disciplines in place and is on the first rung of the TQM ladder. It should be treated as a matter of course, not one for hype.

Executives should be fully aware of the limitations of quality systems. Appendix A deals in more detail with quality systems.

Quality management tools and techniques should be chosen carefully

Whatever the TQM approach chosen, the organization will need to use a selection of quality management tools and techniques to assist with the quality improvement process, from introduction and promotion to fostering its development and advancement. However, it is important not to rush headlong into a plethora of tools and techniques. (These are examined in appendices B, C and D.) CEOs and executives should understand how these tools work and their various uses and applications.

The UMIST research on the quality improvement process found that the application of any tool or technique in isolation and without a TQM strategy and long-range management vision will provide only short-term benefits. For them to be effective over the longer term, major organizational changes in behaviour, attitudes, values and culture are needed. The key factor is not the tools and techniques themselves, but how they are used within a process of quality improvement.

Lascelles and Dale[9] make the point that it is important for managers to address questions such as those outlined below when considering the use of a particular quality management tool or technique:

- What are the purposes of the technique?
- How will it help us to improve the way we manage product and service quality?
- Is it right for our product, processes, people and organisational culture?
- Are we being given the right advice concerning which technique and how to use the technique itself?
- What organisation changes are necessary to make the best use of the technique?
- What resources, skills, information, education, training, etc. do we need in order to introduce the technique successfully?
- Have we the staff, financial resources and commitment to make the technique work?
- How will the technique fit into, complement, or support other techniques, and quality assurance methods and systems that are already in place, and any that might be introduced in the future?

No one tool or technique is a panacea

No one tool or technique should be regarded as more important than another; they all have a role to play in the quality improvement process. It is a mistake to single out one technique for special attention. Senior executives should view with considerable suspicion anyone peddling one technique.

Tools and techniques fulfil a number of roles. For example, planning for quality, improving the design of the product and process, controlling or improving the process, capturing and documenting quality system data, modelling quality systems, solving problems, motivating people and promoting quality awareness. It is important to be fully aware of the main purpose and use of the tools and techniques being considered.

Every person in the organization should be taught and encouraged to use the seven basic quality-control tools: Pareto diagrams, cause and effect diagrams, control charts, histograms, check sheets, scatter diagrams and graphs (see Ishikawa).[10] Simple tools and techniques can be just as effective as the more complex ones, and senior managers must ensure that their staff are not dismissive of them.

Techniques should be used for maximum benefit

When a major customer insists that its suppliers use a particular tool or technique, there are two observable phases in its use. At first it is applied just to satisfy the demand and maintain the business. Suppliers resort to a number of camouflage measures in a bid to convince the customer that they are serious in their application of the technique. The theme of this phase is satisfying the paperwork requirements. The second phase is when the suppliers start to question how they might use the technique to their own best advantage in order to advance the process of quality improvement. Senior managers must ensure that phase two is reached as quickly as possible.

Mission statement on quality

The CEO and senior management need to develop a company vision and mission statement, which should include an organizational definition of quality. It is important that every company employee can identify with the vision and mission statement and that progress towards its achievement can be measured. The vision and mission statements of the Ford Motor Company and Grace Dearborn are outlined below:

Ford Motor Company

Company vision
To be a low-cost producer of the highest quality products and services which provide the best customer value.

Company mission
Ford Motor Company is a worldwide leader in automotive and automotive-related products and services as well as in newer industries such as aerospace, communications and financial services. Our mission is to improve continually our products and services to meet our customers' needs, allowing us to prosper as a business and to provide a reasonable return for our stockholders, the owner of our business.

Company values
How we accomplish our mission is as important as the mission itself. Fundamental to success for the Company are these basic values:

People Our people are the source of our strength. They provide our corporate intelligence and determine our reputation and vitality. Involvement and teamwork are our core human values.
Products Our products are the end results of our effort, and they should be the best in serving customers worldwide. As our products are viewed, so are we viewed.
Profits Profits are the ultimate measure of how efficiently we provide customers with the best products for their needs. Profits are required to survive and grow.

Guiding principles
Quality comes first To achieve customer satisfaction, the quality of our products and services must be our number one priority.
Customers are the focus of everything we do Our work must be done with our customers in mind, providing better products and services than our competitors.
Continuous improvement is essential to our success We must strive for excellence in everything we do – in our products, their safety and value and in our service, our human relations and competitiveness and our profitability.
Employee involvement is our way of life We are a team. We must treat each other with trust and respect.
Dealers and suppliers are our partners The company must maintain mutually beneficial relationships with dealers, suppliers and our other business associates.

Grace Dearborn

Company vision
Grace Dearborn is committed to its customers and their short and long term identified needs, in a flexible and responsive manner.

We recognise that we are in partnership with our customers and seek to earn their total trust and confidence as a primary means of meeting mutually agreed objectives. In so doing, we aim to become, and remain, the most desirable (first choice) supplier in our fields of business.

Company mission
To market on-going specialist/consultancy services involving the use of performance chemical aids and supporting equipment to assist customers in selected fields to solve quality, manufacturing, efficiency and maintenance problems.

Costs of failures

Senior executives should have an indication of the cost to their organization of non-conforming products, processes and services.

What questions to ask

As a final point senior managers should be sufficiently knowledgeable about TQM to know what type of questions on quality improvement to ask their people and to understand the quality improvement mechanisms. They should also be able to query results and the process by which they were obtained.

What senior executives need to do about TQM

The senior executives need to decide on the actions to take to ensure that product and service quality becomes the number one priority for the organization. Leadership and participation from the CEO and senior managers are necessary prerequisites to launching a process of continuous improvement.

Time and commitment to TQM

They need to allocate time and commitment to:

- communicate their views on TQM – executives should take every opportunity to talk and act in a manner consistent with the principles of TQM;
- decide how the company will approach the process of quality improvement;
- assess the improvements made;
- become personally involved in improvement activities; and
- become involved in competitive benchmarking as this will enable them to see, for example, what the superior-performing organizations have achieved and the discrepancies in their own organization's performance.

Executives should consider how they will demonstrate their commitment to TQM to people from all levels of the organization hierarchy. They need to visit every area of the organization to see what is happening in relation to TQM, ask about results and problems, give advice and create good practice through leadership. In relation to this last point they should take the lead in organizational housekeeping with the objective of seeing that the plant is a model of cleanliness and tidiness.

Of course there are considerable demands on senior managers' time and a vast number of projects and matters seeking their attention. However, to leave the launch pad TQM must take precedence over all other activities. The CEO should plan to devote at least one day a week to TQM activities. The experience of the superior-performing companies is that once the process is bedded in, the time devoted by the CEO to TQM may be reduced and he or she can focus on maintenance issues and the promotion of new themes.

Filter quality down

It is the responsibility of the CEO and other senior managers to ensure that everyone in the organization knows why it is adopting the concept of TQM and that they are aware of its potential in their area, department and/or process. The CEO's and senior management's commitment must filter down through all levels of the organizational hierarchy. It is important that all employees feel they can demonstrate initiative and have the responsibility to make changes in their own area of work. Consideration needs to be given to how this should be addressed.

Commit resources

The CEO and senior management need to commit resources to TQM: for example, release people for improvement activities and ensure that key decision-makers are made available to spend time on TQM issues. The CEO needs to delegate responsibility for product and service quality improvement. For this to be effective, however, the CEO must have a good understanding of TQM and the process of quality improvement. The CEO needs to develop an infrastructure to support the quality improvement activities structure in terms of:

- monitoring and reporting the results (there is nothing like success to convert cynics and counter indifference);

- providing a focus and the people to make it happen;
- developing improvement objectives and targets;
- involving people from non-manufacturing areas.

It is helpful to establish a TQM steering committee or quality council to oversee and manage the quality improvement process. The typical role of such a group is to:

- agree plans and goals, and provide and manage resources;
- monitor progress;
- determine actions;
- create an environment conducive to quality improvement;
- facilitate teamwork;
- concur on issues of quality improvement; and
- ensure that firm foundations are laid down.

Long-term planning for quality improvement

From the vision and mission statements a long-term management plan needs to be drawn up setting out the direction of the company in terms of its development and management targets. This plan should be based on the corporate philosophy, sales forecast, current status, previous achievements against plan and improvement objectives. From it an annual policy should be compiled, and plans, policies, actions and improvement objectives established for each factory, division, department and section. Middle managers and first-line supervisors should, at the appropriate point, participate in the formulation of these plans, targets and improvement objectives. This ensures that the policies initiated by the CEO and senior management flow through the organizational hierarchy to enable employees in each function of the business to carry out their activities with the aim of achieving common goals and improvement targets; it is fundamental to the planning for quality improvement.

Policy deployment

The process of policy deployment ensures that the quality policies, targets and improvement objectives are aligned with the organization's business goals. The ideal situation in policy deployment is for the senior person at each level of the organizational hierarchy to make a presentation to his or her staff on the plan, targets and improvements. This ensures their penetration and communication on a step-by-step basis throughout the organization, with general objectives being converted into specific objectives and improvement targets. It is a primary communications vehicle.

As part of this policy deployment some organizations formulate, every year, a plan focusing on a different improvement theme. There must also be some form of audit at each level to check whether targets and improvement objectives are being achieved, and the progress being made with specific improvement projects. This commitment to quality and the targets and improvements made should be communicated to customers and suppliers. The respective reporting and control systems must be designed and operated in a manner that will ensure that all managers co-operate in continuous improvement activities.

Listening to the customer

The CEO must ensure that his or her organization listens to what its customers are saying and what they truly need. This is more easily said than done, but customer information is the starting point of the quality improvement effort. Executives must ensure that they do not disguise things: honesty is the byword in TQM. If they do resort to elaborate camouflage measures, the organization will be, in naval parlance, dead in the water. Every opportunity to join the customers' and suppliers' quality improvement processes must be taken; mutual quality improvement activities can strengthen existing partnerships and build good working relationships.

Senior managers must ensure that corrective action procedures and defect analysis are pursued vigorously and a closed-loop system operated to prevent repetition of mistakes.

Develop positive quantifiable measures of quality

It is important for the organization to have positive, quantifiable measures of product and service quality as seen by its customers. This enables it to keep an outward focus on the market in terms of customer needs and future expectations. Typical performance measures include:

- field failure statistics;
- reliability performance statistics;
- customer returns;
- customer complaints;
- 'things gone wrong' data;
- adverse customer quality communications.

Internal measures such as non-conformance levels, quality audit results, yield results and quality costs should also be developed.

A measurement system to monitor the progress of the quality improvement process is a key necessity; without it improvement will be more difficult. In the words of Scharp (President and CEO of A B Electrolux),[11] 'What gets measured gets done'; consequently people will focus on those actions necessary to achieve the targeted improvements. All the evidence from Japanese companies indicates that improvement targets act as key motivators.[12]

Keep key people informed

Senior managers should never overlook the fact that people will want to be informed on how the quality improvement process is progressing and its effect in the market place. There must be two-way communication, to provide feedback and encourage dialogue, between directors, managers and staff. Executives cannot communicate too often on TQM and quality improvement. Regular feedback through quality action days and key issues conferences needs to be provided for any concerns raised by employees. This will help to stimulate further involvement. These activities are a useful means for every employee to communicate with the CEO.

Learn about statistical methods

The CEO and members of the senior management team should be prepared to learn about statistical methods, use them in decision-making, and demonstrate an active interest and involvement in techniques such as SPC. This ensures that decisions are based on fact not opinion. For example, when passing through manufacturing, operational and office areas they should acquire the habit of inspecting the control charts on display and direct questions to the people responsible for charting and analysing the data. They can also learn, from the data on the charts, of any problem the operator is experiencing with the process. Control charts communicate to senior management the condition of the process – ignoring the message will only cause frustration among those involved with SPC and hinder the process of quality improvement. It should not be overlooked that SPC teaches people to ask questions about the process.

Diffuse information rapidly

Quality improvement can be facilitated by the rapid diffusion of information to all parts of the organization. A visible management system in which a variety of information is collected and displayed is a very useful means of aiding this diffusion. The CEO needs to consider seriously this form of transparent system.

Quality improvement is continuous

TQM is a continuous and never-ending process, and senior management must never become complacent about the progress the organization has made but must strive continually to achieve quality improvements in the product, service system, and associated processes. They need to adopt the philosophy that there is no ideal situation and always room for improvement. Areas of waste need to be identified and ruthlessly attacked.

Executive summary

The CEO and senior managers should become involved in TQM because:

- it is all about good management practices and, through knowledge of the subject and active involvement and leadership, can improve managerial skills and abilities;
- it is a strategic decision;
- the ultimate responsibility for product and service quality rests with the CEO;
- he or she is the main person who can bring about cultural change;
- it ensures credibility and longevity of the process;
- people are influenced by his or her actions.

The following are typical activities in which the CEO and senior managers should become involved:

- identify the major issues facing the organization and become personally involved in their resolution;
- set up and chair a TQM steering committee;
- quality planning, audit and improvement meetings and organizational housekeeping;

- carry out regular audits and diagnosis of the state of the art of TQM and quality improvement in the organization;
- deal with customer complaints and visit customers and suppliers;
- lead customer workshops and panels;
- regularly visit all business areas, units and divisions;
- communicate as never before.

The CEO and senior managers should understand that:

- TQM is a long-term strategy;
- there are no quick fixes;
- there is no one best way of starting a process of quality improvement;
- the concept of TQM depends on people;
- no single quality-management tool or technique is a cure-all;
- quality-management tools and techniques fulfil a number of roles;
- meeting the twenty clauses of the BS 5750/ISO 9000 quality system series is a minimum requirement.

The CEO and senior managers should:

- decide what action to take to ensure that TQM becomes the number one business priority;
- allocate time to understand the concept and principles of TQM;
- ensure that there are clear responsibilities for TQM and everybody in the organization knows the reasons for its adoption;
- devote at least one day a week to quality improvement activities;
- commit resources to TQM and establish an improvement infrastructure;
- develop a company vision and mission statement and put in place a process of policy deployment;
- set up a TQM steering committee;
- aim to create a continuous improvement environment which permeates all departments;
- ensure that the organization listens to all the views of all its customers;
- identify key performance measures;
- use statistical methods in decision-making;
- promote and encourage cross-functional management to break through the barriers of sectionalism.

Notes

1 McKinsey and Company (1989) *Management of Quality: The Single Major Important Challenge for Europe*, European Quality Management Forum, 19 October, Montreux, Switzerland.
2 Lascelles, D. M. and Dale, B. G. (1990) 'Quality management: the chief

executive's perception and role', *European Management Journal*, vol. 8, no. 1, pp. 67–75.

3 Crosby, P. B. (1979) *Quality Is Free*, McGraw-Hill, New York.

4 Deming, W. E. (1982) *Quality, Productivity and Competitive Position*, MIT Press, Cambridge, Massachusetts.

5 Feigenbaum, A. V. (1983) *Total Quality Control*, McGraw-Hill, New York.

6 Juran, J. M. (1988) *Quality Control Handbook*, McGraw-Hill, New York.

7 BS 5750 (1987) *Quality Systems*, British Standards Institution, London.

8 Ford Motor Company (1990) *Worldwide Quality System Standard Q-101*, Ford, Plymouth, Michigan.

9 Lascelles, D. M. and Dale, B. G. (1990) 'The use of quality management techniques', *Quality Forum*, vol. 16, no. 4, pp. 188–92.

10 Ishikawa, K. (1976) *Guide to Quality Control*, Asian Productivity Organization, Tokyo.

11 Scharp, A. (1989) *What Gets Measured Gets Done: The Electrolux Way to Improve Quality*, European Quality Management Forum, 19 October, Montreux, Switzerland.

12 Dale, B. G. (1990) 'Japanese manufacturing efficiency: a study in the electronics industry', *IEE Proceedings*, vol. 137A, no. 5, pp. 293–501.

4

Total Quality Management: Some Common Failings of Senior Management

Introduction

As discussed in chapter 3, it is the responsibility of the CEO and senior management to create the right organizational environment, atmosphere, values, behaviour and culture in which TQM can achieve its potential. This requires changing, through a deliberate, structured and systematic process, the behaviour and attitudes of people at all levels in the organization hierarchy: those who because of the organization culture, tradition, lack of TQM education and training and/or neglect have, in manufacturing industry, regarded product quality as a means of sorting the conforming from non-conforming product and reworking product to prevent non-conforming goods being passed to customers and, in service situations, have adopted a take it or leave it attitude to the consumer.

It is not an easy task to create an organizational culture in which each person in every department is fully committed to improving his or her own performance and is dedicated to satisfying internal customers' needs and future expectations. Implementing quality-management techniques, such as SPC, is much easier. In the final analysis, it is all down to persuasion. Such a change in culture takes many years and requires executives to take a long-term view. On the TQM road it is easy, especially when under pressure, to slip back into the traditional, firefighting way of doing things; many people are more comfortable firefighting than planning and leading improvement activities. There is also the tendency for people to question why the organization is adopting TQM. So it is not surprising that organizations do encounter a wide range of obstacles in pursuing a process of continuous and company-wide quality improvement. In our experience the road blocks often emanate from the CEO and senior and middle management.

This chapter outlines some of the common mistakes CEOs and senior managers make in relation to TQM, and examines the reasons for the apparent lack of TQM commitment, awareness and vision that exists in some organizations. Were executives to do all the things outlined in chapter 3, they would not fall into the traps which are now to be discussed.

Time

TQM – an afterthought

In some organizations the CEO and other key decision-makers are not prepared to devote the time to learn about TQM and take personal leadership. The impression they give is that TQM is not as pressing a priority as financial affairs, marketing and production/technical issues; it tends to be treated as an afterthought. Too little time is given to improvement activities; a typical estimate is less than 5 per cent of each working week. Executives should analyse their weekly activities under the broad categories:

- housekeeping (e.g. reading reports);
- travel;
- firefighting;

- control (e.g. dealing with programme changes, organizational restructuring and the introduction of new products and technology); and
- improvement.

The findings of such an analysis would be most revealing.

TQM is the prime responsibility of the CEO and senior managers and they need to become totally immersed in it; without this total commitment nothing will happen. They often claim that they simply do not have the time. The attitude of those CEOs who have emerged as true quality leaders is that you create time simply by doing every task in a quality manner. Xerox and Milliken won the 1989 Malcolm Baldrige National Quality Award (established in 1987 to recognize the achievements of American companies that make significant improvement to their products and services) for doing just this. The seven main criteria assessed for the Award and on which the winners were selected are:

- leadership;
- information and analysis;
- strategic quality planning;
- human resource development and management;
- management of process quality;
- quality and operational results; and
- focus and satisfaction.

The CEO and Chief Operating Officer at Milliken devote more than half their time to the company's pursuit of excellence process. [1]

Do as I say not as I do

Some CEOs brief their senior staff that the organization is embarking on TQM. These staff are then delegated responsibilities in relation to TQM and told to get on with their allocated tasks, and not to involve the CEO, who will be busy dealing with some financial, marketing, new technology, etc., project. They are, however, told to report back from time to time on the progress made.

The CEO tends to assume that delegated tasks are being carried out in the manner ascribed. This is often not the case. Those to whom the tasks have been delegated have their own day-to-day job responsibilities and it is frequently found that insufficient attention is given to the task. They may misinterpret what the CEO expects of them or the given tasks may conflict with their own beliefs and/or self-interests. On either count, the tasks are sometimes not accomplished as envisaged, and the most unfortunate thing is that some CEOs are never aware of the true situation.

The CEO operating in this passive way is verbally supporting TQM, but neatly sidestepping the issue; quality improvement is seen as something for others. He or she is falling into the trap of 'do as I say not as I do'.

Take others along with you

On the other hand, there is a tendency for the CEO and senior managers who have spent some considerable time assimilating and distilling the received TQM wisdom, developing their personal knowledge of the subject and plotting the organization's course for TQM, to fail to allow sufficient time for other people in the organization to develop the same level of understanding. These senior managers then become frustrated, and cannot understand why staff are not acting in the manner expected of them. This patchy understanding of TQM can in turn tempt the CEO to criticize managers and departments who are perceived not to be making sufficient progress. This should be avoided at all costs as it tends to isolate individuals and functions.

Don't send a substitute

It is a common complaint among middle management that the CEO and members of the senior management team often opt out of TQM training courses and elect a substitute to attend in their place or else they attend the course for only a short time. Any executive who has done this should be aware that the signal being received is that quality is not such a demanding priority.

Before a one-day TQM appreciation course held by UMIST for the board of a blue chip company, the CEO had told his secretary to interrupt the course after an hour and a half with a bogus urgent matter that would occupy him for the remainder of the day. In this way, he had shown some commitment to the TQM training, but matters outside his control had prevented him taking the complete course. However, the first 90 minutes of the course convinced him that it was important to learn more about the subject.

The Ford Motor Company has established, in the UK, three external centres which they approve and support for training suppliers in total quality excellence (TQE) and SPC. The three-day SPC course offered by the centres was designed for members of senior management teams. However, in 1985 all three regional centres reported to Ford that an insufficient number of senior executives were attending this course. UMIST has now held over 120 'open' courses and on-site courses for individual organizations, and company directors comprise less than 5 per cent of the course delegates. Consequently, a one-day TQE and SPC appreciation course was developed to ensure that CEOs and senior management are aware of the 'what and how' of SPC and the need for a strategic plan of implementation within their plants.

In recent times a number of TQM conferences have been held, but have attracted more middle managers than board members. Only those specifically aimed at CEOs and directors lead them to attend. This is unfortunate because they have so much to learn by mingling with quality management specialists and hearing, at first hand, some of their frustrations in trying to pursue a process of quality improvement without sufficient support from company executives.

Resources

Quality improvement activities

In some cases there is a failure to commit the right level of managerial resources to TQM. To start and then develop a process of quality improvement, an infrastructure is required to support the associated tasks. Departments and people need to be able to devote time to quality planning, prevention and improvement activities.

The CEO and other senior managers should understand that day-to-day control and assurance of quality should be separated from improvement and TQM promotion activities. If this is not done, people will naturally focus their efforts on the daily short-term activities and devote little time to longer-term planning and improvements. It is a fact of business life that people will give more priority to the day-to-day activities for which they are accountable. These tasks are more easily recognized and rewarded than are those related to improvement, especially those involving some form of teamwork. People need to be encouraged to take part in improvement activities, and to do this they must be released from their day-to-day routines. A full-time quality co-ordinator and/or facilitator(s) relieved of day-to-day work pressures can help to integrate individual improvement activities under a common umbrella.

Training in quality

The CEO should also be prepared to invest in people through a continuous process of education and training in quality. Too many CEOs and senior managers regard this as negative expenditure rather than investment. In a number of cases senior management have authorized the purchase of a TQM training package, often as a result of customer pressure, which then fails to be used to its full potential because of a lack of resources given to its application.

The ultimate aim is for everyone to take responsibility for the quality assurance of his or her processes and outputs, and the product and service quality offerings of the organization. This state of affairs is not a natural phenomenon and does not happen overnight, and the CEO and senior managers must be prepared to spend time coaxing people along this path. Once the CEO is seen leading the TQM initiative, and respect has been earned, quality leaders will emerge from all parts of the organization.

Road blocks

'Getting things done' is a frequent cause of complaint among those committed to pursuing improvement activities. This complaint appears more with established products and services to which improvements are sought than with products, processes and services that are being planned.

A frequent sticking point in the improvement activity is gaining the involvement of manufacturing engineers, production preparation staff, technical specialists, designers, and the like. Even when simple mistake-proofing devices are pointed out to them, for example, they often claim not to have the time to construct the device and put it in place. In addition, technical specialists and management often fail to recognize and employ some of the simple quality-control techniques. The use of quality-planning techniques such as FMEA is another area where many are not prepared to commit resources, because it encroaches on the time available for carrying out their day-to-day activities. Surprisingly, it is not that they remain unconvinced of the value of such techniques; rather, it is the perceived time taken to use them. Considerable selling activity is needed to progress on these fronts.

The CEO is often not aware of such road blocks and this can act as a serious impediment to the process of quality improvement. The protagonists of these types of improvement have to resort to making presentations to the CEO and senior management team to convince them of the value of advanced quality-planning techniques. This should not have to be the case.

Lack of resources to quality follow-up

Another common problem caused by a lack of resources committed to improvement is insufficient attention and detail given to removing basic causes of errors. People do what is necessary to prevent non-conforming product and services reaching the customer, but do not then devote any effort to long-term corrective action and developing systematic recurrence-prevention measures; thus the chronic problems persist and increase. A related difficulty caused by a lack of an improvement infra-structure, and a failure to manage the improvement activities, is that solving one problem tends to generate several others outside the scope of the original project.

These types of problems would not occur if executives understood the resources required in TQM and involved themselves in improvement and diagnosis activities and in auditing progress made.

Another problem can stem from the cost-cutting or streamlining measures most organizations introduce from time to time. Senior managers need to take care in communicating and implementing these measures; otherwise they are likely to have a negative impact on the process of quality improvement.

The quality crisis currently faced by some European organizations stems from a lack of resources in terms of the calibre of individuals who, in the past, have been appointed to the role of quality manager. This shortage of qualified people is due partly to the relatively low status accorded to the position in the past.

Teamwork is not practised

Today's problems get priority

The CEO and senior management should work as a team to develop improvement objectives and plans, and identify the means by which they can measure organizational improvement. They are responsible for pinpointing opportunities, prioritizing projects and steering the improvement efforts. In some organizations managers seem obsessed with 'events of the moment' and 'today's problems' such as reorganization and technical or marketing innovation – at the expense of the systematic improvement process and teamwork. The CEO and senior managers meet from time to time, but rarely function as a team to identify and consider strategies that will lead to organizational improvement. In extreme cases CEOs play senior managers off against one another, with each senior manager in turn attempting to gain the CEOs attention for his or her particular plan, policy or project.

The purpose of teams

Teamwork is an essential element of TQM, providing an opportunity for co-operative action in pursuit of quality improvement; however, Western organizations do not excel at it. The CEO and senior managers need to give more thought to facilitating teamwork within the organization and recognizing the achievements of effective team members. Teams are a way of involving everyone in quality improvement initiatives. They:

- aid commitment;
- provide an additional means of communicating between individuals and across functions;
- provide a better understanding of processes;
- provide the means for people to participate in the business;
- improve relationships and develop trust;
- aid personal development;
- facilitate awareness, leading to behaviour and attitude change; and
- help to change management style.

For example, Xerox Business Products and Systems (one of two 1989 Malcolm Baldrige Award winners) estimates that 75 per cent of its workers are members of at least one or more of 7,000 quality improvement teams.[1]

There are a variety of teamwork approaches to teambuilding, some of which are discussed in chapter 7.

Fears of middle managers

Middle management may fear that they will be bypassed as a result of quality improvement activities. A number of middle managers shine as trouble shooters (this is how they have achieved promotion), and know nothing else; if there is no firefighting they feel unnecessary and naturally fear for their jobs.

Some CEOs are not good at selecting colleagues who will be good team players in TQM and quality improvement, and one of the 'old guard' as part of the team will have a considerable negative influence on TQM. In a number of cases this has been recognized too late, and the middle or senior manager has had to be moved to a position or site where he or she can do least damage.

Training

The ability of the Japanese to manage the process of quality improvement more successfully and at a faster rate than appears currently possible in European manufacturing, commerce, public sector and service organizations is a key issue in their success story. One of the major factors appears to be the depth of knowledge and training in quality skills, techniques and problem-solving possessed by the Japanese management and supervisory structure. Further details of this are given in chapter 9. Western organizations often do not invest sufficiently in TQM education and training, and in developing their problem analysis skills and expertise.

Quality training should be mandatory

It is important that organizations invest not only in technology and systems but also in their people's education and abilities; *TQM requires new skills*. An increasing number of organizations now provide each of their employees with a basic understanding of business, finance and where they, as an individual, fit into the organization. In this way they are aware of what they can do to improve matters. Regular training is required to reinforce the message in such a way that the improvement concept becomes an integral part of people's day-to-day work and not an additional task. An indication of some organizations' depth of commitment to TQM is that quality-related training courses are mandatory for all employees. Others specify the number of hours' training each employee should receive each year and allow employees to choose the training they need; the effectiveness of the use of training and the results achieved should then be assessed by a formal mechanism.

There is a tendency for senior managers to look for and expect massive benefits arising from the implementation of quality systems and procedures, and quality-management tools and techniques. Any such benefits will be only short lived without major changes in people's behaviour, attitudes and values. A company-wide education and training programme needs to be planned and undertaken to facilitate the right type of changes. The aim of this programme should be to promote a common TQM language, awareness and understanding of concepts and principles, ensure that there are no knowledge gaps at any level in the organizational hierarchy and provide the skills to assist people with improvement activities; this should include team leadership, counselling and coaching skills. A planned programme of training is required to provide employees with quality-management tools and techniques on a timely basis. Many organizations find a good deal of variation in relation to understanding what the process of quality improvement actually involves.

The CEO and directors need to be involved in leading some quality-related training, using a cascade-type approach. Unfortunately, more often than not they do not.

Failures of conventional training for TQM

It is worth considering the points made by Payne and Dale[2] in relation to the disadvantages of conventional training courses. The CEO and senior managers should be – but are often not – aware of the following points:

- Chief Executives, whose actions determine whether or not a company has a corporate culture where quality comes first, rarely attend such [i.e. TQM] courses, in particular 'open' courses.
- The training department, in conjunction with departmental managers, identify individual training needs and delegates are directed to attend a course. This often produces a negative reaction from delegates when they return to work after attending a course, with complaints such as 'a mountain of paperwork', 'the number of queries which require resolving', 'all these telephone calls to return and letters to answer', etc.
- When courses are run in-plant they are often of a 'one-off' nature, with minimum follow-up instruction and advice.
- The typical approach adopted in courses is to first teach principles, techniques and systems, followed by their application through general examples and problems. The courses by their very nature and experiences of the lecturer(s) involved, cannot deal with specifics relating to the delegates' individual needs.
- Prior to taking the course, it is not easy for delegates to assess the expertise of the course leader.
- The people giving the courses are sometimes limited in their know-

ledge of the application of these principles, techniques and systems to industrial problems, and are short of suitable material to use as training examples.

- The delegates are likely to experience a problem of transferring the new knowledge gained whilst on the course and effectively applying it in their own working environment. The course has only changed the behaviour and attitudes of individuals; delegates on their return to their company have to motivate and change the behaviour, attitudes and direction of both their peers and senior management, and it is not uncommon for them to experience resistance from their respective company cultures.

- There is little attempt to integrate the knowledge imparted on the course with controlled projects carried out in the trainees' organisation.

- The problem associated with influencing other people's behaviour and attitudes in conjunction with day-to-day work pressures, results in a lack of practice in applying the new knowledge. This causes a rapid decline in the individual's motivation and in the meantime the course notes have been filed and forgotten.

Just-in-time training

Training is often carried out in a vacuum, little thought being given to how it can assist the process of quality improvement. There is little point in training without clearly specified improvement objectives. The training which is undertaken is often wasted, with no follow-up projects pursued by the trainees and/or people being trained too far in advance of the introduction of particular quality initiatives and techniques; to coin a term, the training should be carried out 'just in time'. Organizations not considering such issues fail to get value for money from their investment in training.

Understanding

The lack of time devoted to learning about TQM means that many CEOs and directors have insufficient understanding of the philosophy and logic underlying TQM and the associated techniques, systems and procedures. These have long been well known, and are very clearly outlined by internationally recognized quality experts such as Crosby,[3] Deming,[4] Feigenbaum[5] and Juran.[6] The main problem is communicating the concepts so that executives understand them. Claiming not to understand is usually the excuse for doing nothing; and doing nothing is easy.

In Europe, at least, this knowledge gap is attenuated by the lack of TQM education at undergraduate and postgraduate level in universities, business schools and polytechnics (see van der Wiele et al.).[7] Among the objectives of the European Foundation For Quality Management (EFQM)[8] are:

Business Schools and Universities are encouraged to develop, implement and up-grade Quality Management education programmes.

EFQM has an objective to intensify Western European research programmes directed at strengthening Quality Management capabilities, programmes and achievements.

The majority of CEOs and senior managers have had little or no exposure in their formal education and professional training to the concept and philosophy underlying TQM and quality improvement. Consequently, many have under-developed quality instincts and beliefs.

Lack of understanding leads to problems

This lack of understanding manifests itself in a number of ways.

1 A lack of TQM organizational vision, mission and guiding principles. This results in a lack of harmony among functions, people and improvement activities, and there are no clear focus, priorities and planning. It also leads to failure to develop a work environment in which everyone is an active participant. People do not have a common understanding and values regarding product and service quality, often because it is insufficiently defined; thus people have different expectations and work to different standards and requirements – in short, there is a lack of cohesion.

2 The CEO and board are not sure of what is required of them in terms of their responsibilities for TQM and company-wide continuous quality improvement, which activities they need to be involved in and how they can help. They often spend time discussing quality-related problems, but frequently do not have the skills to solve such problems on their own.

3 Worries about giving employees more involvement in the business and greater powers of decision-making: executives frequently fail to recognize the detailed know-how and enthusiasm which exist at shop-floor level. Trust and mutual respect are not widespread in Western organizations.

4 CEOs are sometimes shy about exchanging information and ideas with their staff. *TQM demands that there are no secrets.*

5 There is a failure to understand the role each function in the organization has to play in TQM. This frequently leads to a lack of co-operation and collaboration in identifying and solving problems, and ensuring that prevention activities are practised. It also manifests itself in the attitude that it is always someone else's problem. Quality improvement is then restricted to a few individual departments; it is not company-wide.

6 No milestones, checkpoints, phases of activity, key result indicators, criteria and plans are established by the CEO and senior management. So, people within the organization are unsure of what progress has been made and the next steps.

7 TQM is viewed just as a paperwork requirement to satisfy the demands of major customers. It is not uncommon to find quality managers and technical specialists resorting to a number of ruses to convince customers that the organization is serious about TQM, and to show the CEO that they are managing product and service quality effectively. The CEO and other senior managers are often unaware of the measures being used and the state of TQM and quality improvement in the organization.

8 The concept of TQM conflicts with the education and professional training many executives have received and also with their fundamental experience, beliefs, management style and company culture: they do not consider it to be the right way.

9 Some CEOs argue that their organization's particular sphere of operation is different and therefore some particular aspect of the total quality approach is unsuitable and will not work.

10 Too many CEOs isolate themselves in their offices and fail to visit the areas producing the product/service, and have little empathy with what is going on in the plant. This is the case in large organizations, where there are always a certain remoteness and anonymity of management.

11 The CEO is always looking for the next fad: he or she is unaware or remains unconvinced of the competitive edge TQM can provide.

12 The CEO thinks that the principles of TQM can be put in place very easily and becomes frustrated about the lack of progress. Often the full implications of TQM are not appreciated. The difficulties encountered in doing the simple thing well and consistently, the diagnostics required to reach the root cause of problems, the role model, etc. are completely underestimated.

13 Staff are not encouraged to identify factors which prevent them from turning in an error-free performance. Everyone should be encouraged to identify and correct problems that affect product and service quality. Employees' opinions must be sought and carefully listened to. Listening is a key aspect for broad participation in the improvement process.

14 Some CEOs encourage effective systems to manage the rework and scrap; this is not important – the management of continuous improvement *is*.

15 There is a failure to recognize and reward the efforts of individuals and

teams; a process of recognition and celebration acts as a key motivator. This also applies to the communication of successes – reporting real business results tends to boost employees' morale.

16 Insufficient attention is given to the key role of line personnel in the process of quality improvement.

Mistaken beliefs

Some CEOs and senior managers have picked up the wrong signals and are failing to follow the fundamental principles involved in quality improvement. This problem is related to the difficulties caused by the lack of understanding discussed above.

Quality improvement is not *my* responsibility

Quality improvement is seen to be the responsibility and province of the quality manager and his or her department; and TQM as a function of production and operations, to be used only by operating personnel in a manufacturing environment. There is some concern and a lack of knowledge about how to approach and facilitate quality improvement in non-manufacturing areas.

Senior managers believe that the answer to all their quality problems lies in the implementation of a particular quality-management technique, and that *they* need no formal training in the quality skills and techniques required to develop an effective quality improvement strategy.

Quality by response

There is a tendency to respond solely to meet the requirements of customers in terms of quality system standards, and use quality-management techniques such as SPC and FMEA because they are a contractual requirement. Many organizations never achieve much more than this and consequently become stuck at first base. The approach to be recommended is that followed by the CEO of an electronics manufacturing organization: 'Forget the Ford Motor Company and General Motors; we need SPC for our own corporate well-being.'

This will solve it

The CEO and managers frequently expect too much from the introduction and use of a single quality-management tool or technique, quality system or procedure, etc. Consequently, following a short period of usage they tend to believe that such and such technique is not working, and look for the next one (see figure 4.1). The benefits from the use of such techniques, systems and procedures are cumulative; the effect of a single tool or technique should not be viewed in isolation (see figure 4.2).

Operatives' responsibility

Some CEOs still hold the view that organization quality ills can be cured just by changing the operators' behaviour and attitudes to product and service quality. They tend to look for quality-improving changes at the

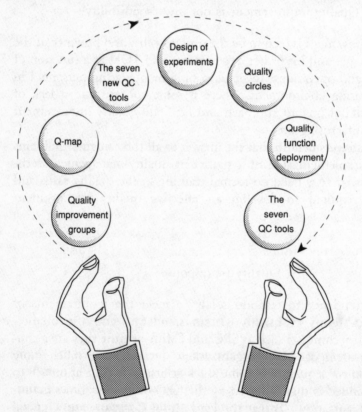

Figure 4.1 The use of quality-management tools and techniques

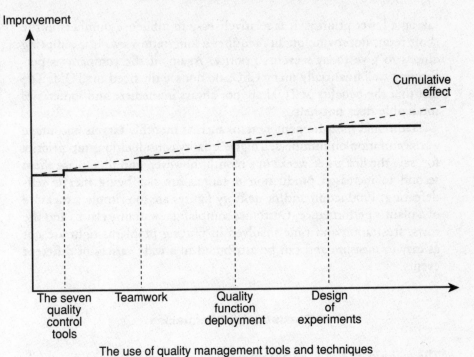

The use of quality management tools and techniques

Figure 4.2 Incremental improvement through the use of quality-management tools and techniques

bottom of the organization rather than at middle and senior management level. The CEO and senior managers should be aware that the degrees of freedom for change are considerably greater at the top of the hierarchy.

The belief that quality problems are caused by people, and that different forms of advanced technology will eradicate the problem, is common. The simple things (e.g. housekeeping) and the influence of people are undervalued.

Output and cost are the main priorities

The CEO and senior management are frequently assessed by shareholders, financial institutions and the main board in terms of numbers: profit, cost, headcount, sales turnover, production levels, stock turnover, etc. This results in their placing considerable emphasis on meeting production, output and cost targets, with product and service quality taking a lower priority. It is relatively easy to influence numbers in the short term; improving quality requires a long-term view. It is tempting always to give today's events priority. Again, if the company is performing well financially many CEOs do not see the need for TQM. The fact that the benefits of TQM are not always immediate and sometimes intangible does not help.

Traditional measurement systems such as monthly targets encourage a concentration on numbers. To give quality considerations top priority for, say, the first three weeks in a month, however, and then place them second to increased production if targets are not being met is self-defeating. Production and/or delivery figures are too simple a measure of a plant's performance. Customer complaints, warranty claims and the costs, frustration and time involved in putting problems right are not as easy to measure and can be attributed to a wide variety of different events.

Statistical inadequacies

The majority of CEOs do not understand process variation and capability. They frequently have concerns about their lack of knowledge of statistical methods and, for fear of exposing their own inadequacies, avoid using statistical techniques in their decision-making. They should be sufficiently knowledgeable about the concepts of variability and statistical thinking to enable them to ask sensible questions about the processes and extract useful answers. The uses and limitations of statistical models should be understood and executives need to be able to interpret statistical analysis.

Appendices B, C and D provide an overview of some of the more popular statistical techniques used in quality improvement.

Conclusion

In the face of all the underlying evidence of TQM's importance in distinguishing an organization from its competitors and the obvious effect on its corporate health and survival, the key question is: why do some CEOs and senior managers fail to be sufficiently committed and dedicated to TQM?

Chapters 5 and 6 address this question.

Executive summary

The main mistakes CEOs and senior managers make in relation to TQM are:

- failing to commit sufficient time to learn about TQM and become personally involved in planning for its introduction and development;
- not allowing sufficient time for people to develop their understanding of the concept and its underlying principles;
- underestimating the resources needed to start and develop a process of quality improvement and setting up the required infrastructure;
- teamwork is not practised and fully understood;
- committing insufficient resources to TQM education and training;
- insufficient understanding of the philosophy and logic underlying TQM and its associated tools, techniques, systems and procedures;
- failing to follow consistently the fundamental principles involved in a process of continuous quality improvement;
- treating output and cost targets as the main business priorities;
- lack of use of statistical methods and understanding of process variation and capability

Notes

1 Feature article (1989) 'Xerox and Milliken get Baldridge Award', *Business America*, vol. 110, no. 23, pp. 2–11.
2 Payne, B. J. and Dale, B. G. (1990) 'Total quality management training: some observations', *Quality Assurance*, vol. 16, no. 1, pp. 5–9.
3 Crosby, P. B. (1979) *Quality Is Free*, McGraw-Hill, New York.
4 Deming, W. E. (1982) *Quality, Productivity and Competitive Position*, MIT Press, Cambridge, Massachusetts.
5 Feigenbaum, A. V. (1983) *Total Quality Control*, McGraw-Hill, New York.
6 Juran, J. M. (1988) *Quality Control Handbook*, McGraw-Hill, New York.
7 Van der Wiele, T., Snoep, P., Bertsch, B., Timmers, J., Williams, R. and Dale, B. G. (1990) 'Total quality management training and research in Europe: A state-of-the-art survey', *Proceedings of the First European Conference on Education, Training and Research in Total Quality Management*, IFS (Publications), pp. 3–20.
8 European Foundation for Quality Management (1989) *Introduction to EFQM*, Eindhoven, The Netherlands.

The material cited in note 2 has been used in preparation of this chapter.

5

Motivating Managers to Accept and Promote Total Quality Management

Motivation Theories

Effort, Performance and Outcomes

Executive Summary

If senior and middle management can appreciate and understand the various theories and methods of motivation, and then internalize these theories and their implications for practice, it will assist them to create an organizational environment which is conducive to TQM. This chapter explores three different types of theories of motivation and their implications for managers and organizations. For a more detailed assessment of these theories see Robertson and Cooper,[1] upon which some of the material is based.

Motivation theories

Problems and issues concerning motivation are frequently of central importance in organizational life. For example:

- Why do talented people who undertake a wide range of activities, some of which require considerable planning and intellect, outside working time 'leave their brains in the car park' when they enter their workplace?
- Why does someone with apparent ability to do a job well consistently fail to perform effectively?

- How can employees (in groups and as individuals) be encouraged to produce and deliver products and services which are free from defects?
- Why do people make apparently silly mistakes and sometimes repeat them?
- Is there any truth in the claim made by some supervisors and managers that some of their staff are incapable of receiving and responding to training?
- Why do some employees respond to any new initiative by saying that they have heard it all before?
- Why do managers treat workers as just a pair of hands?
- How can product and service quality be emphasized in a way that motivates adherence to the concept and principles of TQM at all levels and functions of the organizational hierarchy?
- How do you convert the cynics and sceptics?
- How can continuous and company-wide quality improvement be facilitated?

It must always be remembered that few employees do anything but their best; nobody sets out deliberately to do a bad job and make mistakes; no one likes to be blamed for poor performance, in particular, when the cause is outside their area of control: individuals are, however, often defeated by the system. It is a management responsibility to create the most efficient working environment, and provide the means and mechanisms to enable operators to perform to the best of their ability. The points made by Deming[2] and Juran[3] that at least 85 per cent of quality problems are as a result of the system should be noted here. Who is responsible for the system? – management.

Although many issues of the type listed above frequently have an individual motivational basis, it must be remembered that other factors, such as inadequate training, job experience, personality characteristics, unsuitable organizational structure and culture, inadequate supervision, poor working environment, and bad previous experience of management behaviour, may also be involved – these are also the result of the system. Thus, while motivation is unquestionably an important topic, many other factors are involved in successful performance, and managers must resist the notion that all performance problems can be understood and resolved by addressing motivational issues. Just as attempts to understand human personality emphasize both internal and external factors, explorations of motivation also recognize a distinction between them. One method of explaining people's motivation to behave in certain ways is to propose the existence of certain internal, motivational states of drive or need.

Some theories of motivation focus on the 'content' of motivation and attempt to uncover needs such as hunger, security, affiliation, self-esteem, which underlie and control behaviour. Others focus on the 'processes' by which goals or needs exert their influence. Examples of both are now discussed.

Hierarchy of human needs

One of the most influential content theories of motivation is the need hierarchy formulated by Abraham Maslow.[4] He identified five distinct need categories:

1 physiological needs;
2 safety and security needs;
3 belongingness and love needs;
4 self-esteem needs;
5 the need to self-actualize.

Furthermore, he proposed that these needs are organized into a hierarchy (see figure 5.1); needs higher up the hierarchy emerge to play a prominent role in the control of behaviour only when needs lower down the hierarchy are satisfied. Thus, someone who is hungry (a physiological need) will take risks and ignore safety needs to obtain food. Someone who is tired will lose concentration and make mistakes. In the work context, safety needs such as job security, safe and attractive working conditions, etc., need to be satisfied before turning to the development of friendships and good relationships with others,

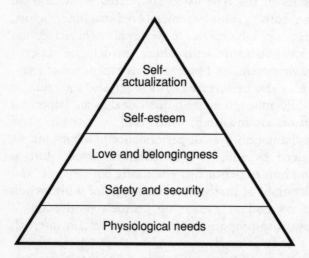

Figure 5.1 Maslow's need hierarchy (needs lower down the pyramid must be at least partly met before higher needs become important)
Source: Maslow, A. H. (1954) *Motivation and Personality*, Harper, New York.

including teamwork. The highest level in the hierarchy, self actualization, concerns the needs for self-fulfilment and the achievement of one's full potential. What Maslow attempts to emphasize with his need hierarchy is the positive side of human nature, by stressing that despite the requirement for the satisfaction of lower-level needs, humans will, whenever possible, strive to achieve their potential and attain the satisfaction to be derived from using one's personal abilities and attributes to the full.

Some possible implications of the need hierarchy for organizations are fairly clear, which may be one of the reasons Maslow's theory has been so popular with management. First, the incentives or goals that will motivate employees will depend on their current level of need satisfaction. Second, it is probably in the best interests of the organization to attempt to arrange working conditions and tasks so that lower-level needs are met, basic frustrations are removed and employees are motivated by their own needs for self-actualization. Deming[5] also makes the point about the need to remove barriers that prevent people from doing a good job.

Motivation and work

Attempts to explain motivation in terms of human needs can be of value in organizational contexts only if the job factors involved in the satisfaction of such needs can be identified. Frederic Herzberg's[6] 'two-factor theory' represents an attempt to examine the role of various job factors and how they relate to needs. His theory is based, to a large extent, on investigations of the factors in jobs that give rise to satisfaction or dissatisfaction. In an early study[7] of a fairly small sample of engineers and accountants in the Pittsburgh area of the United States, employees were asked to describe incidents in their jobs which made them feel particularly good (satisfied) or bad (dissatisfied) about them. This study, and later similar studies[8] indicated those factors that were related to good feelings about the job (such as achievement, recognition, the work itself, responsibility), and those related to bad feelings (such as company policy and administration, working conditions, supervision). These data led Herzberg to his two-factor theory, which proposes that two different types of factors contribute to satisfaction and dissatisfaction at work: motivators, associated with good feelings about the job, are mostly derived from the job itself; hygiene factors are mostly external to the job and involve aspects of the physical or psychological environment. Some of the most important implications of

y concern ideas about how satisfaction and motivation
by restructuring or enriching jobs, so that they provide
ding experiences. Examples include increasing the
rs, job rotation, giving 'ownership' of the process to
onal personnel, and providing the opportunity to be involved in
selecting new machinery.

The core of Herzberg's proposal is that it will not be possible to motivate people by improving hygiene factors alone. Improvements in, say,
working conditions may decrease dissatisfaction but will not improve
motivation. True motivation, according to Herzberg, derives from
factors associated with the job itself and relies on offering opportunities
for achievement, recognition, involvement, responsibility, empowerment, etc. These features have been referred to in earlier chapters.

Job characteristics model of motivation

More recently, Hackman and Oldham[9] have proposed a 'job characteristics model' that identifies five core job characteristics involved in job
satisfaction and motivation (see figure 5.2): skill variety, task identity,
task significance, autonomy and feedback. According to the model, satisfaction and motivation are controlled by the critical psychological
states: meaningfulness of the work, responsibility for the outcomes of
work and knowledge of the results of work.

Managers should note, in particular, this latter point with respect to
response, feedback and communication of the results and progress of
quality-improvement initiatives and actions, and celebration of achievements. As already mentioned in earlier chapters, communication is a
key component of TQM. Management cannot communicate too much
about TQM, and should use all the means at their disposal; this is
especially the case in a multi-locational environment.

The critical psychological states are linked to the core job dimensions.
Skill variety or multi-skilling is concerned with the extent to which the
activities of the job call for a selection of abilities and skills. Task identity and significance concern the extent to which the activities of the job
form an identifiable whole, and to which the job has an impact on the
lives or work of other people. Autonomy relates to the freedom and
independence the job-holder has, and feedback to the extent to which
knowledge of results concerning individual effectiveness is provided. For
example:

- Learning and practising problem-solving skills used in quality-improvement

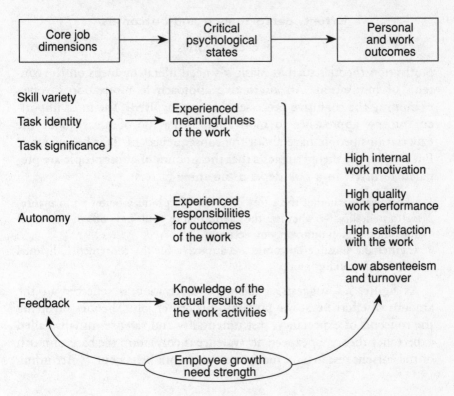

Figure 5.2 The job characteristic model
Source: Hackman, J. R. and Oldham, G. R. (1976) 'Motivation through the design of work: test of a theory', *Organizational Behaviour and Human Performance*, Academic Press, Florida.

projects, either individually and/or through teamwork, the use of quality-management tools and techniques, and ownership of the process help to enhance these three core job dimensions.

- Statistical process control (SPC) gives control over processes to the process owner.
- The audit and management review in the BS 5750/ISO 9000 series of standards[10] should give control over the working procedures in a formalized way to the process owner.
- These two preceding aspects give a degree of empowerment, communication and feedback.

Hackman and Oldham have also produced the job diagnostic survey[11] which provides measures of the job dimensions and other variables involved in the model.

Effort, performance and outcomes

Process theories

Motivation theories such as Maslow's need hierarchy focus on the contents of motivation. An alternative approach to motivation involves examining the cognitive processes that are involved. The most important process approaches to motivation make use of ideas about the expectations people have about the consequences of their behaviour.[12] Put simply, the theory suggests that the amount of effort people are prepared to invest in a task depends on three factors:

1 expectancy – whether the effort involved will produce better performance;
2 instrumentality – whether the performance will pay off in terms of outcomes, e.g. promotion, job security;
3 whether the possible outcomes are attractive for the concerned individual and/or the working group.

As figure 5.3 suggests, a person's motivation is reflected in the amount of effort he or she puts into his or her job. Theories involving the concepts of expectancy, instrumentality and valence (usually called expectancy theory, or expectancy/valence theory) form the basis of much of the current research on motivation and work behaviour.[13] According

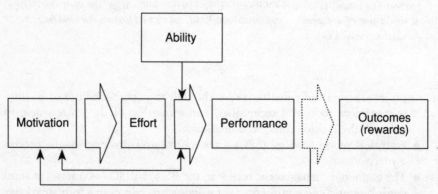

Figure 5.3 The basic motivation–behaviour sequence according to expectancy theory. A person's motivator is a function of: (a) effort-to-performance expectancies; (b) performance-to-outcome expectancies; and (c) perceived valence of outcomes
Source: Hackman, J. R., Lawler, E. E. and Porter, L. W. (1977) *Perspectives on Behaviour in Organizations*, McGraw-Hill, New York. The material is reproduced with permission of McGraw-Hill Inc.

to expectancy theory, the following factors are involved in determining motivation, effort and, eventually, job satisfaction.

1 The perceived relationship between effort (E) and performance (P): this concerns the belief that extra effort will lead to better performance.
2 The perceived relationship between performance and outcomes (O): this concerns the belief that improved job performance will lead to outcomes such as promotion, extra pay, bonus, more responsibility, increased job autonomy, job security, recognition, etc.
3 The attractiveness of valence (V) of the possible outcomes: this concerns the value of the possible outcomes for the person concerned, such as the elimination of dangerous and dirty aspects of the job, the job being made easier, more interesting, etc.

Other points worthy of note are:

4 Even if motivation is high, this may not be reflected in performance, perhaps because of barriers such as a lack of ability or training, inadequate materials, machinery, aids and tools, an inappropriate strategy for doing the job, a system and organizational environment which are not conducive to continuous improvement, etc.
5 The beliefs that the person holds about links between effort, performance and outcomes are modified as a result of experience – hence the feedback loop. For example, an initial belief that good performance will lead to positive outcomes, such as promotion, recognition, improved working conditions and salary, may not be borne out by experience and this may result in a reassessment of the performance outcome relationships; this would include such things as suggestions for improvement being rejected by management without adequate explanation, key issues identified from a quality action day or key issues conference not being followed through, or a useful quality-related initiative being cancelled as part of a cost-cutting drive.

Attractiveness and payoffs

Two points are worth mentioning in connection with such theories. First, they emphasize the fact that the attractiveness of specific outcomes or rewards is a very individualistic matter. What is important and attractive for one person may be irrelevant for another. Thus, although expectancy theories seek to provide a general model of the factors involved in determining effort and performance for all employees, the individual differences between people are an integral part of the theory. The recognition of employees' achievements and celebrating successes are key features in the process of quality improvement, and organizations need to work out which are the best methods for them; a change is required from highlighting problems to celebrating successes. The second and related point is that although expectancy theories concentrate on the common processes involved, the contents of each individual's motivational system (e.g. whether increased pay, flexibility of working arrangements, more involvement in decision-making, and increased participation have higher valence) are also important.

Implications for individual managers

Among the chief implications for managers are those put forward by Nadler and Lawler.[14] These are discussed below, and warrant serious consideration in the development of a process of continuous quality improvement.

1 *Find out what particular outcomes or rewards are valued for each employee.* The theory proposes that different people will value different rewards.

2 *Be specific about the precise behaviours that constitute good levels of performance.*

3 *Make sure that the desired levels of performance are attainable.* According to the theory, people are prepared to put the effort in if they feel they can achieve their objectives. If an employee feels that it is not possible to reach the performance level, even with high effort, his or her motivation will be low.

Deming's[15] Point 10, 'Eliminate slogans, exhortations, and targets for the workforce asking for zero defects and new levels of productivity', should be noted. He also examines in his Point 11, 'Eliminate numerical quotas for the workforce and numerical goals for management', the implications of management setting numerical targets without providing the means to achieve them (e.g. from objectives through strategies and to action plans). Deming is of the view that if the targets are too low, employees will achieve them easily and will not be encouraged to improve. On the other hand, if they are too high employees will become disillusioned when they fail to achieve them. This may attract losses and lost opportunities. It is interesting, however, that in Japan improvement targets are set deliberately high in order to motivate employees – but the targets are not imposed, they are set in conjunction with employees and reached by consensus as part of the policy deployment process (see chapter 9).

4 *Ensure that there is a direct, clear and explicit link between performance at the desired level and outcomes and rewards.* In other

words, employees must be able to observe and experience the perform-ance–outcome connection. If this is unclear or is seen not to work, there will be no motivation and this is likely to restrict employees' quality-improvement efforts. The way in which organizations appraise performance can lead to this type of problem. The appraisal methods employed often need to be rethought and revised, particularly in large organizations where they are often decided by head office personnel and then imposed on local management.

5   *Check that there are no conflicting expectations.* Once the motiv-ating expectancies have been set up and employees have a clear grasp of the effort–performance and performance–outcome relationships, it is important to check that other people, processes, systems and procedures within the organization are not encouraging alternative expectancies and that employees are not receiving mixed messages. For example:

- In multinational companies, local management sometimes receive different messages from head office and from their own top management, and a common complaint is that to understand them they have to read between the lines.
- Some managers put all their efforts into meeting production schedules and targets, with quality improvement taking second place; this is typical in a traditional firefighting environment.
- Middle managers are often confused as to how they should commit their time, energy and resources to the key corporate strategies (quality, manufac-turing, logistics, technology, etc.) and as a result pursue their own pet project. This produces conflicting messages to their subordinates and is detrimental to the improvement process. Well-thought-out and clearly com-municated objectives and strategies are essential.

6   *Ensure changes in outcome are large enough to justify the effort.* As Nadler and Lawler[16] put it, 'trivial rewards will result in trivial amounts of effort and thus trivial improvements in performance'. How-ever, rewards may be trivial in a financial sense but significant in terms of recognition, satisfaction and empowerment. Managers should not aim for quantum leaps in improvement; small incremental steps make attainable targets and should warrant recognition and reward.

7   *Check that the system is treating everyone fairly.* The theory is based on the idea that different rewards will need to be used for different people. Nevertheless, 'good performers should see that they get more of the desired rewards than do poor performers, and others in the system should see that also'.[17] In other words, despite the use of different rewards the system should appear equitable to those involved.

In the pursuit of quality improvement great emphasis is placed upon the manufacturing and producing part of the business yet a large percentage of indirect labour is employed ostensibly to aid these departments. It is therefore important that efforts and improvement tools and techniques should be embraced by all managers and employees in every function of the business.

Implications for organizations

Some of the main implications for organizations proposed by Nadler and Lawler[18] are listed below. These too need to be considered in planning for quality improvement:

1 Design pay and reward systems so that:
   (a) desirable performance is rewarded (e.g. do not reward mere 'membership', by linking pay with years of service);
   (b) the relationship between performance and reward is clear. Whatever the rewards in terms of pay, promotion, learning new skills, education and training, job flexibility, involvement in improvement activities, etc., that result from good performance, they should be made clear and explicit.
2 Design tasks and roles so that people have an opportunity to satisfy their own needs through their work, but do not assume that everyone wants the same things. Some may want 'enriched' jobs with greater autonomy, feedback, etc., others will not.
3 Individualize the organization. Expectancy theory proposes that people have different needs, values, etc. It is important therefore to allow people some opportunity to influence not only the type of work they do, but any other aspects of organizational life, such as reward systems, the format of the suggestion scheme or the fringe benefits offered by the business.

Executive summary

- Management must attempt to understand the theories and methods of motivation, and apply them to their organization's continuous quality-improvement process.
- The following motivation theories are worthy of study:
  o Maslow's hierarchy of human needs;
  o Herzberg's two-factor theory;
  o Hackman and Oldham's job characteristic model.
- Management should realize that the vast majority of problems relating to

product and service quality are of their own making and the solution is in their hands.

- The barriers that prevent people from doing a good job should be identified and removed.
- Process theories of motivation indicate that the amount of effort people are prepared to invest in a task depends on expectancy, instrumentality and attractiveness of the outcomes.
- A number of factors are involved in determining motivation, effort and job satisfaction, including:
  ○ relationship between effort and performance;
  ○ relationship between performance and outcomes;
  ○ the value of the possible outcomes to the individual.

Notes

1 Robertson, Ivan T. and Cooper, Cary L. (1983) *Human Behaviour in Organisations*, Macdonald & Evans, Plymouth.
2 Deming, W. E. (1986) *Out of the Crisis*, Massachusetts Institute of Technology, Center for Advanced Engineering Study, Cambridge, Mass.
3 Juran, J. M. (1988) *Quality Control Handbook*, McGraw-Hill, New York.
4 Maslow, A. H. (1954) *Motivation and Personality*, Harper, New York.
5 Deming, *Out of the Crisis*.
6 Herzberg, F. (1968) 'One more time: how do you motivate employees?', *Harvard Business Review*, vol. 46, pp. 53–162.
7 Herzberg, F., Mausner, B. and Snyderman, B. B. (1959) *The Motivation to Work*, John Wiley, New York.
8 Robertson and Cooper, *Human Behaviour*.
9 Hackman, J. R. and Oldham, G. R. (1975) 'Development of the job diagnostic survey', *Journal of Applied Psychology*, vol. 6, pp. 159–70.
10 BS 5750/ISO 9000 (1987) *Quality Systems*, British Standards Institution, London.
11 Hackman and Oldham, 'Development'.
12 Lawler, E. E. III (1973) *Motivation in Work Organisations*, Brooks/Cole, Belmont, California.
13 Steers, R. M. and Porter, L. W. (1979) *Motivation and Work Behavior*, McGraw-Hill, New York.
14 Nadler, D. A. and Lawler, E. E. III (1979) 'Motivation: a diagnostic approach', in Steers and Porter, ibid.
15 Deming, *Out of the Crisis*.
16 Nadler and Lawler, 'Motivation'.
17 Ibid.
18 Ibid.

6

Managing the Process of Organizational Change

Introduction

Total quality management requires the introduction and acceptance of individual, group and organizational change throughout a company's operations: a complete change in the way a business is managed, as out-lined in the earlier chapters. TQM provides real opportunities to make and influence behaviour and attitudes, which have real effects on internal and external relationships and the way the organization conducts its business. Any changes and restructuring will have to be achieved by a process of continuous and ongoing change. To build cul-ture change into all a company's processes is a time-consuming task, never a part-time activity; not once-off, but continuous in the spirit of never-ending improvement. It is also important to note that to make and sustain the necessary change in company culture, and at the same time run a day-to-day business operation, is far from easy.

Changing people's behaviour and attitude is one of the most difficult tasks facing management. 'Resistance to change' is a term often used by managers to describe the situation when the quality-improvement process enters a trough and becomes stagnant. Many managers use the excuse that the workers' attitudes are the main stumbling block to improvement and are impossible to change. Probably, such managers have themselves not made the necessary long-term commitment to quality improvement, and have failed to give the necessary leadership. They sometimes forget that seeing is believing and practising is understanding. As already stated, TQM needs real and effective leadership by management.

It is important that managers who are serious about TQM and quality improvement understand the issues and factors in the process of organizational change. They should be prepared to accept the more participative approach which TQM most certainly requires. As already discussed, TQM is all to do with making incremental improvements. This is also true in the case of culture change, the aim being to make many small things happen in a consistent manner. If dramatic and unplanned changes are made, the culture will almost certainly never revert to its original state. The necessary changes do not happen by themselves; they need to be clearly thought out, tangible and structured, and mechanisms are needed to see that each small step is firmly in place before others are taken.

Today, many managements have set themselves the objective of developing their organization towards a 'total quality culture'. Unfortunately, this is capable of wide-ranging interpretation within the organization. To appreciate fully the task and implications of changing to such a culture, managers must understand not only assumptions about individual motivations and learning, but also about the process itself, various strategies for change and about individual resistance to change. This is what this chapter sets out to do. Some of the material is drawn from *Managing People at Work*, by Peter Makin, Cary Cooper and Charles Cox,[1] which explores in some detail the issues and concerns of managers in the process of organizational change.

Individual change

Organizational change can take place at three levels: the individual, the group, and the organization.

Individual change is the basis for all change: unless individuals change in some way, nothing changes. Those responsible for managing change need to involve people, to discuss and foster ideas. At management level, management development programmes are the main method of encouraging such change, and provide the necessary assistance. Their focus is typically on developing the skills individual managers need to cope with their present jobs, helping them accept the need to delegate power as a key step in making full use of their subordinates' knowledge, ability and skills, and developing skills for the future. Any planned programme of organizational change will need to include plans for individual change.

Senior and middle management must understand that through a process of continuous quality improvement the thought processes, decision-making, suggestions, initiatives, communications and presentation skills of their subordinates will improve. They must also learn to trust them, be prepared to shift the focus of responsibility, be consistent in their decision-making and actions, and listen more carefully to what people are saying. Likewise, subordinates need to understand that with TQM they will be more accountable for the processes within their direct control and take ownership for their own quality assurance and making improvements. Another major change with TQM is that individuals have to base their decisions on facts and data, not on opinion and sixth senses. It is also important to understand that there is usually a time lag between executives and middle managers talking about TQM and quality improvement, and their resulting behaviour and actions; this often confuses.

The establishment of a company-wide TQM education and training programme will depend on the assumptions that those responsible for it make about how people learn. These same assumptions are also fundamental to the strategy taken for any other level of change, so they are worth examining in relation to their implications for the design of change interventions. As Makin, Cooper and Cox[2] suggest, there are three broad sets of assumptions about learning on which social scientists tend to work.

Assumptions about learning

The behaviourist approach

The behaviourist approach is based on the work of Skinner.[3] A change agent working on these assumptions would look for those 'reinforcements' which are producing the current behaviour. Having specified precisely the new behaviour, the object would be to set up a schedule of reinforcement, to encourage the necessary change. Behaviour modification can be carried out in this apparently manipulative way, but it does not have to be. It is quite possible to discuss the desired change with participants, and to help them set up their own specification and requirements of new behaviour and schedules of reinforcement, so that control and the necessary changes are very much in their own hands.

Cognitive assumptions

The behaviourist approach assumes that change is best brought about by considering external factors. The cognitive approach, on the other hand, is based on a belief that behaviour is controlled by internal factors, such as the individual's beliefs, prejudices, assumptions and theories about the situation. To change his or her behaviour, therefore, you have to change these internal theories. There are various views about how this is done. One, known as the structuralist approach, considers the mind as rather like a computer, training being a matter of 'reprogramming' via well-designed courses that feed in appropriate new information. Such courses will be effective only if the individual is prepared to accept the new ideas, which is by no means certain. In recognition of this, an alternative, known as the functionalist approach, is based on the belief that people will learn once they realize that they have a practical need for the information offered. This will occur when they are given the opportunity to experiment and learn things for themselves. Training involves a range of activities, from courses designed around case studies and practical exercises, problem-solving skills and methods to long-term real-life projects.

The humanist school

The third set of assumptions which has had considerable influence on change processes derives from the humanist school, one of whose most influential members was Abraham Maslow.[4] Humanists believe that, given the right conditions, human beings are naturally committed to personal growth and development, the potential for which is unlimited (this theory has been discussed in chapter 5). Japanese companies seem able to make this work for the ongoing development of each individual. The role of the trainer or change agent then becomes that of providing the right conditions. Some insights on how this is done are provided by

Carl Rogers.[5] Originally a psychotherapist, his ideas have been widely accepted and used in education and training. In his view, it is impossible to 'teach' anything of value to another person: 'It seems to me that anything that can be taught to another is relatively inconsequential, and has little or no significant influence on behaviour ... I have come to feel that the only learning which significantly influences behaviour is self-discovered, self-appropriated learning.'

This may seem a little extreme, but it does draw attention to the fact that it is impossible to teach someone who does not want to learn: people will learn (and change) only if they want to. The role of the trainer or change agent is to try to bring about conditions where they will want to change. In terms of TQM-related training, the ideal situation is when the CEO or another senior manager introduces the training course and articulates the reasons for the organization embracing the concept and principles of TQM, and the importance of education and training in the process of continuous quality improvement. It is also recommended that the TQM training is cascaded down through the organization, with managers training their immediate subordinates; this also aids a change in culture. Once a critical mass of people has received training, peer pressure becomes important and useful – anyone not wanting training is the odd one out. Another important factor is to evaluate how effectively the training is transferred to the workplace by the trainee. Integrating activities and projects with training is a key aspect.

Self-development

Thinking along humanist lines has brought about an approach to training known as self-development. In this approach, individuals become responsible for directing their own development. They define their own learning objectives, decide for themselves the best way to achieve them, and evaluate their own progress. The training department staff become consultants, providing help and support. Much of the development under this system comes from 'real life', for example by taking on more challenging work to gain new experience and skills. People may still attend courses, but only when they, themselves, decide that this fulfils the needs they have identified. The use of the self-development approach stems from the fundamental belief that people are responsible and will organize their development in a way that is compatible with the needs of the organization, and will be committed to achieving organizational goals.

The values of the humanist movement have had a very strong influence on current practice in training and organizational development generally. They are equally compatible with support and achievement cultures in organizations. Self-development consequently requires a high degree of interdependence between the individuals involved. In the more traditional training systems, either cognitivist or behaviourist, there is more likely to be mutual dependence or straight authority/ dependence. In general, trainees involved in these systems are relatively passive and learn (or fail to learn) what is presented to them within the framework provided.

In order to make clear the assumptions underlying each of these approaches, the differences between them have been emphasized. It is, however, important to note that they are all quite compatible with one another. People learn as the result of reinforcement. They also have internal maps and theories about how the world and their own organization work, and changing these will change their behaviour. Their internal maps will, in fact, change as a result of changes in reinforcement patterns. There is also overwhelming evidence that learning is, in general, more effective if people are in charge of it themselves. The Lasermedia interactive SPC videodisc training package[6] is but one good example of this, together with rapid development of this medium of training. The wise change agent will, therefore, use all the approaches as appropriate.

Organizational change

In order to deal with the introduction of TQM in an organization, it is important to understand the process of organizational change. This is frequently referred to as organizational development (OD), which usually refers to changing the total organization. Richard Beckhard[7] suggests that OD interventions usually have five characteristics. They are:

- planned;
- organization-wide;
- managed from the top;
- attempting to increase the organization's effectiveness;
- usually involved in changing not only the structure but also the organization's processes and attitudes.

All five characteristics are relevant, and can be observed in the development of a total approach to the management of product and service quality. Warren Bennis[8] summed this up by saying that 'organizational development is a response to change, a complex educational strategy intended to change beliefs, attitudes, values and the structure of organizations so that they can better adapt to new technologies, markets and challenges, and the dizzying rate of change itself'.

For senior managers to understand organizational change, they must be aware of the process of change, the strategies available for change and the resistance to it. The rest of this chapter deals with these issues.

The change process

Breaking down barriers

Whatever type of change strategy is being used, change takes energy, time and resources since there is always inertia in the system to be overcome. By their very nature organizations are not meant to change; they are social structures intended to make employees' behaviour more predictable and efficient by rationalizing it in the form of a bureaucracy. In relation to TQM, Lascelles and Dale[9] identify six change forces or triggers:

- the CEO;
- demanding customers;
- competition;
- the need to reduce costs;
- a restart situation venture;
- a greenfield venture.

They go on to make the point that demanding customers are the key external change agent and the CEO the key internal one.

In 1947 Kurt Lewin[10] suggested that change is a three-stage process, whether individual, group or organization level. He describes the stages – termed unfreezing, change and re-freezing – as follows.

Unfreezing

Before any change can take place, the established methods and patterns of behaviour must be broken down. People may be unaware of these established procedures until their attention is directed to them, and only then may their effectiveness be challenged. This demonstration of current ineffectiveness is essential for change to take place. People will willingly become involved in a change process only when they have accepted the need for change. The early activities of an organizational change programme are usually designed to bring about this unfreezing.

Change

Once current behaviours and attitudes are unfrozen, it is possible to work on the change process. This can be done using any of the following interventions: strategic planning activities, goal setting, coaching and counselling, team building (including the development of cross-functional teams), techno-structural changes, a formal programme of TQM education and training, etc.

Re-freezing

For people to operate effectively, their behaviour must be reasonably stable. An individual or organization in a state of constant change will achieve little. This means that the new behaviour must be allowed to stabilize. Usually people are very good at doing this for themselves. All that is needed is time for re-freezing to occur naturally. Sometimes activities are included towards the end of a change programme that are designed to enable participants to look forward and review the effects of the planned changes. If these are perceived as beneficial, this review will aid the change process.

Top-down change

An important point to note is that change does not happen by itself. As Makin, Cooper and Cox[11] suggest, there must be a source that initiates the change, and it must have sufficient power to be able to influence others in the direction of the desired change. In organizational change programmes the source is usually located somewhere in the management hierarchy. There is, in fact, a view that any organizational change will be successful only if it is initiated by top management. This, it is suggested, is the only group with sufficient power to make the change programme happen and is usually referred to as the 'start at the top and work down' approach.

This is certainly true in the case of TQM. However, a few successful organizational change projects have started at the bottom and worked up; the introduction of quality circles and the use of quality management tools and techniques, such as statistical process control (SPC) and failure mode and effects analysis (FMEA) are examples of this. This bottom-up approach in relation to TQM, while easier to start and involving little risk, is not ideal and cannot be recommended. Only top management have the authority to initiate and standardize real irreversible change. In some organizations, however, this approach has worked and succeeded in changing management style and behaviour, leading them to drive and empower quality-improvement initiatives. Experience with TQM indicates that a bottom-up approach is very difficult to sustain, more than likely to fizzle out and should be treated with extreme caution. Some organizations in their approach to TQM have used a top-down and bottom-up methodology and this pincer movement has involved middle management and brought them into the quality improvement process at a much quicker rate.

Strategies for change

While openness, trust, truth and care remain the ideals of many change agents, it is recognized that most organizations do not operate on these principles. TQM does help to build these principles into the organizational culture. There are a number of ways this can be achieved. Chin and Benne[12] have defined what they call 'general strategies for effecting change in human systems'. They suggest there are three of these that provide a good framework for defining change strategies, both in organizations and, more widely, in society as a whole, as Makin, Cooper and Cox[13] outline.

Empirical–rational strategies

This approach assumes that people are basically rational. Change can be effected, therefore, by showing that it is in the individual's own interest to change. This is sometimes referred to as 'enlightened self-interest'. Change is achieved by the use of data and rational persuasion. The assumptions underlying this strategy lie deep in traditional education, and include a belief in the benefit of research and the general dissemination of knowledge. The communication and discussion of the quality requirements of customers can help to facilitate this change, as can participation in the quality improvement teams of both customers and suppliers.

Normative–re-educative strategies

This group of strategies does not deny the rationality of human beings. It places more emphasis, however, on the belief that behaviour is determined largely by the social and cultural norms of the group or society to which people belong. Individuals have a strong commitment to conforming to, and maintaining, these norms. Successful change is therefore accomplished by changing them, using a mixture of education, training, persuasion and peer pressure.

Power–coercive strategies

These involve the use of physical, resource or position power to coerce individuals into changing. Physical power is widely used by governments when adopting this strategy. At the organizational level, resource or position power is more usual. Chin and Benne[14] point out that passive resistance, along the lines used by Gandhi, is also an example of a power–coercive approach.

Seat belts and quality improvement: the strategies in use

To help understand the use of strategies outlined above, the British government's attempts to get both drivers and front-seat passengers to wear seatbelts are outlined, followed by some quality-improvement examples.

A considerable amount of time and money was spent using empirical–rational strategies: advertising campaigns giving information on safety factors – 'You know it makes sense.' All this had little effect. The government then switched to a power–coercive strategy: not wearing a seatbelt became an offence. Seat-belt usage leapt overnight to in excess of 90 per cent. The maintenance of this high level is now most probably due to normative–re-educative influences: wearing seatbelts has become the norm. While the threat of a fine is still in the background, it is suspected that most people would, even without this, continue with the new behaviour. In Kurt Lewin's terms, power–coercive strategies were necessary for the unfreezing and change processes; Normative–re-educative strategies produced the re-freezing.

Several examples of the three strategies are evident in the process of quality improvement. In the majority of cases the process has been started by the power–coercive strategy, since many companies have adopted an aggressive or positive stance in improving the quality of their products and service only with outside pressure.

1 Lascelles and Dale[15] stress the importance of a demanding customer as a major external change agent by, for example, imposing a contractual requirement that its suppliers should use SPC and provide it with process capability data, or requiring their quality system to meet the BS 5750/ISO 9000[16] series of quality standards before being allowed to bid for business.
2 Suppliers to the Ford Motor Company must meet Ford's Q1 requirements (by 1 January 1992 to win new business, by 1 August 1993 to maintain carryover business. To qualify for a Q1 award, a supplier must meet or exceed a number of criteria, including:[17]
    (a) scoring 80 per cent overall (and 70 per cent per item) in Ford's twenty-item Quality System Survey;
    (b) in particular, scoring 80 per cent in the five questions pertaining to statistical methods in the survey;
    (c) having had all initial samples approved or no self-certification anomalies during first-time presentation within the previous twelve months;
    (d) secure a minimum 90 per cent rating during the previous six months for ongoing quality performance without any quality concerns, validated and reviewed with the supplier as its responsibility, that result from variation from engineering requirements and/or cause customer dissatisfaction.
3 Motorola requires all its eligible suppliers to sign a statement of their intent to apply for the Malcolm Baldrige National Quality Award, and those not wishing to compete are disqualified as suppliers. (This initiative stimulated considerable debate: see, for example, the letters column of *Quality Progress*, November 1989.)

Minimum criteria such as these have now become the order-qualifying standard in many markets and customer–supplier situations: normative–re-educative strategies. In many cases the results achieved and the stimulus of prestigious quality awards such as the Deming Application Prize in Japan, the Malcolm Baldrige National Quality Award in America and the European Quality Award in Europe have caused some organizations to undertake quality improvement in their own self-interest – empirical–rational strategies.

Individual adaptation

So far change strategies have been considered from the point of view of someone trying to change others. To complete the picture, *how* change takes place within the individual needs to be considered. Kelman[18] has provided a social influence model for this. He suggests that there are three mechanisms for change. These can be seen as responses to the attempted influence of others, as Makin, Cooper and Cox[19] outline.

Compliance

Individuals change simply because they are unable to resist the pressure being placed upon them. This is a common response to physical, resource or position power. In some cases, if there are rewards, or at least no costs, for the individual, the change may become internalized and hence relatively permanent. Often, however, this is not a good way to create change, since the response is, at best, relatively passive. When the pressure is removed, the original behaviour and attitudes are likely to recur. At worst, it results in counterdependence, and individuals may expend considerable energy and ingenuity in finding ways to avoid changing.

Identification

Identification is a frequent response to personal power. The person being influenced changes because of a desire to resemble the source of power, due perhaps to admiration of or being inspired by the individual concerned. The lifetime of change by identification may be long, with the change becoming internalized. Equally, it may be quite short lived, particularly if less admirable aspects of the source of influence suddenly become apparent. A charismatic CEO, committed to TQM, has considerable influence on his or her staff; problems can be experienced with sustaining the momentum when the CEO has been promoted or changed companies.

Internalization

Internalization is the most effective form of change, since the individual accepts the change and adopts it as part of his or her self-image. Inevitably, this form of change is likely to take longer than compliance and identification, and time must be allowed for it to occur. If there are strong pressures for change, the process may be even slower. Individuals must be allowed to develop commitment in their own time. Once this commitment has developed, however, the change is relatively permanent.

Resistance to change

Finally, we need to look at resistance to change, particularly as there are two popular myths concerning it. The first is that people dislike change, and will attempt to avoid it. While certainly true that change programmes (including TQM) occasionally provoke resistance, this is by no means a universal reaction. Indeed, on many occasions people enjoy change and look forward to it. If this were not so, the rapid rate of change in relation to quality improvement that has happened in many European organizations would not have taken place. The reality is that the majority of the population of the developed world has happily adapted to enormous changes, both in technology and their way of life, over the last few decades. It may be, however, that people differ in their readiness to accept change. Rogers and Shoemaker[20] have suggested that people fall into five different types: innovators, early adopters, majority (early), majority (late) and laggards.

- Innovators are quick to adopt new ideas and to change accordingly. They are also risk takers, as some of the new ideas may prove to be mistaken and/or difficult to adapt and put into place.
- Early adopters follow closely behind the innovators, but are rather more respectable and tend to conform with societal norms. They are not seen by the rest of society to be as non-conformist as the innovators.
- The early majority take on change once it has started to become accepted.
- The more conservative late majority wait to see all the effects before adopting change.
- Finally, the laggards are very suspicious of change and are slow to adapt.

Rogers and Shoemaker suggest that most people fall into the two 'majority' classifications, with far fewer occupying the two extreme positions. Individuals may also vary according to the nature of the change.

The other myth is that resistance to change is necessarily a bad thing. Sometimes such resistance may be healthy. Both people and organizations need periods of stability to re-freeze and absorb the changes that have already taken place. Also, the existence of resistance may be an indicator that, for some reason, a particular change is not considered desirable. In such cases a closer look is needed at the root causes for the resistance.

Another issue which needs to be considered is where top management joining a company instigate change for change's sake in order to make their personal mark on the organization. This type of change can be disruptive. Conversely, if the organization is running efficiently and they take the sensible approach and keep the business on its current course, they risk being criticized for *not* achieving or changing anything.

Reasons for resistance

Where beneficial change is resisted it may be for a number of reasons. Sometimes people believe that the change is likely to be to their disadvantage and even, in a few cases, to the organization itself. On occasion this may indeed be true. If an individual's job is at risk or he or she has worries about coping with the new concepts, procedures, systems, skills, practices, etc., resistance to the related changes is not surprising. A good example is the concern of some shop-floor operatives that SPC would expose their lack of numeracy and literacy, and that their day-to-day production routines leave insufficient time to measure process parameters and/or product characteristics, carry out calculations and plot the data on control charts. Fear of change is often enhanced by the secrecy in which change programmes are planned and implemented; fortunately this rarely happens with the introduction of TQM. In some cases, quality-improvement projects may not be publicized if there is any doubt about their successful outcome. This failure to communicate is often due to management's fears that people will find ways of blocking the changes if they are aware of them in advance, and at the early planning stage they too are unsure of the likely outcome of the change. Paradoxically, the secrecy itself makes people suspicious and often leads to the very blocking behaviour management had hoped to avoid. Secrecy thus becomes a self-fulfilling prophecy.

Change will always involve some effort, as new ways of doing things have to be learnt. For some people the fear of the unknown will be a major factor, especially if there are high levels of insecurity and dependency. Again using the example of SPC, when it is being introduced on a particular process as part of a pilot programme, there is a tendency for operators and first-line supervisors to cry, 'Why us and not them' and sometimes, 'Why them and not us?'

Other sources of resistance may lie in the social system. The existing norms of the group or organization will usually be very powerful. These are necessary, of course, as they provide the rules within which people relate to one another and work together. Change may require these norms to be changed in some way. Problems may also arise if change programmes are instituted in only one part of an organization: any imbalances elsewhere will breed resistance as a means of restoring the balance. Other resistances, of a social nature, may be due to the change agent threatening vested interests or 'sacred cows'. Where programmes are carried out by outside consultants, personnel may be suspicious of outsiders and ask: 'What can they teach us?' or 'What do they know about the industry?' Many organizations use management consultancy packages to start a process of quality improvement and this suggestion of suspicion needs to be recognized.

Overcoming resistance to change

There is overwhelming evidence that the best way to reduce resistance to change is to involve those who will be affected in the decision-making process. Individuals who have been involved in planning, devising and implementing change are far more likely to feel positively about it. In general, they will feel more committed, which will lead to speedier implementation. When managing a process of change the human trait of people wanting to support their own ideas should never be forgotten. Natural leaders within a business can also assist with breaking through resistance to change.

The ideal situation is where all the necessary information is freely available and decisions are then taken by consensus. There will, however, be occasions when it is not possible to be totally open (for example, if some of the information is commercially sensitive). As Makin, Cooper and Cox[21] continually emphasize, good communication and feedback channels should be established between the source of change and those who are to be affected. Even where there are short-term costs, such as retraining, it is necessary to show that there will be long-term benefits, such as improved pay, better working conditions, avoiding a takeover, etc. Obviously, it will be easier to effect change if there is a general climate of trust in the organization, where people feel that their fears will be listened to and their problems recognized and dealt with sympathetically. Ideally, the programme itself should be open to change in the light of such feedback.

Managing the process of change

In drawing this chapter to a close, it is useful to quote the process developed by Daniels and Dale[22] in examining the relationship between TQM and corporate culture. They have developed a simple three-step process which they claim is applicable in assessing and managing cultural change in most organizations.

Step 1 Establish a number of key cultural parameters to provide the basis for a common understanding throughout the company as to the style or way of working the organization is seeking to encourage. The parameters should be selected with considerable care and forethought, and must be applicable to all levels of the organization. They should highlight fundamental as opposed to superficial aspects of management style.

Step 2 Devise a means of measuring the parameters and assess the current position against these parameters. Relate the extent of the presence or absence of the key behaviour parameters identified to the effectiveness of the organization and/or individual departments. The connection between organizational effectiveness and corporate culture would strongly support the efforts to bring about cultural change. Identify a desirable future situation.

Step 3 Develop an action plan which will address the weaknesses and achieve the transition. This could be done away from the workplace, in a traditional training forum, or at the workplace by means of facilitative support.

Executive summary

- A study of organizational culture prior to the introduction of TQM will provide some useful clues to the likely areas of difficulty.
- Organizational change to operate a business in line with TQM principles is a time-consuming and long-term task and requires a wide range of management skills.
- Management should not underestimate the time needed to make the organizational changes which are conducive to TQM.
- Executives who are serious about TQM need to understand the key issues and factors involved in a process of organizational change.
- TQM requires the acceptance of individual, group and organizational change.
- Individual change is the basis of all change.
- Management development programmes can encourage changes and provide assistance.
- Organizational changes and developments have five characteristics. They are:
  - planned;
  - organization-wide;
  - managed from the top;
  - attempting to increase the organization's effectiveness;
  - involved in changing not only the structure but also the organization's processes.

- Change, whether it be attitudes, individuals, groups or organizational, is a three-stage process involving unfreezing, change and re-freezing.
- Change strategies must be adapted to suit the prevailing circumstances that exist within the organization.
- People differ in their readiness to change, and fall into five categories:
  - o innovators;
  - o early adopters;
  - o majority (early);
  - o majority (late);
  - o laggards.
- The best way to reduce resistance to change is to involve those who will be affected in the decision-making process.
- Recognize, in the planning process, the factors, influences and personalities that may contribute to resistance to change.

Notes

1 Makin, P., Cooper, C. L. and Cox, C. (1989) *Managing People at Work*, The British Psychological Society, Leicester; Routledge, London.
2 Ibid.
3 Skinner, B. F. (1953) *Science and Human Behaviour*, Macmillan, New York.
4 Maslow, A. H. (1971) *The Farther Reaches of Human Nature*, Viking, New York.
5 Rogers, C. R. (1967) *On Becoming a Person*, Constable, London.
6 Lasermedia (1988) *Statistical Process Control: Interactive Video Course*, Bognor Regis, West Sussex.
7 Beckhard, R. (1969) *Organizational Development: Strategies and Models*, Addison-Wesley, Reading, Mass.
8 Bennis, W. G. (1969) *Organizational Development: Its Nature, Origins and Prospects*, Addison-Wesley, Reading, Mass.
9 Lascelles, D. M. and Dale, B. G. (1989) 'What improvement: what is the motivation?', *Proceedings of the Institution of Mechanical Engineers*, vol. 203, no. B1, pp. 43–50.
10 Lewin, K. (1947) 'Group decisions and social change', in T. Newcomb and E. Hartley (eds), *Readings in Social Psychology*, Holt Rinehart & Winston, New York.
11 Makin, Cooper and Cox, *Managing People*.
12 Chin, R. and Benne, K. D. (1976) 'General strategies for effecting changes in human systems' in W. G. Bennis, K. D. Benne, R. Chin, and K. E. Carey (eds), *The Planning of Change*, 3rd edn, Holt, Rinehart & Winston, New York.

13 Makin, Cooper and Cox, *Managing People*.

14 Chin and Benne, 'General strategies'.

15 Lascelles and Dale, 'What improvement?'

16 BS 5750 (1987) *Quality Systems*, British Standards Institution, London.

17 Ford Motor Company (1990), Q1 Preferred Quality Award for Suppliers to the Ford Motor Company, Corporate Quality Office, Dearborn, Michigan.

18 Kelman, H. C. (1958) 'Compliance, internalization and identification: three processes of attitude change', *Journal of Conflict Resolution*, vol. 2, pp. 51–60.

19 Makin, Cooper and Cox, *Managing People*.

20 Rogers, E. and Shoemaker, F. (1971) *Communication and Innovation*, Free Press, New York.

21 Makin, Cooper and Cox, *Managing People*.

22 Daniels, J. M. and Dale, B. G. (1992) 'The impact of TQM on cultural change', (in press).

7

Team Building

Introduction

The development of people and their involvement in improvement activities individually and through group activity is a key feature of TQM. There are a number of ways in which involvement through team-working can be facilitated. Quality circles and quality improvement teams are perhaps the most familiar examples but there are many others. Some teams are formed from members of one functional area and have a narrow focus; others are cross-functional, have a much wider focus and deal with some of the deep-rooted problems between internal customers and suppliers.

The effective solution of problems through any of these group activities facilitates the process of team building and this, along with improved communication and understanding and people involvement and development, is often more important than the result. Team building is a primary building block in the development of TQM, and should be encouraged within any organization. The Japanese are much more comfortable with the use of teams as part of their quality-improvement efforts than are most European companies, which often pay little attention to team activity. This may be due to the divisive nature of Western industry: 'them and us', 'management and unions', etc. It is often the case in European organizations that management will decide to launch some form of team activity as part of a quality-improvement initiative, throw the members together and expect the team to work in an effective manner without any form of coaching, direction or counselling.

It is important for managers to know something about the types of teams typically used in quality-improvement activities, and the various methods of or approaches to team building that have been used in a range of organizational change situations. Some of these team-building efforts rely heavily on experienced training consultants/facilitators, either internal or external change agents, for their effective implementation.

This chapter opens by discussing the operating characteristics of quality circles and other types of problem-solving groups such as quality improvement groups. It then reviews some of the management training techniques that have been used in team building in the workplace, which may be of benefit, in adapted form, for the development of teamwork within a process of quality improvement (for a detailed account of team-building methods see Makin, Cooper and Cox,[1] on which some of this material is based).

What are quality circles?

Quality circles are a direct form of employee participation in the business of any organization. A typical quality circle is a *voluntary* group of six to eight employees from the same work area (smaller and larger circles do exist, but this is the average). They meet usually in company time, for one hour every week or fortnight, under the leadership of their work supervisor, to solve problems relating to improving their work activities and environment. [Quality circles are a means of providing employees with the opportunity to solve problems, and implement and monitor their solutions.]

Quality circles appear to work because of three main factors:

1 members like talking about their work;
2 members are interested in their work and want to contribute; and
3 members welcome the opportunity to identify and solve, using their skills and experience, the problems they have to live with and nobody seems to care about.

The typical operating characteristics of a quality circle (based on Dale and Oakland)[2] are:

- The members join a Circle voluntarily and can opt out as and when they wish.
- The members select the problems and projects which they wish to tackle.
- The solutions are evaluated in terms of their cost-effectiveness.
- The findings, solutions and recommendations of the Quality Circle are presented to senior management for comment and approval.
- The Circle implements, where practicable, their recommendations. If this is not possible, the departments responsible for putting the recommendations into place should maintain a dialogue with the Circle concerning the progress being made and the likely date of implementation.
- Once implemented, the Circle monitors the effects of the solution and considers future improvements.
- The Circle carries out a critical review of all activities related to the completed project. This enables the members to identify ways by which they might improve their problem-solving activities.

A number of these features give quality circles a special character quite different from those of other methods of group working and group problem-solving.

Characteristics of other types of quality-improvement groups

Superior-performing companies operate a variety of teamwork related to quality-improvement activity. They often define the characteristics of their different forms of team activity, in particular separating our quality circle activity from that of their other teams. The following example from Grace Dearborn (manufacturer of speciality chemicals) is typical.

In deciding which quality improvement approach to use, the following three major factors should be taken into account:

- Where the idea for the improvement originated.
- The strategic significance of the improvement.
- Whether the improvements affects more than one major area of the company's operation.

These approaches, coupled with those improvements brought about by individual employees, provide the basis for continuous quality improvements.

1 *Management Action*
The characteristics of quality improvement which is driven through by management action are as follows:

- The need for change may have been identified at any level in the company.
- The improvement objective has been defined by management.
- The process of quality improvement is management led.
- The objective can address both improvement and strategic issues.
- The process to be improved is owned by one department.

2 *Quality Project Team*
The characteristics of project teams are:

- The need for change can have been identified at any level within the company.
- The objective has been defined by senior management.
- The project team is management led.
- The project team addresses strategic change.
- Achievement of the objective requires that a number of different functions within the company be represented on the team.
- The process to be improved is owned by more than one department.

3 *Quality Improvement Teams*
Characteristics of quality improvement teams are:

- The improvement need has been identified at a non-managerial level.
- The improvement objective has been defined and agreed with senior management.
- The process of quality improvement is employee led within the objective agreed above.
- The objective addresses improvement issues rather than strategic changes.
- The process to be improved is owned by one (or more) department.

In *summarizing* the operating characteristics of teams used in the process of quality improvement the following points must be noted:

- The key issue is not the name of the team activity, but the structure of the team, its operating characteristics, remit, accountability, and ability to facilitate improvements.
- If management initiate any form of improvement activity, be they circles, quality improvement teams, suggestion schemes, they have an implicit

responsibility to investigate and evaluate all recommendations for improvement – otherwise there is demotivation.

Team building strategies

As Makin, Cooper and Cox[3] suggest, group or team building is the second most frequent form of change intervention. Indeed, a review by Porras and Berg[4] estimated that 40 per cent of all organizational change interventions involved team building. As already mentioned, teams are an essential part of organizations and, in particular, are valuable in helping to foster and develop TQM. They exist wherever several people need to co-operate to complete a task and/or to seek improvements. The emphasis in team building is usually on the manager or first-line supervisor and his or her immediate group of subordinates, and focuses on improving the way that teams operate together. It may also be used at a more casual level, for example with people who work together occasionally but are not part of a formal team (e.g. as part of joint problem-solving between external customers and suppliers).

The origins of team building go back to the work of Elton Mayo, who built on the early work of the Hawthorne studies to demonstrate the importance of social relationships at work. Other influences are the work of Kurt Lewin at the National Training Laboratories, and the development of the T-group movement. To improve a team's effectiveness, it is common, in practice, to concentrate on one or more themes:

- increasing mutual trust among team members;
- increasing awareness of both your own and other people's behaviour;
- developing interpersonal skills, such as listening, giving feedback, bringing others into the discussion.

Deciding which themes to develop will depend on a number of factors, in particular the theoretical orientation of the consultant, trainer or facilitator who may be working with the team, together with the diagnosis of weaknesses in the team. Ideally, this diagnosis should be made in co-operation with the team members.

A variety of approaches are used in team building. These derive largely from different assumptions about how people best learn (i.e. change), and about the best environment for effective teamwork. A discussion of some of these approaches will help organizations wishing to develop the potential of their team activity in quality-improvement efforts.

T-groups

Sensitivity training, T-groups and other forms of experimental training are very broad and hence difficult to define precisely. T-groups (T stands for training) involve a wide range of activities, many of which are similar to those used in other approaches, such as encounter groups. In general, the T-group consists of eight to ten people, and the aim is for them to learn from their own behaviour and interactions. Emphasis is placed on developing a climate of trust and openness, thus fostering a high level of interpersonal feedback and the acceptance of feelings. The trainer or facilitator is there to help the group achieve these objectives, not as a formal expert teacher; he or she operates non-directively. The focus of the group can be at the level of personal learning and growth, or the understanding of group activity, or learning at the organizational level, or any combination of the three.

T-groups are firmly rooted in the values of the 1960s and early 1970s. Much emphasis is placed upon authenticity – being open and expressing inner feelings. Unfortunately, these values are often in conflict with the norms of most organizations, even those which claim to embrace the TQM ethic. Chris Argyris[5] has pointed out that the organizational norm is to value rationality as effective, and suppress feelings as ineffective. This is based on the belief that as individuals start expressing feelings they become more emotional, less rational, and therefore less effective. But individuals' natural reaction to this norm is to suppress the expression of their feelings, even those that are perfectly reasonable. This becomes so automatic that they may not even realize they are being suppressed. Since these emotions are not recognized or expressed, they gradually build up until they burst out, often as anger. The trigger that sets off the outburst may often be a very minor event. Because they are now so emotional that they are out of control, they may be ineffective. This can confirm the organization's assumption that feelings and emotions are bad. The individuals therefore resolve not to give vent to their feelings in future, and the cycle starts again. According to Argyris, people need to recognize their feelings as they develop, and deal with them in some way. In classic T-groups, this would be by openly expressing them.

Mainly because of the difference between the values of T-groups and those of most organizations, this approach had fallen into disuse by the 1980s. Such a clash of values led to poor transfer from the training situation to the 'real world' of the organization. There was even some evidence that people were less effective after such training, although a minority did show positive change. This was most probably because open and supportive behaviour was inappropriate in political and formal organizational cultures. Other problems concerned the unpredictable nature of T-groups themselves – because of the open structure, anything could happen (or sometimes not happen). There were also ethical problems. Because T-groups are both powerful and personal, there is a strong case for participation being voluntary. There are, however, strong group and organizational pressures on the individual in such a 'voluntary' situation. In addition, if some members did not choose to attend, effectiveness might of necessity be reduced.

Most organizational change practitioners in the late 1960s and 1970s saw T-group values as the way organizations ought ideally to be: with a climate of high openness and trust. However, despite emphasizing this approach for some twenty years, nothing has changed in the real world of organizations. They have not become more trusting and open. Most practitioners have, therefore, abandoned these values and espoused the contingency model of 'horses for courses'. The valuable and valid legacy of T-groups in current thinking is to have emphasized that humans are both rational and feeling beings.

Continuous improvement through TQM can be achieved only by openness, trust, honesty and sincerity. Therefore, as more organizations embrace the principles of TQM, experimental techniques such as T-groups might be considered a valid option for building group cohesion.

Role negotiation

Role negotiation is, in a way, at the opposite end of the scale to T-groups, as Makin, Cooper and Cox[6] highlight. It was developed by Harrison[7] in order to take account of the issue of power in organizations.

In preparation for the negotiations implied in the technique's name, each team member considers each of the other members and prepares a list of items under the following three headings:

It would help me increase my effectiveness if you would:

- do more of, or do better, the following . . .
- do less of, or stop doing, the following . . .
- keep on doing (i.e. maintain unchanged) the following . . .

Members then meet in pairs to negotiate the changes they would like to see, and those they are themselves willing to make. Negotiations continue until both parties are happy and agreement has been reached, written down and signed by both parties. It is part of the agreement that if one of the parties does not keep to the bargain, the other can use the sanction of withdrawing. The intention is that the negotiations should be done in such a way that there is an incentive to keep to the agreement, so as to gain the benefits promised by the other. Harrison makes the point that it is not legitimate, or necessary, to probe into individual feelings. What is required, however, is honesty. Threats and pressures, on the other hand, may be used, but it should be remembered that their use may lead to defensiveness. The role of the consultant/ trainer/facilitator is to help the negotiators understand and keep to the guidelines, and to help them clarify the requirements for change. It is, of course, important that they do not actually influence the items, but simply help the individuals clarify their own ideas.

The ideas involved in role negotiation can also be used in developing the internal-customer relationship discussed in chapter 1.

Structured approach

This is based upon assumptions that change is best brought about by providing information so as to understand the processes within groups – a cognitivist approach. The core of this approach is a team-building workshop or training course. This comprises a series of exercises, each designed to focus on some aspect of team working. The exercises are usually of a type known as substitute task exercises: tasks not related in any way to the normal work of the group, but designed to highlight some aspect of group process, such as competitiveness, goal clarity, use of quality management tools and techniques, decision-making, etc. The fact that the task is unrelated to normal work makes it easier for the group to focus on the process, and avoids undue attention being given to the task itself. On the other hand, there could be a lack of motivation due to the non-reality or artificial nature of the tasks. It is common to use short questionnaires and other measures to bring out key aspects of team processes. These activities, assisted by interventions from the consultant/trainer/facilitator, help the group and individuals to gain a better understanding of how their present methods of working could be improved.

Team-development packages

Packages provide a virtually ready-made team-building programme, which can be used as needed. They are usually fairly highly structured and based on a particular theoretical framework. Often they are aimed more at developing the skills of the team leader than at total team development. A good example is the use of Blake and Mouton's[8] managerial grid. The approach can be used to enable the manager or team leader to clarify his or her current style in terms of 'concern for task' or 'concern for people'. Exercises are then available to enable the individual to develop towards the optimal style, which is high on both concerns. The package can also be used to explore team members' preferences for different styles.

Another widely used package is provided by John Adair.[9] This is also mainly directed at the team leader. Adair argues that there are three sets of needs which must be met if a team is to work effectively:

- task needs – practical things to do with getting the work done;
- group needs – concerned with keeping a cohesive team;
- individual needs – the personal goals which each individual hopes to achieve through membership of the team.

It is important that attention is paid to all three of these. For a fully effective team, all must be fulfilled. If ensuring these needs are met is seen to be the leader's responsibility, training concentrates on team leadership. Alternatively, if the view is taken that responsibility is shared by all team members, the concepts are used as a framework for reviewing how effectively the group is functioning. Exercises are used to highlight the importance of each set of needs, and how well they are being fulfilled.

It is important that the trainee team leader has a real team-leader task to perform in the workplace; otherwise the training is likely to be forgotten very quickly.

Team interaction analysis

Interaction process analysis is the fourth strategy of team building suggested by Makin, Cooper and Cox.[10] Interaction process analysis is an approach that enables participants to analyse the type of contribution each person is making to the group, and the implications for group effectiveness. It is based on the work of Bales[11], who designed a rather complex classification of the types of interaction which take place

Table 7.1 Example of categories for interaction process analysis

Managing people at work

Category/definition	Example
Gives support	
Raises others' esteem	Great idea!
Gives reward	You're looking fine.
Shows solidarity	I'm with you on this one.
Gives help	What was your point, Dave?
Builds on suggestions	. . . and then we could . . .
Agrees	Yes, let's do that then.
Shows acceptance	Okay then.
Understands	I see what you're getting at.
Complies	If that's what you want.
Gives non-verbal signs of encouragement	Mm; *nod*
Gives suggestion	
Makes proposals	It could be in the by-pass value.
Suggests direction	Let's begin with looking at the sales figures.
Offers autonomy for others	What do you think about it, Geoff?
Gives opinion	
Evaluates	That's not very helpful.
Analyses	The way I see it, the problem is . . .
Expresses feelings	I'm annoyed by it.
Expresses wishes	I hope to get through it all this morning.
Interprets	It seems to me that the situation is . . .
Imposes	Look, let me tell you.
Gives information	
Informs	It's 4.30.
	I was amazed.
Repeats	What I said was . . .
Clarifies	I meant the same thing.
	That's what I'm saying.
Confirms	Yes, that's right.

(*continued*)

Table 7.1 (*Continued*)

Managing people at work

Category/definition	Example
Asks for information	
Seeks facts	Where are the figures?
Seeks information	How did you do that?
Asks for repetition	What was that?
Asks for opinion	
Seeks feelings	How do you feel about that?
Seeks wishes	What do you want to do?
Seeks interpretations	How do you see it?
Seeks evaluations	Do you think that's a good idea?
Asks for suggestions	
Seeks direction and ways of taking action	How can we go about this? Anybody got any ideas?
Shows disagreement	
Shows resistance, rejection	No, I'm not too sure about that.
Withholds help	*Silence, non-verbals*
Defends and asserts	Not at all!
Antagonizes others	You really believe that!
Attacks others	You're wasting my time!

In developing appropriate categories of interactions between group members it is almost impossible to give absolute definitions of what should be included in each. Nevertheless, these definitions and examples should be of assistance for a trainer developing his or her observational and analytical skills.

Source: Adapted from Bales, R. F. (1950) *Interactive Process Analysis*, Addison-Wesley, Reading, Mass.

between individuals in groups. The original classification is too complex to master and use quickly, so various simpler versions, such as that shown in table 7.1, have been devised.

One way in which interaction process analysis can be used is for team members to take it in turns to observe the group, either when it is working normally or in special training sessions, and classify and count the types of contribution made by each team member. Alternatively, the consultant can undertake this task. The results are fed back to the group, who consider their implications, both for individuals and the group as a whole. It is not uncommon to find that certain individuals' contributions tend to be predominantly of one or two types. They are often surprised to discover this. Sometimes this is true for the group as a whole. There may, for example, be a great deal of giving opinions and suggestions, but not asking. Sometimes categories such as gives support are noticeably lacking. If this is the case, it is necessary for group members to widen the range of contributions they are making.

Team roles

There are a number of theories which suggest that, for a group or team to operate effectively, a number of specific roles must be represented. Much of the early research into role differentiation has suggested that there are two basic roles in all human groups: the task leader and the social emotional specialist. [12] Effectively, one person in a group takes on the various behaviours necessary for achieving the goals of the group, and another takes on the role of resolving interpersonal differences, releasing tension, showing solidarity, etc. This has been termed the 'hypothesis of two complementary leaders' theory. The approach has been elaborated on by many. For example, Wallen [13] has suggested that there are three roles in groups, played by a number of different people in a group: friend/helper, strong fighter and logical thinker. This approach tends to divide the Slater role of task leader into two: strong fighter and logical thinker. Wallen argues that all groups need a combination of these three roles to be effective; overemphasis on any one can have detrimental effects.

Most researchers involved in group behaviour would accept that the essence of Wallen's and Slater's differentiation is probably present in all groups. They would, however, also suggest that many other roles are present in human groups. For example, Handy [14] highlights at least three other very important adjunct roles to the standard two or three: the comedian, the commentator and the deviant.

- The comedian is the person who acts as a 'willing butt for other members of the group and in particular the Chairman'.
- The commentator, on the other hand, is a threat to the group, because he 'takes it upon himself to maintain an occasional commentary on the proceedings'.
- The deviant tends to draw attention to himself by disagreeing with group decisions or the group leader. This serves a very useful purpose in the group, since it provides the group with a focus for their own coherence.

It is important that management understand roles such as these when selecting team members for quality teams. In a study into the characteristics of the members and leaders of active and inactive quality circles, for example, Makin, Eveleigh and Dale[15] found that the absence of individuals with two role preferences (plant and complete finisher as described by Belbin)[16] differentiates between active and inactive circles.

The difficulties many people experience in groups occur when there is role ambiguity or conflict.

Role ambiguity exists when an individual has inadequate information about his or her role, for example in the context of work where there is a lack of clarity about the work objectives associated with the role, about colleagues' work expectation of the work role, and about the scope and responsibilities of the job. French and Caplan[17] found at one of NASA's bases, in a sample of 205 volunteer engineers, scientists and administrators, that role ambiguity was significantly related to low job satisfaction and to feelings of a job-related threat to one's mental and physical health. This was also related to increased blood pressure, pulse rate and physiological strain.

Role conflict, on the other hand, exists when an individual in a particular work role is torn by conflicting job demands or by doing things he or she really does not want to do, or does not think are part of the job or role specification. The most frequent manifestation of such conflict is when a person is caught between two groups of people who demand different kinds of behaviour, or who see the job as entailing different functions. A case in point is headquarters versus site requirements. In organizational terms, the most potentially conflicting roles are those of the shop steward or foreman. Indeed, Margolis and Kroes[18] found that foremen are seven times more likely than shop-floor workers to develop ulcers.

Which of the team-building methods should be used?

The question arises, of course, as to which of these different approaches to use to develop the effectiveness of quality improvement group activity. This will depend upon a number of factors:

- the type of team;
- the constituents of the team;
- the objectives of the team;
- how long the team has been in operation;

- the situation;
- the projects to be tackled;
- whether a consultant/facilitator is to be used;
- the skills and preferences of the consultant/facilitator; and
- the assumptions about how change takes place.

One of the most important situational determinants will be the organizational culture. In a power culture, role negotiation may be appropriate; in a role culture, a structured approach might work better. In relation to the skills and preferences of the consultant, although there is evidence to suggest that all the techniques described above can be effective, people do, obviously, tend to do best that at which they are most skilled. This is a legitimate factor to take into account when choosing a technique.

There is, of course, no harm in taking an eclectic approach, and mixing assumptions and approaches as appropriate. With a process of quality improvement, as in other contexts, it is important to be flexible and prepared to use a variety of methods and analyse the effects on the team and its outcomes.

Executive summary

- There are a number of types of teams, each with different operating characteristics, which can be employed in quality-improvement activities – some teams are drawn from one functional area and have a narrow focus, others are wider and tend to be cross-functional.
- Quality circles have a special character quite different from other methods of group working or problem-solving.
- Superior-performing companies operate a variety of teams to facilitate their continuous quality-improvement efforts.
- Team building is a primary building block in TQM
- Team building includes building mutual trust, developing interpersonal skills and adapting to people's needs.
- A variety of approaches are used in team building: T-groups, role negotiation, structured approach, team development packages and team interaction analysis.
- For a team to function effectively a number of roles must be represented, for example task leaders, social-emotional specialists, logical thinkers and strong fighters.

Notes

1 Makin, P., Cooper, C. L. and Cox, C. (1989) *Managing People at Work*, The British Psychological Society, Leicester; Routledge, London.
2 Dale, B. G. and Oakland, J. S. (1991) *Quality Improvement Through Standards*, Stanley Thornes, Cheltenham.
3 Makin, Cooper and Cox, *Managing People*.
4 Porras, J. I. and Berg, P. O. (1978) 'The impact of organizational development', *Academy of Management Review*, vol. 3, no. 2, pp. 249–66.
5 Argyris, C. (1962) *Interpersonal Competence and Organizational Effectiveness*, Dorsey, Alabama.
6 Makin, Cooper and Cox, *Managing People*.
7 Harrison, R. (1987) *Organization Culture and Quality of Service*, Association for Management Education and Development, London.
8 Blake, R. R. and Mouton, J. S. (1964) *The Managerial Grid*, Gulf Publications, Houston.
9 Adair, J. (1968) *Training for Leadership*, Macdonald, London.
10 Makin, Cooper and Cox, *Managing People*.
11 Bales, R. F. (1951) *Interaction Process Analysis: A Method for the Study of Small Groups*, Addison-Wesley, Reading, Mass.
12 Slater, P. (1955) 'Role differentiation in small groups', in P. Hare (ed.), *Small Groups*, Knopf, New York.
13 Wallen, N. (1963) 'Analysis and investigation of teaching methods', in N. Gage (ed.), *Handbook of Research in Teaching*, Rand McNally, Chicago, Ill.
14 Handy, C. (1976) *Understanding Organisations*, Penguin, Harmondsworth.
15 Makin, P. J., Eveleigh, C. W. J. and Dale, B. G. (1991) 'The influence of member role preferences and leader characteristics on the effectiveness of quality circles', *International Journal of Human Resources Management*, vol. 2, no. 2, pp. 193–204.
16 Belbin, R. M. (1981) *Management Teams, Why They Succeed or Fail*, Heinemann, London.
17 French, J. R., and Caplan, R. D. (1970) 'Psychosocial factors in coronary heart disease', *Industrial Medicine*, vol. 39, no. 3, pp. 383–97.
18 Margolis, B. L. and Kroes, W. H. L. (1974) 'Work and the health of man', in J. O'Toole (ed.), *Work and the Quality of Work Life*, MIT Press, Cambridge, Mass.

8

Involvement at Work

Introduction

Much has been said in the last couple of years about the need to demo-
cratize or humanize the workplace in British industry, to improve the
quality of working life by providing workers with greater participation
in the decisions involving their work. This can be achieved in a number
of ways, for example by including employees on company boards and
involving them in long-term policy-making issues or by allowing them
greater freedom in deciding how to organize and conduct their own jobs
and involvement in the range of team activities, as outlined in chapter
7. These two approaches to industrial democracy, which are not mutually exclusive, have been respectively termed distant and immediate
participation by Strauss and Rosenstein.[1] There are also a number of
indirect forms of participation, such as improved communication and
provision of information through briefing groups or annual employee
reports, and consultation through joint councils at departmental, plant
and company levels.

Recently, there have been developments in European companies to
establish the mechanisms of greater industrial democracy or distant participation. This chapter considers the work that has been done in the

field of *immediate* participation for, at least in the initial stages of the 'participative revolution',[2] these developments are likely to have most impact on increasing people's job satisfaction, performance and quality of working life, thus helping to create the organizational environment in which TQM and the process of quality improvement will flourish.

TQM does not work without effective employee involvement and participation, at all levels of the organization. As a concept, TQM concerns realizing the potential of people.

Employee participation objectives

Over the last decade a substantial number of employee or immediate participation programmes have been introduced throughout Europe and elsewhere under different labels: autonomous work groups, self-managing teams, job enrichment schemes, work restructuring, quality circles, quality improvement teams, manufacturing cells, etc. Each of these approaches to employee participation is attempting to meet any one or more of what Herrick and Maccoby[3] have put forward as the four principles of humanization at work:

1 Security – employees need to be free from fear and anxiety concerning health and safety, income and future employment.
2 Equity – employees should be compensated commensurately with their contribution to the value of the service or product.
3 Individuation – employees should have maximum autonomy in determining the rhythm of their work, and in planning how it should be done.
4 Democracy – employees should, wherever possible, manage themselves, be involved in the decision-making that affects their work, and accept greater responsibility in the work of the organization.

Experiments in the humanization of the immediate work environment vary enormously, from those which emphasize participative decision-making to those that attempt to nurture work autonomy, from those which have been thoroughly conceived and planned to those which have developed out of political crises and expediency, and from those which have been systematically monitored to those which have been uncritically praised. Since the European Community are likely to move increasingly toward greater participation in industry, for a variety of political and socio-pyschological reasons, it is worthwhile exploring some of the examples and results of the recent work undertaken to improve the quality of work life and, therefore, assist the organizational development of TQM. One aspect of TQM is the involvement of people in a more focused way.

Methods of involving people

A wide variety of methods can be used to help establish immediate participation, or workplace involvement, that would create a TQM environment. These include job enrichment, job enlargement, autonomous work groups, empowerment and other motivational strategies, as discussed in chapter 5.

Job enrichment, job enlargement and job rotation

Job enrichment was derived from Herzberg's theory of motivation, where he emphasized the importance of motivators (such as recognition, advancement and responsibility) at work. This theory was extended by Hackman and Oldham's[4] job characteristics model, which suggested that, if you want to motivate or involve people in their work, task variety, task significance, autonomy in the job and a feedback mechanism are essential; participation is a form of job enrichment. Job enrichment, therefore, involves developing the job in such a way as to provide these four essentials.

Job enlargement, on the other hand, might include a number of these characteristics but tends to emphasize task variety, that is, extending the number of activities in which an individual worker is involved. The Japanese concept of total productive maintenance (TPM) is a good example of this. In a natural work group machine operators can take on basic first-time servicing and maintenance, setting, self-checking, etc. TPM is discussed in chapter 9 and more details can be found in Nakajima.[5]

A variation on the theme would be job rotation, where employees move from one job to another and perform all or most of the tasks involved in a process, whether in an office or factory. This can present the problem of generating 'Jacks of all trades and masters of none'. To be effective it needs excellent initial and refresher training, plus clear procedures and working instructions.

A good quality-improvement example of involving people to make their work and processes more efficient and easier is mistake-proofing, discussed in chapter 9, details of which are found in Shingo.[6]

The success of these schemes is well documented.[7] For example, in a Dallas plant of Texas Instruments, maintenance workers were organized into nineteen-strong cleaning teams, with each member having a say in planning, problem-solving, goal setting and scheduling. This form of job enlargement and enrichment decreased employee turnover from 100 to 10 per cent, a cost saving of over $103,000 a year. In the 1970s Shell UK introduced job enlargement and enrichment in the micro-wax department at its Stanlow Refinery, where morale was low, costs high and maintenance poor. A major restructuring of job tasks was introduced, whereby employees worked as a team to complete all the job tasks as opposed to only part of them. The workers were given more decision-making power about their jobs and in respect of running the plant generally. Both commitment and morale increased. In objective terms, sickness and absenteeism were halved, off-plant wax testing was reduced by 75 per cent, output increased by between 30 and 100 per cent in various units, and occasionally significant reprocessing costs were saved.

Although job rotation, enlargement and enrichment can have some real benefits, the reorganization of the whole work environment, from top to bottom, is far more successful and long lasting. This has been shown continually since the 1970s, in the job restructuring called *autonomous work groups* in both manufacturing and administration.

Autonomous work groups

Much of the autonomous work group movement began in the 1950s and 1960s at the Tavistock Institute in the UK.[8] As Wall and Martin[9] describe them,

> a key feature of autonomous work groups is that they provide for a high degree of self determination by employees in the management of their everyday work. Typically, this involves collective control over the pace of work, distribution of tasks within the group, and the timing and organisation of breaks; also participation in the training and recruiting of new members.

This differs from job rotation, enlargement and enrichment in that the work group itself decides details of production, distribution and work group norms to a much larger extent than the former job restructuring schemes. In addition, these approaches have been more thoroughly researched than the former techniques, and have played a prominent role in the quality of worklife movement.

There are many examples of its success in the workplace. The most extensive and interesting examples of work redesign and participation programmes in Europe come from Philips, the manufacturer of electrical appliances and other equipment, mainly in its assembly operations, but there is also an example from among clerical workers. Most of these experiments took place during the 1960s. For instance, autonomous work groups were set up in the bulb assembly and finishing departments, where thirty individual jobs were combined into groups of four, with a certain amount of job rotation. It was found[10] that production costs were reduced by 20 per cent, defect levels were halved and output increased; workers' satisfaction was no higher, but they indicated a strong preference for the new job design. Philips had similar results with the autonomous work groups introduced in the black and white television factory in the 1970s. It formed seven-person work groups with twenty-minute work cycles and multiple job tasks (e.g. quality control, work distribution, material ordering). The evaluation programme revealed significantly lower absenteeism, lower waiting time for materials, better co-ordination and improved training, and component costs reduced by 10 per cent; unlike the bulb department, greater job satisfaction was expressed as well.[11] Also worthy of note was Philips's white collar experiment: the order-processing department was reorganized by product – three operational lines became three product lines. Within each product line every employee learnt all the tasks and rotated them; and each unit decided on their work group leader who, in conjunction with his or her team, was responsible for delivery of a complete product. Productivity doubled and the majority of employees expressed a preference for the new system, although some indicated that supervision was too close.

The most widely known example of work redesign in Italy took place at Olivetti's Ivres plant in the parts workshop and two assembly departments. Olivetti abolished the long assembly line on two product lines, and introduced what it called 'integrated assembly units' or 'assembly islands'. These are composed of a group of thirty people whose job is to assemble, inspect and maintain the whole product. The entire output needed is produced by a number of identical integrated units. A detailed account and assessment of its success can be found in Butera.[12] Briefly, the following changes were evident:

- increased speed of product throughput and decreased in-process time, to less than a third of the time of the line system;
- quality of product improved significantly; lower wastage;

- increased job satisfaction and worker motivation;
- there was a greater flexibility in the system for allocating human resources in the plant;
- per capita costs and training costs increased.

It can be seen that almost all the outcomes were positive, with the exception of increased per capita and training costs, which were to be expected. The activities are still in progress in Olivetti and, indeed, other departments are experimenting with new work systems.

In Sweden, where in recent times unemployment has been almost non-existent, absenteeism has been a particular difficulty in both Volvo and Saab, and the development of autonomous work groups is an initiative taken to counteract it. One of the best-documented examples is the Saab engine assembly line (at the Sodertalje truck and bus plant). The move toward autonomous work groups began in 1969 with the expansion of the works council and the development of information groups and small production teams of seven or eight – with job tasks being decided by foremen and workers in collaboration. By the early 1980s the plan had 90 development and 200 production groups, where decisions about work organization were jointly reached. In the first year of the programme, capital costs were higher and absenteeism and staff turnover were about the same as previously, but significantly more labour was attracted into the plant (and a more flexible work system was materializing). By the third year, labour turnover was reduced from 70 to 21 per cent, unplanned stoppages were down from 6 to 2 per cent, production had increased, costs were 5 per cent below budget, and absenteeism was markedly improved.[13] Another interesting Swedish example, which involved a comparative analysis of two different forms of work restructuring was carried out in Granges AB, a die-casting foundry near Stockholm. A job enrichment scheme was introduced in one unit of the plant and autonomous work groups in another. Labour turnover rose from 60 to 69 per cent and productivity fell by 7 per cent in the first unit, but in the other productivity rose 20 per cent and labour turnover decreased from 60 to 18 per cent (in addition, absenteeism fell by 5 per cent and defect levels by 2 per cent).

Finally, the type of programme carried out in the United States is best illustrated by Corning Glass, which introduced autonomous work groups in the electric hotplate assembly department at its Medfield, Massachusetts factory. Groups of six workers assembled an entire electric hotplate and had the freedom to schedule work any way they chose. Absenteeism dropped from 8 to 1 per cent, defect levels from 23 to 1 per cent and job satisfaction levels rose dramatically.

What can be learned from work humanization and employee participation schemes?

After surveying briefly some examples of work humanization and employee participation schemes, it is important to attempt to answer a number of more general questions raised by them. First, why were these programmes undertaken in the first place, that is, what did they hope to achieve? Second, how successful were they in achieving their object-ives. Third, what problems are raised by the implementation of such innovations in industry and how might they be improved in the future, particularly for assisting with the quality-improvement process?

Reasons for implementing quality of working life experiments

If we examine in detail most of the published work in this field,[14] we can begin to answer the first question posed above: what organizations hope to achieve. A survey of the best-documented and most quan-tifiable of the available studies reveals a wide range of reasons given for making such changes: recruitment difficulties, high levels of absence, high costs, high defect levels, low productivity, demarcation disputes, high labour turnover, automation, introduction of new technology, etc. The two most common reasons by far are low productivity and high absenteeism/labour turnover, together representing around half of the reasons stated by organizations. The next category, accounting for some 25 per cent of problems, comprises inadequate product quality per-formance and lack of job satisfaction. The remaining 25 per cent com-prises the following reasons (in order of frequency of expression):

- industrial relations difficulties (e.g. poor worker–management com-munication);
- experiments with new work designs;
- to encourage participation;
- unnecessarily high costs;
- inability to recruit;
- introduction of new equipment, productivity deals, etc.

It can be seen that most of these innovations apply to manufacturing or assembly-type operations with few white collar, clerical or middle-management programmes. This supports Taylor's[15] survey of the 100 best-documented international cases of work restructuring, in which he found that most of them were in assembly operations (33 per cent), semi-skilled machine tending (23 per cent) and process operating (21 per cent), while only 9 per cent were among white collar workers and maintenance tasks were a poor fifth at 3 per cent.

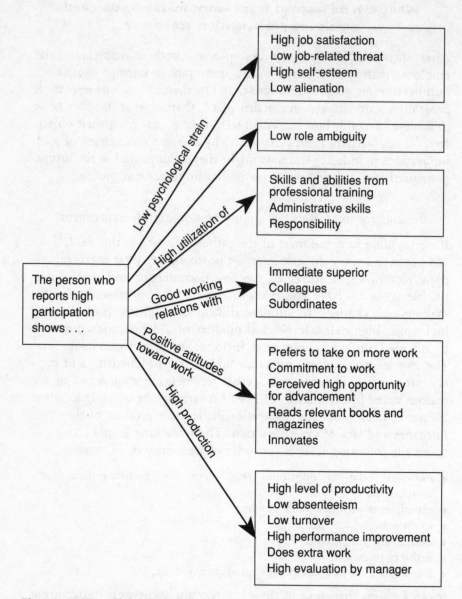

Figure 8.1 The effect of participation on work-related criteria measures
Reprinted by permission of the publisher, from French, J. R. P. and Caplan,
R. D., 'Organizational stress and individual strain', from *The Failure of Success*,
A. J. Marrow (ed.) © 1973 AMACOM, a division of the American Management
Association. All rights reserved.

This situation is due to lack of initiative by management for there is nothing to prevent clerical processes being reorganized. Lucas Industries and Girobank, to give two recent examples, have analysed their information flows in clerical and paper-processing activities and have restructured into both natural working groups and flowlines. In this way the internal 'supplier and customer' are brought closer together.

How successful are these quality of working life experiments?

For several reasons it is unwise to draw any firm generalized conclusions about the efficacy of the quality of working life and participation projects available today:

1 we may hear about only the successful interventions, while those which are less successful or of only marginal benefit are buried under piles of reports or forgotten altogether;
2 that not enough of the reported work has objective criteria measures by which we can confidently judge them;
3 insufficient work in this area is comparative, that is, where one approach, to reducing absenteeism for instance, is compared to other possible approaches.

Nevertheless, given these caveats, there remains convincing evidence that many of the participative and work humanization projects (which meet some of the criteria discussed above) have had positive individual and organizational consequences. The empirical work associated with these types of experiments was recently summarized by two University of Michigan researchers[16] in figure 8.1.

It can be seen from the figure that many of the sources and manifestations of stress for the individual at work are minimized (e.g. job-related threat, alienation, etc.), and many of the organizational objectives are achieved (e.g. lower absenteeism, high productivity, etc.), when the conditions for improving the quality of working life through involvement and participation at the workplace are introduced.

Problems associated with work humanization

In spite of the fact that quality of working life experiments have many beneficial outcomes, a number of problems and difficulties are associated with their implementation. The following are only the tip of the proverbial iceberg of potential problem areas.

1 Difficulties associated with the consequent changing roles of management

and workers occasioned by these interventions: this should not present a problem in an organization where TQM has taken root.

2 Problems of designing and recreating training programmes to meet the specific needs of the different varieties of work humanization projects: in short, training is a problem in many Western business situations and needs improving.

3 Coping with the fears of first-line supervisors and middle management: the involvement from the outset of supervisors and middle managers is important as is discussing with them the redefinition of roles.

4 Dealing with the resistance of the unions, who may feel that some of these approaches threaten to affect the number of jobs and manning levels: this is very much dependent upon the skills of management, positive work environment and the opportunity of redeploy excess personnel.

5 Increasing costs during the initial phase of these interventions: benefits will appear later (see chapter 2 on quality costs reduction).

6 Organizations may have to pay more for workers taking increased responsibility: this will lead to increased involvement and loyalty.

Because of all these potential problem areas, a number of stages should be gone through in introducing employee participation and quality of working life schemes, as discussed by Ottaway.[17]

1 Vital to any successful change project is that there is a pyschological contract between those changing and those advocating or implementing the change. This will involve all employees concerned with the change, discussing the 'what', 'how' and 'when' of the change programme. One way to ensure success at this stage is the formation of a working party of all interested participants, to oversee the quality of working life intervention to fruition.

2 It is important to diagnose the quality of working life problem areas: job design, style of management, the required quality improvements, industrial relations difficulties, etc., and then to introduce a small-scale project as a pilot scheme.

3 To design the change effort with the full participation of those who will be involved in the change programme.

4 Before implementing the new programme, it is essential to take back any possible proposal for change to top management and the unions, who first contracted the change programme and established the working party, to endorse the suggested project.

5 Once the programme has been accepted, training must be introduced to prepare those concerned with the skills necessary to carry through the experiment successfully. Shop-floor workers may need to learn, for example, how to make decisions in groups, or first-line supervisors how to facilitate greater worker involvement or relinquish decision-making power.

6 In addition to helping to create the work structure in which change can take place and preparing people for the change by training, it is necessary to reinforce the appropriate new behaviours that emerge.

These six steps should ensure that many of the potential difficulties associated with humanizing the workplace are minimized or to some extent contained. In addition to these stages, and permeating the whole process of change in this field, are four underlying principles, emphasized by French and Caplan,[18] which must be adhered to throughout.

1 The participation or change programme is not illusory, that is, it is not used as a manipulation tool (for example, when management asks employees for advice and then ignores it).
2 The decisions on which participation are based are not trivial to the people concerned (e.g. management asking workers to decide on the colour of the paper to be used for the company's newsletter).
3 Those aspects of the work environment on which participation is based are relevant to the needs of the workers.
4 The decisions in which people participate are perceived as legitimately theirs to make.

These conditions are critical guidelines in designing and developing processes which encourage involvement and work sharing, as major steps toward TQM.

Executive summary

- TQM will not function effectively without the total commitment and involvement at all levels of the organizational hierarchy.
- TQM is all about realizing the potential of people.
- The vast majority of a company's employees are, in general, keen to contribute to a process of continuous quality improvement.
- Management need to design strategies for developing and encouraging involvement.
- Security, equity, freedom of action/autonomy and democracy are the four principles of humanization at work.
- Job enrichment, job enlargement, job rotation and autonomous work groups can all assist the involvement of people in the workplace.
- Teamworking, flexibility and quality improvement are key involvement ingredients.

Notes

1 Strauss, G. and Rosenstein, E. (1970) 'Worker participation: a critical view', *Industrial Relations*, vol. 9, no. 2, pp. 197–214.
2 Preston, L. E. and Post, J. E. (1974) 'The third managerial revolution'. *Academy of Management Journal*, vol. 17, no. 3, pp. 476–86.
3 Herrick, N. Q. and Maccoby, M. (1976) 'Humanising work: a priority goal of the 1970s', in L. E. Davis and A. B. Cherns (eds), *The Quality of Working Life*, Free Press, New York, vol. 1, pp. 63–77.
4 Hackman, J. R. and Oldham, G. R. (1976) 'Motivation through the design of work: test of a theory', *Organizational Behavior and Human Performance*, vol. 16, no. 2, pp. 250–79.
5 Nakajima, S. (1988) *Introduction to Total Productive Maintenance*, Productivity Press, Cambridge, Mass.
6 Shingo, S. (1986) *Zero Quality Control: Source Inspection and the Poka-Yoke System*, Productivity Press, Cambridge, Mass.
7 Cooper, C. L. and Mumford, E. (1979) *Quality of Working Life in Western and Eastern Europe*, ABP London; Wall, T. and Martin, R. (1987) 'Job and work design', in C. L. Cooper and I. T. Robertson (eds), *International Review of Industrial and Organizational Psychology, 1987*, John Wiley Sons, New York and Chichester: pp. 69–91.
8 Trist, E. L. and Bamforth, K. W. (1951) 'Some social and psychological consequences of the long-wall method of coal-getting', *Human Relations*, vol. 4, no. 1, pp. 3–38.
9 Wall and Martin, 'Job and work design'.
10 Den Hertog, F. J. (1974) 'Work structuring Philips' Gloeilampen-fabrieken', *Industrial Psychology*.
11 Ibid.
12 Butera, F. (1975) 'Environmental factors in job and organization design: the case of Olivetti', in Davis and Cherns (eds), vol. 1, pp. 166–200.
13 Norstedt, J. and Aguren, S. (1974) *The Saab–Scania Report*, Swedish Employers Confederation, Stockholm.
14 Davis, L. E. and Cherns, A. B. (eds) (1975), *The Quality of Working Life*, vols. 1 and 2; Wilpert, B. and Sorge, A. (1984) *International Yearbook of Organizational Democracy*, John Wiley, Chichester.
15 Taylor, J. C. (1972) 'Quality of working life: annotated bibliography', unpublished paper, University of California, Los Angeles.
16 French, J. R. P. and Caplan, R. D. (1973) 'Organizational stress and individual strain', in A. J. Marrow (ed.), *The Failure of Success*, Amacom, New York.
17 Ottaway, R. (1975) 'Working in the right direction', *The Guardian*, 15 September 1975.
18 French and Caplan, 'Organizational stress'.

9

The Japanese Approach to TQM

Introduction

Most experts are agreed that quality is the dominant factor in the success of Japanese companies in world markets, and much has been written about this during the last decade or so. In any text dealing with the subject of TQM it would be a serious omission not to discuss the ways in which Japanese companies manage quality. In the pursuit of TQM, learning from best practice can afford considerable benefit. It is possible to discover pointers to the future strategic directions in which organizations should move if they are to gain competitive advantage.

Total quality control (TQC) is undoubtedly the integrative strategic framework of the Japanese company. The concept of TQC (which also readily translates to total quality commitment or total quality care) is accepted without question by the Japanese, and it is the qualifying criterion in their home market. TQC is not perceived as desirable; it is considered to be *essential for continued survival*. By their considerable efforts over the last twenty-five to thirty years a number of Japanese companies have the principles of TQC firmly in place and are totally committed to sustaining the process of continuous improvement.

The chapter is structured under the following broad headings:

- customer satisfaction;
- long-term planning;
- research and development;
- organizing and planning for quality assurance and improvement;
- management of improvement;
- visible management system;
- involvement of people;
- education and training;
- total productive maintenance;
- just-in-time.

The data on which the chapter is based have been collected by Barrie Dale from leading four study missions of European manufacturing executives to Japan to examine the approach to TQC in a selection of their major manufacturing companies.

Customer satisfaction

In Japan the internal market place is dominant and competition fierce. Organizations need to be totally dedicated to satisfying customers and this effort must be long term and continuous; otherwise they will be overtaken by the competition. The market is saturated and demands ever-increasing product diversification and attractiveness, speedy response to market needs, rigorous reliability and quality of conformance. Japanese companies believe that bringing new products to the market place quickly will sustain their competitive edge. 'The customer always comes first' is a term they use to describe their market-orientated spirit. They are always looking at the needs of the market. They also comment that their customers' quality requirements are becoming increasingly rigorous, and that these requirements are a moving target. It is also interesting to note that Japanese companies concentrate on increasing market share and net sales, and not the rate of return on investment.

There is a total belief that business operations and efficiency can be improved by reflecting customers' needs and requirements. Japanese organizations have a variety of systems and procedures by which they can properly identify these needs and keep focused on the market. They go to considerable lengths to collect information on the wants and needs of customers. For example, a manufacturer of ceramic products has 4,500 fixed points of observation from which data are collected. It is also common practice for Japanese organizations to use quality function deployment (QFD) to translate customers' wants into design requirements, and build in quality at source. Detailed information is also developed on customer profiles, their current needs and future expectations. The databanks Japanese organizations have built up on this are far in excess of anything witnessed in European companies.

Long-term planning

Quality, cost and delivery

Quality (including service), cost and delivery (accuracy and lead time) (QCD) are the main objectives and organizations strive to become the best at them – a prime consideration in company vision, mission and policy statements. Extensive use is made of mottoes expressing some appropriate message on QCD. This helps to keep the theme in the forefront of employees' minds. The mottoes, often suggested by employees, are changed at least once a year. It was stressed by the representatives of companies visited that this policy of quality first has remained unchanged since their formation. They believe that their corporate strength is built up through TQC, and quality is foremost in every aspect of corporate policy. This view is encapsulated in the point made by one organization that even if only one out of 10,000 products failed, the failure rate for that customer would be 100 per cent.

Planning, feedback and decision-making on TQC are long term, often extending at least ten years ahead, and then a series of middle-range plans are formulated to assist in meeting the long-term business plan and strategic themes.

Policy deployment

One of the main TQC planning activities is the deployment of the

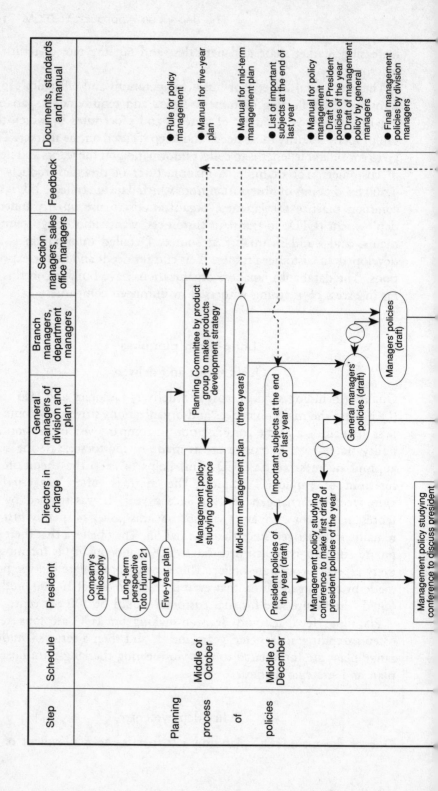

Step	Schedule	President	Directors in charge	General managers of division and plant	Branch managers, department managers	Section managers, sales office managers	Feedback	Documents, standards and manual
Planning process of policies		Company's philosophy						● Rule for policy management
	Middle of October	Long-term perspective Toto Human 21						● Manual for five-year plan
		Five-year plan	Management policy studying conference	Planning Committee by product group to make products development strategy				● Manual for mid-term management plan
	Middle of December	Mid-term management plan (three years)						● List of important subjects at the end of last year
		President policies of the year (draft)	Important subjects at the end of last year					● Manual for policy management
		Management policy studying conference to make first draft of president policies of the year		General managers' policies (draft)	Managers' policies (draft)			● Draft of President policies of the year ● Draft of management policy by general managers
		Management policy studying conference to discuss president						● Final management policies by division managers

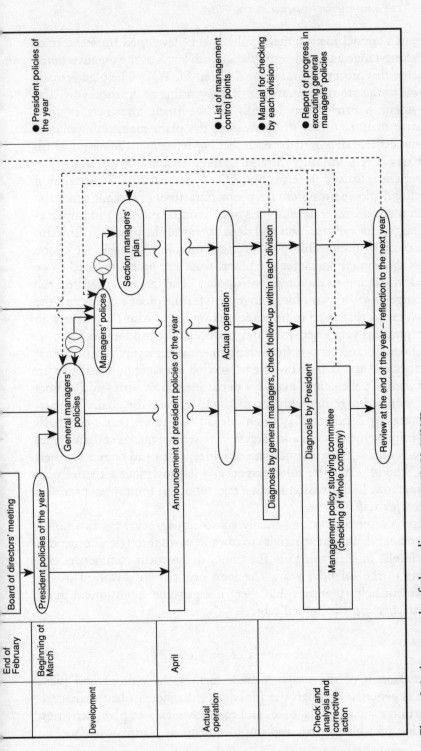

Figure 9.1 An example of the policy management system

Source: Toto Ltd, Chigasaki Works, Chigasaki City, Japan.

president's annual management policy plan (developed from the company's long-range and mid-term plans) to all levels of the organizational hierarchy; this process provides the skeleton for TQC. The plan is made available to the group companies at the beginning of the fiscal year. The deployment is carried out initially by the plant managers to their respective manufacturing divisions, and the plant manager's policy is then successively deployed by each section/department manager to his or her area of responsibility through to foremen and line operators. The deployment is usually in terms of QCD. Figure 9.1 is an illustration of the policy deployment system from a manufacturer of ceramic products.

Each plant manager develops his or her annual policies and improvement targets for every section and department of the plant(s) within his or her remit of responsibility to meet the president's policy. He or she decides the annual policy for the plant, what key problems need to be tackled in relation to the president's policy. The target is based on the long-range business plan, long-range plan for the plant's operation, the improvements that need to be made, taking into account an evaluation of the previous year's activities and performance, production forecasts and schedules, and reports from departmental managers. This target is fully discussed and debated with each section manager in relation to his or her annual policies and plans for departmental activities until a final target is agreed together with the methods to reach the goal. This particular activity is called 'Play catch'. It is usual to set yearly and half-yearly improvement plans and targets. The section manager then agrees with each of his or her foremen the activities, plans and targets for their group, who in turn agree roles, targets and improvement activities with ᵕᵕh operator. Each division keeps a register of the improvement action agreed with staff.

There is a set time scale (usually six to eight weeks) for this policy management deployment activity to cascade down through all organizational levels. In each company the policy deployment commences at a set time in the calendar year. The long negotiations involved in the deployment help to ensure that there is a genuine commitment at all levels to meeting the agreed targets.

Assessment of progress

The assessment of the progress made against the policies and plans agreed is generally through the president's diagnosis; plant managers' and section managers' diagnoses and monthly review of plant activities; discussion of achievements and improvements at plant conferences on

QCD; and for each section its daily management and records in terms of clarity of the section's function in the organization and the role of each person, clear points of control, activities for improvement, standardization and taking corrective action. The plan–do–check–action (PDCA) cycle is extensively used in all these diagnoses (see figure 9.2).

It is usual for the plant manager to audit quarterly the progress being made by each section to achieve its improvement objectives, and for the section manager to undertake a diagnosis of his or her section quarterly and monthly. Line operators carry out a self-estimation of their achievements, against the agreed target, which is commented upon by the foreman and followed up by a personal interview. The foreman then reports to the section manager on his or her achievement, the outstanding problems and the priority actions to be taken, and this reporting procedure is continued up through the organizational structure. If achievement against target is low, a full discussion will take place with all concerned to determine the reasons for this and to decide the corrective actions to recover the situation.

In some organizations the process of policy deployment is also subject to diagnosis by outside experts such as Union of Japanese Scientists and Engineers (JUSE) and/or university professors. Any reports relating to the diagnosis are subjected to an in-depth examination. It is argued that the process of deployment is itself important, not just the results.

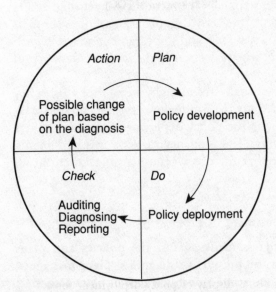

Figure 9.2 The plan–do–check–action cycle

It is usual for each section to have a visible display of this policy deployment, as part of its visible management system. Figure 9.3 illustrates the key points of the typical format of such a display. The left-hand side of the figure shows the tree of policy deployment from the plant manager down to each section, which makes its own plans for improvement based on existing problems. The overall rate of imperfection for each section is related to the different processes, with information being provided on individual problems. A proportion defective (p) control chart is used to monitor the rate of imperfection against the set target. The right-hand side of the chart displays annual improvement targets, for quality, delivery, cost, safety and morale. A slogan relating to the improvement is displayed on the board at the head of

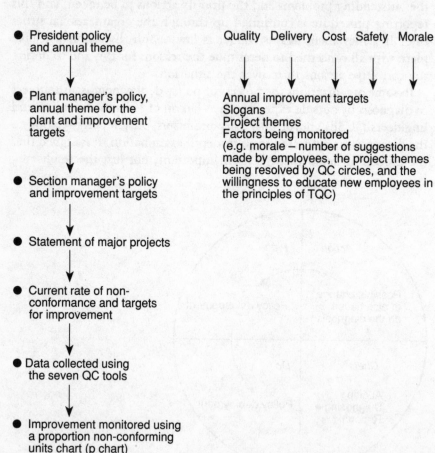

Figure 9.3 Key points of the visual display of policy deployment for a section

the problem to be solved. The names of the workers responsible for the various activities relating to the policy deployment are also displayed. All these plans include a number of provisions for the involvement of employees in the quality-improvement process. Positioned at right angles to the board and completing the policy deployment 'corner' are pictures of typical imperfections in the section together with an improvement book. This book logs each improvement made, and helps to promote standardization and serves as a point of reference for people on the type of improvements made in the past.

Within each section there is an effort to solve each year at least two major projects, registered as themes and derived from the policy deployment. This is in addition to the activities of quality circles (QCs). European companies tend to try to solve too many problems at the same time, and as a consequence the improvement effort tends to be too thinly spread.

In European companies the job of CEO is a lonely one, and managing directors, plant managers and other middle managers often filter out information to the CEO. In Japan the policy deployment and its visible display at shop-floor level not only ensure that the president can see what is happening in each section of each division under his or her control, but also that all personnel know the details of the president's policy and what is required by their section and themselves to make the necessary contribution to achievement of overall policy. The discipline of policy deployment and the agreement at each organizational level of achievable targets ensure that line operators' and section managers' energies are directed to the same ends, and likewise up to the level of president; this is often termed a spiral upward movement.

There is little doubt that the policy deployment method facilitates both the attainment of corporate goals and the operation of the organization in a systematic manner. It also assists in integrating the quality-improvement process with organizational long-term strategic plans.

Commitment of senior management

The total commitment and leadership of senior management on a long-term basis is always stressed by the Japanese as a key point for successful TQC activities. The role of senior management includes:

1 ensuring that the entire organization is committed to TQC and establishing corporate quality systems;
2 promoting TQC activities continuously;

3 participating in such activities as:
  (a) membership of the committee for quality planning;
  (b) quality assurance meetings for design and manufacture of quality into the product;
  (c) quality audit, quality improvement and corrective action meetings;
  (d) quality audits and diagnoses of the improvement activities of site locations (in relation to these audits and diagnoses, senior management study, prior to the actual visits, information on factors such as the quality-improvement plans, targets, achievements and problems; these data are provided by the TQC promotions office);
  (e) motivating employees;
  (f) involvement in quality-related education and training.

Research and development

Japanese companies believe that research and development (R & D) is the main way to sustain their competitive edge, and this is the major focus of their efforts. They invest heavily in R & D and vigorously pursue new product development. Japanese companies are engaged in short- and long-term R & D. Long-term R & D tends to relate to materials development, and how to combine and integrate different types of technologies. The less innovative short-term R & D is geared to the development of new product features, process development, etc. It is interesting to note that, in what Western companies may regard as the maintenance department, it is not unusual for Japanese companies to undertake R & D in machine technology, using in-house expertise and/or through collaboration with external specialists. They tend to engage in pure research as opposed to leasing this to universities.

Japanese companies aim to bring an increasing number of attractive high-value added products to the market in the shortest possible time. To them this is a key issue and one to which they commit considerable time and resources. Product life cycles in Japanese markets are growing shorter and shorter, and there is an ever increasing demand from the market place for new products. Considerable efforts are concentrated on reducing the cycle time for product development. The Japanese market is continually looking for products with more unique features. Japanese companies believe that if they produce standard products with only a minimum of diversification they will not survive in the market place. Some companies have combined the R & D and marketing functions, to facilitate the creation of new market demands, develop their present market share and exploit technology know-how.

Corporate prestige = R & D

Japanese companies have a systematic approach to R & D, and this helps to reduce the time between product concept and market launch. They have a considerable R & D database on their accumulated experiences from product development to full-scale production from which their designers can draw to satisfy customer needs. This typically contains a variety of information on such aspects as design features, QFD carried out on previous products, product development, design for manufacturability, FMEA, fault tree analysis (FTA), success tree analysis (STA), reliability, and the product shapes and features which appear to customers. This resource certainly provides a competitive advantage by enabling them to produce new designs and products at a faster and faster rate, which Western European companies find hard to emulate. Japanese companies thrive on their reputation for leading-edge technology, and corporate prestige is measured in terms of the R & D activity.

R & D to production

The R & D project team steers the product concept through the various stages from R & D to development to trial production and ultimately full-scale production. Therefore, the team ensures that the design intent is being planned into the product, helps the production division understand the product, assists with operator training and deals with problems as and when they arise during each stage of the manufacturing process. A commonly expressed view is that the research laboratory is the teacher and the factories are the students. The R & D centres also tend to select and prove the equipment before it is used by the factory in full-scale production.

At one research centre, a supplier of components to the automotive industry was developing advanced electronics for use in automotive components, and in turn these developments are driving design developments in the major motor manufacturers. In general, the reverse is true in the European motor industry, with suppliers manufacturing to an original equipment manufacturer's design and carrying out little development work of their own.

Organizing and planning for quality assurance and improvement

Japanese companies take a company-wide approach to quality assurance, from product planning through to sales and services. They usually have a TQC promotions office at head office and sometimes at each plant. As the name suggests, it is used to promote TQC, through a variety of activities such as:

- establishing a TQC policy;
- education and training (inside and outside the organization);
- promoting standardization;
- facilitating QCs and cross-functional teams;
- involvement in steering committees;
- analysing and co-ordinating improvement activities; and
- communicating and exchanging data with suppliers.

The Japanese are great advocates of the lateral management of major functions, and typically have committees dealing with quality assurance, development, cost, delivery, supply, policy and standardization. For example, a typical quality improvement committee will meet three or four times each year and will establish improvement policies and deal with issues such as the organizational activities of QC and how to develop the skills of employees. A quality assurance committee will analyse, catalogue and discuss any day-to-day problems, non-conformance problems in the field and make decisions on how to resolve problems.

The manufacturing department is responsible for maintaining quality; the quality assurance department for:

- providing guidance to manufacturing and other sections in terms of problem analysis and developing improvement plans;
- evaluation of product quality performance;
- audits of the manufacturing division;
- product inspection;
- quality-related training; and
- ensuring that people follow up the plans decided by the TQC promotion office or TQC committee and assisting in cascading these plans down to all levels in the organization hierarchy.

Corporate quality assurance department

In large organizations there is usually a corporate quality assurance department (CQAD). Its role, at a major manufacturer of electronic products for example, is to:

- give guidance on TQC to all companies in the group;
- set a long-term and medium-term policy for the manufacturing divisions;
- provide quality education and training;
- undertake quality auditing;
- maintain a quality performance system for each division and to grade divisions according to performance;
- assess whether the product is easy to use;
- determine that the product is safe if used incorrectly;
- carry out inspections of the company's products on a component by component basis;
- examine packaging;
- carry out endurance tests;
- undertake comparative studies and evaluation of the company's and competitor's products, and other tests to anticipate problems before they occur;
- undertake life style research; and
- study how to produce readable instruction manuals.

General managers are responsible for TQC

The general manager of each division is responsible for TQC, and the TQC promotion office and quality assurance department work together to facilitate continuous quality improvement. Each section and division is responsible for QCD planning at source. They submit a report on their improvement activities to the quality assurance department, which then compiles a report for the TQC promotion office which in turn is passed to the president for consideration in his annual audit of the division.

Source control

The Japanese believe that quality assurance is the central core of TQC, and without effective quality assurance procedures, TQC is difficult. When problems occur they are analysed in considerable detail, using a defect analysis sheet. The Japanese place considerable emphasis on finding out *where* and *why* they are doing things wrongly. The usual procedure is to put in place an emergency measure followed by individual and then systematic recurrence-prevention measures. They are very careful not to repeat failures. When anything unsatisfactory *is* detected, it is fed back to the appropriate upstream stage and preventive action taken to counteract the trouble.

The emphasis is on *source control*, and typical activities employed to assist this include:

- quality assurance tables (e.g. control plans) for in-company and sub-contractor's work;
- design review to prevent any failure on the part of designers;
- the production of operating procedures by the foreman and line operators; and
- standards and instructions for daily control.

In addition, a variety of aids are provided to afford operators all the help required to get it right the first time and to prevent errors:

- checksheets;
- operating instructions;
- product identification cards;
- mistake-proof devices;
- process operation sheets;
- particular features and parameters requiring attention; and
- machine vision systems.

At one manufacturer, every line worker produces a working instruction entitled 'What I know about my job – the knack of doing my job'; these are prominently displayed.

Taking notes – the Japanese way

In planning for quality from the R & D and design stages, considerable attention is given to listening to the customer and a variety of means are employed for this purpose. During planning and production preparation, trial production and full-scale production and field experience, detailed notes are kept of any problems encountered and the counter-measures taken. *Taking notes is part of the Japanese management style.* These notes are always referred to and used in planning new products. All the necessary preparations are made in advance of actual production and considerable resources are committed to this activity. In European organizations, the production preparation stage is rushed in the hope that any problems can be sorted out later, and even if notes are made they are often not analysed and used to prevent recurrence of problems in future products; there is little learning from past mistakes.

Resident engineer system

In the development and design stage, engineers from the quality assurance and inspection departments take up residence in the development and design department (this is termed the resident engineer system). The designs are evaluated for potential difficulties at the volume production stage. Consideration is given to the preventive measures taken to counter problems, and efficient means of production to ensure design quality. Then, in the production preparation stage, development and design department engineers take up residence in the production and inspection departments to ensure that the design requirements are interpreted correctly, pass on know-how gained during the design and development stage and promote the implementation of countermeasures against troubles, including mistake-proofing.[1] These cross-functional teams facilitate the process of simultaneous/concurrent engineering, which not only reduces product development times but also ensures that the designs are suitable to be manufactured and reduces the number of late engineering changes.

Major suppliers also join in at the design stage (they are called guest designers), to ensure that their specialist expertise is used; improvements are identified early in the design cycle. Suppliers are also encouraged to suggest cost levels for their products.

Feed-forward approach

To help assure product quality, there is feedback and/or feed forward of quality information in production planning, product design, prototype evaluation, pre-production planning, purchasing, quality audit, evaluation of pre-production products, volume production, inspection, evaluation of the products from volume production and sale and field-service operations. The objective is to build in quality at each stage before sending work to the next process. There is total collaboration and co-operation between R & D, technical, quality assurance and manufacturing departments to eliminate problems and ensure that processes are mistake-proof.

In order to identify defects early in the design process and to assure design quality, techniques such as design reviews, design of experiments, quality assurance meetings, QFD, FMEA, FTA, quality audits and reliability tests are common. In the production preparation phase the production engineers endeavour to predict failures for the process and to take collective action before machine and process sequences are finalized. FMEA and process capability studies are employed to assist with this. It is usual to carry out a process capability study every time new production facilities are used, when a new design is produced on existing facilities and in the mass production of established products.

Immaculate housekeeping

In all the companies visited, housekeeping was immaculate. At a steel mill, for example, the mission members wore white gloves, which when discarded were hardly discoloured. When touring the photosetting department of a printing company, members had to tie plastic covers over their shoes. Little dust was found on window ledges in any of the organizations visited. Japanese companies believe in having clear gangways: any necessary equipment relating to processes is placed on racking located on an outside wall. It is not uncommon to see the space between the gangway and the outside wall painted green to represent grass, with potted plants placed on the paint. Cleanliness and housekeeping are prerequisites for effective quality assurance, and should be pursued more vigorously by European companies. The general impression is of a working environment which is clean and comfortable and in harmony with employees.

Management of improvement

It was quite clear from the presentations made by the Japanese managers and technical specialists that they form part of a totally committed management team who are enthusiastic, enjoy their jobs and work vigorously on continuous improvement in pursuit of perfection. They believe in the future and have a long-term vision of their company's direction. The companies visited exhibit the typical profile of high growth: one such company had increased sales by 21 per cent during the previous three years, the new products to sales ratio by 25 per cent and labour productivity by 50 per cent. Most companies were planning to increase sales by 20 to 25 per cent over a period of three years.

Japanese management articulate very effectively what they are doing and are highly confident that their strategy and course of action are right. The aim of each company is to be the market leader and the best, whereas in the West the majority of companies appear satisfied with second or third place.

Quality culture

The Japanese have developed a corporate style which, based on the evidence of their worldwide production facilities, can operate successfully anywhere. Their success is not just a matter of national culture, which is simply one factor, but stems directly from management and creating an organizational culture which is conducive to continuous improvement. They appear to have developed a standardized method of managing companies and the improvement process, a method that can be applied to most cultures. They are expanding on a worldwide basis in order to maintain their high sales growth, and most companies visited have made a series of moves to internationalize their base of operation.

An uncomfortable number of European manufacturing companies have a fundamental management problem, characterized by those managers, at all levels, who give the impression that they are just going through the motions. In such companies, if a small number of key people leave, the improvement process stagnates and finally disappears. The Japanese, on the other hand, appear to have moved to a situation of autonomous improvement. All employees manage for themselves the improvement effort, which proceeds in a common direction with each person accepting responsibility. Their efforts are helped by the Japanese tendency to bring all improvement initiatives together under a single banner (TQC or just-in-time, for example), which is then translated into a company-wide effort. This gives their improvement activities and teams a clear focus. In European companies the initiatives being pursued tend to be segmented and somewhat fragmented, and, are the responsibility of individual departments and people.

Through their involvement with individual initiatives, QC and/or through the suggestion scheme, Japanese operators are constantly engaged on problem prevention and improvement activities. They also pay keen attention to the quality of their machinery, through total productive maintenance (TPM). When problems arise emergency teams assist the operator to rectify the situation. There are regular meetings between groups of operators, supervisors and technical specialists to discuss problems and improvement actions. In Western companies there are usually a number of organizational layers between spotting the problem, its solution and recovery of the situation.

Japanese manufacturing managers do, however, operate in a more favourable environment than their Western counterparts. Japanese companies have a bias toward manufacturing in general and engineering in particular. Companies employ huge numbers of engineers. The majority of European manufacturing companies employ insufficient engineers and consequently have not the resources to solve problems. Every Japanese with whom discussions took place during the course of the study missions appreciates that manufacturing is the key to their national economy; improving manufacturing efficiency and productivity is discussed all the time. Work occupies the collective consciousness of the Japanese, and they all realize that their future depends on it.

Investment in people and equipment

Japanese managers and technical specialists exhibit a caring attitude towards production and what is happening on the factory shop floor. Senior and middle managers regularly visit the shop floor to see what is happening, they ask about results and problems, they give advice and help to create good habits through leadership. In European companies most senior managers tend to isolate themselves in their offices.

The Japanese investment in equipment without having to worry about short-term payback periods and know that this will be beneficial over the longer term. This willingness to invest must be a considerable feature in the motivation of their managers and engineers. In the main, the investment is to reduce labour costs. The last thirty or so years have proved the wisdom of this policy. The typical payback period for equipment is three to five years, compared to the one year in European companies; interest rates are also lower.

European manufacturing management are frequently heard to complain that their engineers always want computer equipment and software for their projects. By contrast, while making extensive use of computer-aided design and manufacturing systems, Japanese engineers concentrate a considerable amount of their improvement effort on doing the simple things well. They also spend more time on the shop floor than their European counterparts. Much of the equipment employed by Japanese companies is relatively basic. The key factor is not the equipment itself but how it is used to improve manufacturing efficiency; it is not simply a matter of investing in new technology. All the Japanese companies visited had their own internal machinery manufacturing division and a vast amount of the equipment seen during the factory tours is customized. The proprietory equipment is often employed to eliminate waste and transportation between processes and to facilitate good internal logistics.

Visible management system

Japanese companies place considerable emphasis on their operating data being visible on the factory shop floor. They believe that everyone in the company benefits from an open information system. A complete range of information, in a variety of formats, is displayed. These data assist managers, technical specialists and operators to manage their processes more effectively, facilitate the process of continuous incremental improvement, and identify and publicize the improvements made. The system keeps employees in touch with what is happening, provides a focus to help concentrate efforts, indicates when events are not going to plan and provides warning signals of all kinds of different events. Display devices are often created by operators and first-line supervisors. In some cases, the display is related to a specific manufacturing section (e.g. who is responsible for specific activities, TPM achievements, QC members and projects and a skill matrix including the picture of operators), and in others to a particular topic (e.g. policy deployment, mistake-proofing, education and safety). The following are examples of this visible management system.

- One company, as part of a campaign to improve plant safety performance, displayed on a noticeboard the safety actions to which each operator had committed himself or herself together with the operator's photograph.
- A schematic layout in the sub-assembly and assembly areas of one organization indicated the flow of work and, using different colours, the zone position of different types of operators and their role: red – full-time employees; brown – casual employees; blue – operators responsible for the supply of parts; yellow – employees assisting a section which has fallen behind its scheduled production target.
- A complete wall of one plant was covered in charts relating to a variety of issues, including details and pictures of improvements made, safety achievements and performance, attendance statistics, quality issues, suggestions, production targets, and QC and TPM activities.
- In a refrigeration unit assembly line, quality-control checksheets were displayed at each workstation indicating the product characteristics to which attention is needed, the important processes, and the self-inspections and tests to be carried out.
- In one organization, a number of sub-assembly areas were supplying assembly lines, across a gangway. Each sub-assembly area and line had scheduled production targets for specific times of the shift. If production was on schedule a grey card was displayed across the gangway; if production was two units behind schedule a red card was used.

Team spirit and common ground

There is little doubt that this sharing and diffusion of information helps to ensure that everybody is working together for the good of the company, and will inevitably reduce organizational conflict. There is total openness about concepts such as TQC, TPM and JIT. Everybody in the company knows why they are doing it, the strategies and objectives, techniques employed and successes and failures; this encourages team spirit. In a number of companies, the information displayed indicated that the improvement objective was to reduce the number of operating staff in a production section. Any staff affected in this way are transferred to other sections and to subsidiaries. Transfers are made openly and in consultation with the company labour union. Japanese workers become far more flexible as a consequence, and have the opportunity to broaden and improve their skills. All the companies visited stressed this point and said workers accepted job rotation and movement from one job to another very readily. Job flexibility and job rotation help to eliminate departmental boundaries, which are often a major stumbling block to improvement activities, and diffuse new technologies, approaches and systems to every corner of an organization. Most workers are in multi-skilled groups and able to do all jobs in an area; there are no detailed job descriptions and the salary is paid for the person and not the job. Japanese companies firmly believe in developing generalists and not specialists. The system of lifetime employment and single-company labour unions obviously facilitates flexibility, job rotation and long-term education and training programmes.

Involvement of people

The mission statements of all the organizations visited stressed that their greatest asset is people, and all employees are encouraged to participate in quality improvement. More than one company said that because of the lifetime employment situation they were always searching for ways to motivate and revitalize their staff. The usual means was through QCs, suggestion schemes, other small group activities, a variety of presentations, job rotation, and continuous education and training.

Quality circles and suggestion schemes provide the mechanism and motivation for involving everyone in an organization in continuous improvement. Considerable importance is attached to these two activities and they are seen as complementary. QC can submit suggestions and also have their projects evaluated by the scheme. A variety of award schemes, contests and prizes are used to recognize employees' efforts and to provide direct rewards. Great kudos are attached to these awards. The quantity and quality of suggestions are seen to be important and reflect the department manager's ability to create an environment conducive to improvement.

In a typical suggestion scheme, a suggestion is submitted and evaluated the same day by the foreman of the section; the person making the suggestion is awarded 100 to 300 yen. If the suggestion is considered to have potential it is written up in more detail. At this stage it is evaluated by the section manager and his or her assistant or the QC committee and can qualify for a reward of 1,000 to 10,000 yen. If considered of special merit it can be put forward for annual evaluation and the President's Prize of between 10,000 and 20,000 yen; the evaluation is carried out by the TQC promotion and QC committees.

Quality circles

Without exception the organizations visited had thriving QC programmes involving a large proportion of the total workforce, and suggestion schemes through which a considerable number of suggestions were obtained and most of them implemented. QCs can be considered a natural part of Japanese working life, and in this respect it is perhaps not advisable to make a close comparison with their use by Western organizations. Within each section, the line workers are involved with their foreman in making day-to-day improvements in their routine work activities. They do not appear to separate out, as is the case in the West, QC activities and day-to-day work activities; it is one unified improvement effort at shop-floor level. QCs generally tackle projects which are related to their section's improvement objectives for meeting the president's, plant manager's and section manager's policies and they tend to be managed by the section manager. It was stressed that QCs, while essential, are but a small part of the quality-improvement process.

In most Japanese companies all non-managerial employees belong to a QC. There is some suggestion that membership is not voluntary, with considerable peer pressure to be involved. The effectiveness of QCs is usually assessed at annual or six-monthly intervals, at which time good performance is recognized.

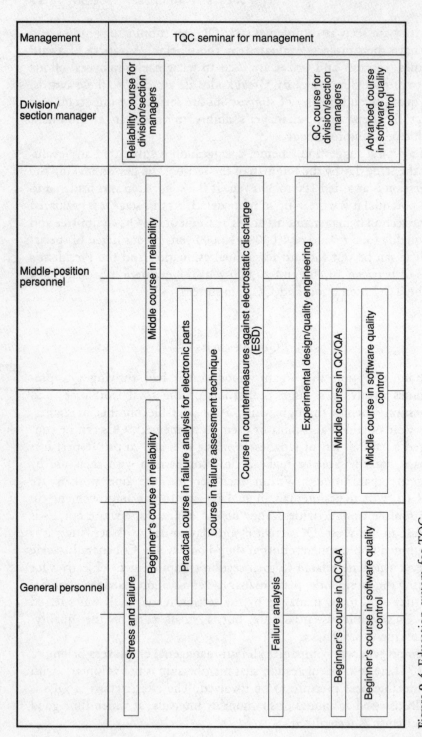

Figure 9.4 Education system for TQC
Source: Omron Corporation, Kusatsu-City, Japan.

Typical objectives of QCs and suggestion schemes in the organizations visited are:

Quality circles
- to provide opportunities for self-improvement of knowledge and skills through co-operative team efforts;
- to create a rewarding work environment; and
- to create a workplace where total participation in quality control is a reality.

Suggestion schemes
- to improve the power to work and individual abilities;
- to promote friendly and healthy human relations among all employees and to vitalize activities; and
- to improve the company structure and operations.

There is a considerable effort to create a work environment in which staff are active participants. The Japanese companies visited treat their workers as human beings and not as tools, and they go to considerable lengths to promote harmony between personnel and technology.

Education and training

Japanese companies believe that everyone in an organization must understand TQC, and that this can be achieved only by education and training. They take a long-range view of quality education and training and tend to have a master training schedule and curriculum to develop the skills of all their employees. The schedule recognizes the different training requirements of people in different functions and levels in the organizational hierarchy (see figure 9.4). Senior managers take a personal interest in the content of the training programme.

Education and training programmes are developed to increase each person's knowledge and skills. The majority of companies encourage their employees to suggest the professional training they wish to undertake. The Japanese firmly believe that better education makes for an improved worker. In one company's training programme two machine operators were undertaking training in computer-aided design and computer-aided manufacture, and the plant director had enrolled for a course on gas welding techniques.

An outline of the training given at supervisory level by one mechanical engineering organization covers:

- self-development;
- effective use of time;

- education of subordinates;
- labour and personnel management;
- safety and health management;
- enhancement of production efficiency;
- understanding costs;
- quality consciousness/tools and techniques;
- process control;
- maintenance; and
- environmental control.

Supervisor training

Both the breadth and depth of the same company's supervisor training programme are worthy of comment. For example, in the section on understanding costs, the supervisors are given detailed information on both fixed and variable costs in their area, plus an understanding generally of everything in a production operation that influences costs (e.g. assembly line balancing). The depth of knowledge would be unusual at much more senior levels in European organizations. The breadth of training is illustrated by the information given on what would generally be regarded as other people's jobs. In this way the supervisors are given a total picture of business operations. The majority of the training material was in the form of checklists that the supervisor was expected to refer to before and after taking action.

In general, European companies give little real training at supervisor level. By contrast, Japanese companies regard supervisors as the first level of management and give them the skills to match this responsibility. All senior managers have been through the same training and so have shared knowledge and beliefs. This approach has tremendous power.

Everyone in a Japanese organization is trained to use the seven original quality control tools and there was ample evidence (as displayed on the quality noticeboards discussed earlier) that these tools were well developed during all stages of production. A variety of training is given in techniques, and presentation and leadership skills to deepen TQC consciousness among employees and to improve their problem-solving ability; the most intensive training is given to design and production engineers.

In the West, people are usually trained by one company, often then moving on to another company which benefits from the training and development already done. Companies in the West must be willing to adopt a broad-minded approach and expect to gain as much as they lose from this turnover of people skills; otherwise there is a danger that investment in education and training will be inhibited. This also frequently results in a failure to develop training strategies; rarely do European companies set improvement objectives for training programmes.

In Japan the quality training programme is typically carried out by staff from corporate and divisional quality departments, engineers, invited lecturers from outside the company and by institutions such as JUSE. Almost without exception the instructors carry out an audit to assess the effective use of newly acquired skills by the people they have trained.

Lifetime employment, lifetime training

Because of the lifetime employment practices of large Japanese organizations, it is possible for them to invest heavily in a long-term programme of education, training and retraining to develop their employees' capabilities. A programme of initial training prepares them for work with the organization in terms of mission, philosophy, systems, procedures and job skills. The fact that all new employees, from junior to senior high school and university, begin employment in an organization at the same time each year helps the planning of the training and forms the basis for relationships which will last for a very long time.

Total Productive Maintenance (TPM)

The concept of TPM is now very much in evidence in Japanese companies. Nippondenso (a subsidiary of the Toyota Motor Group) has achieved considerable success with TPM, which every company in Japan is now trying to emulate.

Japanese companies are very much motivated by national prizes. They have the Deming Award, which recognizes outstanding individual, divisional or company achievement in quality strategy, management and execution, the Japan Quality Control Medal for companies which have won the Deming Application Prize and can thereafter demonstrate five or more years of continuous improvement, the Ishikawa Prize for new methods or new systems for the modernization of management and achievement by their application and the Japan Institute of Plant Maintenance Award for TPM. These awards are regarded as extremely prestigious. More than one company commented that the TPM award was the hardest one to win.

Among the companies visited there was a range of views on the meaning of TPM. The widest definition was total productive maintenance, which encompassed the more narrow total prevention maintenance. Therefore, TPM is seen as a total method of management. Full details of TPM can be found in Nakajima,[2] who developed TPM by combining the key features of preventive, productive and predictive maintenance with TQC, QCs and employee involvement.

It is clear that TQC and TPM are similar concepts, with the common goal of improving product quality. TPM is considered as an additional driver which is complementary to TQC. At one company it was suggested that TQC concerns 'how to' and TPM 'why'. A number of Japanese companies started TQC twenty-five to thirty years ago but the majority have become involved with TPM only during the last three or so years. The consensus view is that, in their experience, TQC has only a limited influence on machine performance and so they have introduced TPM to focus on the machines. The condition of the equipment has a considerable influence on the quality of production output and is a key element in manufacturing a product which meets the needs and expectations of customers. The machine needs the input of people to keep it clean and to improve its efficiency and operation. This is the purpose of TPM.

TPM is a scientific company-wide approach in which every employee is concerned about the maintenance and the quality and efficiency of his or her equipment. The objective is to reduce the cost of machinery and equipment throughout its useful life by more efficient maintenance management. Teamwork is a key element of TPM: it focuses on reducing manufacturing losses and costs and establishes a system of preventive maintenance over a machine's working life. The emphasis of TPM is to improve the skills of operators in relation to machine technology and to train and educate them to clean, maintain and make adjustments to their machines. Training and education are carried out by maintenance and engineering staff. In this way machinery is kept at optimal operating efficiency. The Japanese five Ss – *seri, seiton, seiso, seiketsu* and *shitsuke* (disposal, orderliness, cleaning, neatness and discipline) – are essential activities in TPM. They also promote housekeeping and visible management.

As well as QCs, Japanese companies operate TPM circles to focus on the production facility.

In one battery manufacturing company, the three-year TPM programme has seven key steps:

Step 1 initial cleaning,
Step 2 countermeasure at the source of problems,
Step 3 cleaning and lubrication standards,
Step 4 general inspection,
Step 5 autonomous inspection,
Step 6 orderliness and tidiness,
Step 7 full autonomous maintenance.

After each TPM step has been achieved a TPM sticker is issued and placed on a machine. TPM was introduced to improve supervisors' efficiency, quality, control and ability. Each employee receives a twenty-hour education programme on TPM. The operating personnel devote some eight to ten hours of paid overtime each month on TPM activities, and produce TPM study sheets to educate and involve their peers. Twice a year the best ideas are selected for an award. Silver stars are affixed to machines that have operated at 100 per cent efficiency during a period of two-shift operation. Examples of TPM efficiency improvements are a 20 per cent increase in machine performance for the battery plate-making line and a 100 per cent increase on the battery assembly line.

Just-In-Time (JIT)

JIT is considered a key feature of TQC, and so merits a mention of how it is being developed. Most companies said that their systems were still developing and each day they try to make progress to one-by-one production (i.e. a batch size of one). The aim in all cases is to eliminate the seven *mudas* (wastefulnesses):

- excess production;
- waiting;
- conveyance;
- motion;
- the process itself;
- inventory; and
- defects.

This is to ensure that all actions carried out are adding value to the product. The typical cycle employed to eliminate waste is: identify waste, find its cause, make improvements, and standardize the improvement to hold the gains.

The main factors currently surrounding the deployment of JIT by Japanese companies are:

1 *Customer service.* The main purpose of JIT is not inventory reduction but improved delivery of products to customers. The first aim is to reduce waste and the second is to reduce lead times.

2 *Selective use.* JIT is not applied universally to all products and components. The Japanese investigate each piece produced and determine if JIT can be used. For example, JIT was found difficult to apply in the case of semiconductor manufacture. To cater for fluctuating demand stocks of diffused wafers are kept which are then customized.

3 *TPM essential.* TPM is crucial to the effective operation of JIT.

4 *Pilot projects.* When JIT is initially applied a production/assembly line is chosen as a pilot, where it is developed and refined before being extended to other production/assembly areas.

5 *Reduced set-up times.* For example, on the lead oxide grid pasting lines of a battery manufacturer it previously took two operators thirty minutes to change the dies; this has now been reduced to one minute for one person.

6 *Selective use of kanbans.* A variety of *kanbans* are used – cards, small boxes, *kanban* squares and lights. *Kanbans* are used only in certain parts of the production system, and to order some parts from suppliers.

7 *Flexible supply chains.* A feature of the production system is that if operator A is being supplied with product by operator B and A is not meeting the production schedule, B stops supplying product and comes to A's assistance. Some operators are dedicated to the supply of parts to manufacturing and assembly line personnel and others are responsible for coming to the production line and assisting with emergencies as and when they occur.

8 *Logistics.* Contrary to the belief that Japanese suppliers are located close to their customers, the majority of one typical company's suppliers are 50 to 60 kilometres from the factory. Delivery frequency depends on the quantity and varies from daily to every three days. Another company delivers three times a day to original equipment manufacturers and, on average, its own suppliers deliver twice a day. One company provides a three-month forecast to its suppliers and each day picks from suppliers' production lines and/or stores the parts it requires. It is interesting to note that one wire harness manufacturer commented: 'Like it or not we have to be a JIT supplier to Honda,

Nissan and Toyota.' This comment is echoed by European automotive component suppliers.

Suppliers tend to work to a specific scheduled delivery time on the day in question and use small lorries which deliver right into the factory. The same truck often carries a mix of parts from different suppliers. This also happens with delivery of finished product to the customer. The serious traffic congestion in Japan's principal cities has no doubt been exacerbated by the transport of small quantities of goods at frequent intervals. Koshi[3] claims that 43 per cent of motor vehicle traffic in Japan carries freight, and proposes an underground network for the distribution of goods.

9 *Supplier audits*. Some parts are supplied direct to the line without inspection, while others are inspected. The decision is based on the previous quality performance of the parts and the supplier's quality system. An audit to assess a supplier's quality system, manufacturing processes and parts quality is usually carried out. There are three types of audit: new supply, periodic and emergency. The results of incoming inspection and non-conformances found on the line are evaluated each month and fed back to suppliers. Information between customer and suppliers is regularly exchanged using computer-aided quality-information systems. Quality-improvement meetings are usually held once a month with the aim of improving the quality of supplied product. It is interesting to note that, in general, QC control charts are requested from suppliers only when non-conformances occur. The considerable attention European companies give to SPC is not seen in Japan: they tend to use SPC only when proving capability and when experiencing problems. The absence of 'visible' SPC is indicative of the progress made in quality improvement. If an organization has very capable processes (process capability index (Cpk) values greater than 3) the continued charting may be considered superfluous.

10 *Dual sourcing*. A mix of single and dual sourcing is employed by the companies visited, and in both cases relationships with suppliers are long term. Among the reasons for dual sourcing was to keep some flexibility in a customer's dealings with its suppliers, competition in terms of QCD and the capacity of suppliers. One manager, when asked about the sourcing of wire harnesses by major Japanese motor manufacturers, said: 'Of course Honda, Nissan and Toyota employ dual sourcing.' These three motor manufacturers divide their requirements between the two competing suppliers, depending on capacity, demand and schedule. At regular intervals the supplier confirms its capacity to these three major customers.

11 *Manufacturing technology.* The Japanese employ the same machinery and technology as their European counterparts. However, because of activities such as TPM, reduced setting-up time and integrated materials handling their machine efficiency and effectiveness are much higher. Not all their machinery and equipment is new: one company had die-casting machinery that was over fifteen years old. A number of their production system improvements have come from developing and applying small, inexpensive customized equipment for the handling and transfer of parts between processes, processing itself and the application of mistake-proofing devices. In general, they employ modern production layouts without huge visible investments – apart, that is, from computer-aided design, manufacturing and simulation systems.

12 *Production system development.* Examples of some of the means employed by Japanese companies in developing their production systems include:

- product and cellular layouts tend to change to reflect changes in product mix;
- the use of mixed model production and assembly lines;
- the employment of cycle time conveyors;
- operators stand at workstations to facilitate easy movement and production flow;
- considerable efforts are made to smooth production in relation to volume, variety and capacity. They carry out a number of iterations of the sales and production plant to achieve this. Most organizations give their annual production programme to suppliers;
- when human operation is more efficient and effective than machines, the Japanese use it – on a number of occasions it was said that on some tasks people can work faster than machines; and
- in assembly situations jobs are kept together in kit form.

Executive summary

A number of simple facts can be learnt from the Japanese experience.

- Total quality management depends on a systematic approach which is applied consistently throughout the entire organization.
- There are no short cuts to the success of the Japanese manufacturing companies. Western executives are always on the lookout for the universal panacea –unfortunately there is none – and this attitude is often an irritation to the

Japanese. Their success is the result of the application of a combination of procedures, systems, tools, improvement actions and considerable hardwork and dedication from all employees.

- Senior and middle managers must believe in TQM as a key business strategy and be prepared to stay with it over the long term.
- There must be a permanent managed process which examines all products, processes and procedures on a continuous basis, and all employees must be trained to accept that there is no ideal state. Self-assessment against criteria such as the Deming Application Prize, the Malcolm Baldrige National Quality Award and the European Quality Award is an invaluable means of assessing progress.
- Planning for improvement must be thorough.
- Improvement is a slow incremental process. Companies should not expect quick and major benefits from the application of any single method, system and/or tool and technique. To be effective the quality control tools must be used together.
- There must be an obsession with pursuing perfection and finding out what went wrong and putting in hand corrective action.
- The concept of TQM is simple. Defining, introducing and fostering the process is, however, a tremendous task and requires total commitment from all employees.
- TQM is about common sense. The Japanese put common sense into practice; they manage and apply it in a disciplined manner. Western companies claim that you cannot teach common sense – the Japanese have done just that.

Notes

1 Shingo, S. (1986) *Zero Quality Control: Source Inspection and the Poka-Yoke System*, Productivity Press, Cambridge, Mass.
2 Nakajima, S. (1988) *Introduction to Total Productive Maintenance and TPM Development Program*, Productivity Press, Cambridge, Mass.
3 Koshi, M. (1989) 'Tokyo's traffic congestion can be unravelled', *The Japan Times*, 14 November, p. 5.

The following material has been used in the preparation of this chapter:

Asher, J. M. and Dale, B. G. (1989) 'The Japanese approach to quality', *The TQM Magazine*, November, pp. 275–8.

Dale, B. G. and Asher, J. M. (1989) 'Total quality control: lessons European executives can learn from Japanese companies', *European Management Journal*, vol. 7, no. 4, pp. 493–503.

Dale, B. G. (1990) 'Japanese manufacturing efficiency: a study in the electronics industry', *IEE Proceedings*, vol. 137, no. 1, 5A, pp. 293–301.

Dale, B. G. and Tidd, J. (1991) 'Japanese Total Quality Control: a Study of Best Practice', *Proceedings of the Institution of Mechanical Engineers*, 205, B6, pp. 221–32.

10

Epilogue

As we have seen throughout this book, total quality management is not simply meeting the requirements of a quality system standard or using some quality-management tool or technique to retain the business of a key customer, but is about 'never having to say sorry to a customer' (John Wybrow, Technical Director of Philips emphasizes), appreciating that 'every mistake is a pearl to be cherished and learned from', 'continually searching for improvements and better ways of doing things', 'creating a sense of personal pride in products and services', 'being a part of a team that really cares about what they do and what they produce and deliver to the customer!' In other words, it is about the total involvement of employees at all levels in terms of their own development, participation in the business and in helping to eliminate problems. The focus is directed to giving complete customer (internal and external) satisfaction.

To achieve these goals, it is essential that executives at the highest level create a TQM organizational climate. Large-scale change is inevitable, with all its attendant problems; as Machiavelli suggested in *The Prince*:

It should be borne in mind that there is nothing more difficult to arrange, more doubtful of success and more dangerous to carry through than initiating changes... the innovator makes enemies of all those who prospered under the old order, and only lukewarm support is forthcoming from those who would prosper under the new.

On the other hand, product and service quality which delights the customer is not cheap. Time, energy and resources are money, but the pay-offs can be enormous. It takes a dedicated team of top management to push TQM to its limits, but there are a number of guiding principles that can be followed to ensure some degree of success.

Principles to be adopted

1 Accept that the ultimate responsibility for TQM rests with the CEO and top management – commitment comes from the top.
2 TQM should not be an issue on the management agenda, it *is* the agenda.
3 TQM is a long-term strategy.
4 There are no quick fixes.
5 TQM is a total culture concept, involving everyone in the organization.
6 TQM is not just a matter of meeting minimum ISO 9000 quality-management system standards, but is about individual and organizational exertion to extend limits, boundaries and improvement objectives.
7 No *single* quality-management tool or technique, procedure, system, etc. can act as a cure-all.

Top management activities to ensure TQM

1 Allocate time to understand the concept and principles of TQM.
2 Make sure that TQM becomes the number one business priority.
3 Take responsibility for leading the quality-improvement process, and become a role model.
4 Ensure that everybody in the organization knows the reasons for its adoption and understands their role in the improvement process.
5 Commit resources to TQM. As Roger Milliken of Milliken and Company says, 'Walk the talk', and 'Our people must believe that we mean what we say.'
6 Establish an improvement infrastructure.
7 Identify key internal and external performance measures and agree improvement objectives.
8 Personally devote at least one day a week to quality-improvement activities.
9 Every so often deal with customer complaints yourself.
10 Visit all business areas, units and divisions regularly.
11 Communicate as never before.

Introduce organizational changes to support and develop TQM

1 Develop a company vision and mission statement and establish a process of policy deployment.
2 Set up and chair a TQM steering committee or quality council.
3 Develop a strategic quality plan to meet the business objectives.
4 Aim to create a continuous improvement environment which permeates all departments.
5 Encourage participation and people development and ensure you listen carefully to what your people are saying. As Roy Polson, Managing Director of Manchester Circuits Ltd puts it, 'Build quality into people.'
6 Facilitate teamwork.
7 Institute quality planning, audit and improvement meetings and organizational housekeeping.
8 Ensure that the organization listens to *all* the views of all its customers.
9 Promote and encourage cross-functional management to break through the barriers of sectionalism.
10 Establish a formal TQM educational programme for all employees.
11 Recognize accomplishments.
12 Employ best-practice benchmarking.

TQM means changing the climate in the organization, involving everybody and, for top management, doing jobs never previously considered, at least in the majority of Western organizations dealing personally with customers, frequent visits to production areas, 'hands-on' management, as well as all the quality-related activities described in this book. Communication is crucial to the success of TQM, and nobody can do this better than the CEO and top management. Saul Gellerman once said:

Nothing is more central to an organization's effectiveness than its ability to transmit accurate, relevant, understandable information among its members. All the advantages of organizations – economies of scale, financial and technical resources, diverse talents, and contacts – are of no practical value if the organization's members are unaware of what other members require of them and why. Nevertheless, despite its overwhelming and acknowledged importance, the process of communication is frequently misunderstood and mismanaged.

This book has clearly established the need for top management to be committed to TQM and why they must demonstrate and exercise effective leadership and become totally immersed in it. Are you ready to accept the challenge?

Appendices: Quality Systems and Tools and Techniques

Total Quality and Human Resources: An Executive Guide contains four appendices:

A Quality Systems
B Quality Management Tools and Techniques: An Overview
C Statistical Process Control
D Failure Mode and Effects Analysis

The material they contain has been separated in this way to facilitate easier reading of the main text.

The appendices are essentially different from the ten chapters forming the central core of the book, and concentrate mainly on the systems and technical aspects of TQM. This is not to say that the material in them is less important. We have mentioned on numerous occasions in the text that executives need to understand more about the systems, tools and techniques of quality management, in particular statistical methods.

Each of the chapters in the book provides an overview. The aim has been to promote understanding of a topic without going into detail. The appendices provide an executive guide to quality systems, tools and techniques and, if desired, can be used independently of the main text.

Appendix A

Quality Systems

What Is Quality Assurance?

What Is a Quality System?

The Development of Quality System Standards

The ISO 9000 Series of Standards: An Overview

Implementation Guidelines for the ISO 9000 Series of Standards

Quality System Assessment and Registration

Benefits and Limitations of the ISO 9000 Series of Standards

Executive Summary

Appendix A opens by examining the concept of quality assurance and the responsibilities of people within an organization for carrying out the activity. A quality system is defined and the background of quality system standards is traced, the key features of the BS 5750/ISO 9000[1] series are examined, and its benefits and limitations reviewed. Much has already been written *about* quality systems and standards[2] over and above the standards themselves. The appendix is therefore limited to an overview of the key features and issues.

What is quality assurance?

Quality assurance is defined in ISO 8402[3] as: 'All those planned and systematic actions necessary to provide adequate confidence that a product or service will satisfy the given requirements of quality.' Quality assurance is often treated as something involving only policing by the quality assurance department. Not so: that department's ideal role is to oversee the whole process within an organization, provide guidance, advise on the assignment of roles and responsibilities to each function and person, and to address weaknesses in the system. Quality assurance needs to be integrated into all processes and functions, from the conception of an idea and throughout the life cycle of the product or service – determining customer needs and requirements, planning and designing, production, delivery and after-sales service.

The objective should be for every person to take personal responsibility for the quality assurance of the processes for which he or she is accountable. This includes treating later processes as customers and endeavouring to transfer conforming products, services and documents to those customers, monitoring quality performance, analysing non-conformance data, taking corrective action to prevent repetition of mistakes, and feeding data backward and forward. The emphasis should be on pursuing thoroughly corrective action procedures and non-conformance investigation, with closed-loop effectiveness. Tasks must be performed as defined by the quality system.

The main objective of quality assurance is to build quality into the product/service during the upstream design and planning processes. Quality function deployment (QFD), failure mode and effects analysis (FMEA), design of experiments, design reviews, design for manufacturability and quality audits are of considerable assistance in pursuing this goal.

Quality assurance planned and managed along these lines will strengthen an organization's TQM efforts.

What is a quality system?

ISO 8402 defines a quality system as the 'organizational structure, responsibilities, procedures, processes and resources for implementing quality management'. Details of the documentation required of a quality system are contained in BS 4891.[4] The three levels of documentation, which is hierarchical in nature, are:

1 quality manual – provides a concise summary of the quality management policy and quality system;
2 procedures manual – describes how the system functions;
3 work instructions, specifications and detailed methods.

The quality system should define and cover all facets of an organization's operation: identifying and meeting the needs and requirements of customers, design, planning, purchasing, manufacturing, packaging, storage, delivery and service, and all relevant activities carried out within these functions. It deals with organization, responsibilities, procedures and processes. Put simply, a quality system is good management practice. To be comprehensive and effective, it must be developed using a reference base (a quality system standard) against which its adequacy can be judged and improvements made.

A documented quality system which embraces quality management objectives, policies, organization and procedures and which can demonstrate, by assessment, compliance with the ISO 9000 series of quality system standards (or those of a major purchaser) provides an effective managerial framework on which to build a company-wide approach to quality improvement.

The development of quality system standards

Irrespective of the approach taken to TQM and the progress made, an organization will need to demonstrate to its customers that its processes, procedures and systems are both capable and under control. This need led to the development of quality system standards.

The early standards were provided by major purchasers to their suppliers. They were customer-specific and designed to be used in contractual situations in the industries for which they were designed and operated. Each purchaser developed its own methods of assessment, visiting suppliers to examine the degree to which their operating procedures and systems followed the requirements of the standard (second party certification).

Most of the current quality system standards evolved from military standards. A United Kingdom standard for quality systems was first published in 1973 by the Ministry of Defence (MOD): the DEF-STAN O5 series (O5-21 to O5-29). These were virtual copies of the American-derived NATO Allied Quality Assurance Publications (AQAP-1 to AQAP-9), used by NATO in defence procurements. The MOD used the DEF-STAN O5 series to approve potential suppliers and audit current suppliers. Suppliers were required to develop their quality systems to meet the criteria set out in the standards in order to be included on the list of MOD contractors. The O5 series were withdrawn in 1985 and MOD assessments were carried out using the AQAP standards. From September 1991 the MOD will be relying mainly on third-party assessment against the ISO 9000 series. It will assess only suppliers/contractors who are outside the current scope of the accredited certification bodies. This type of situation relates to specific military applications such as aircraft construction, ammunition and explosives, packaging and software. A new set of defence standards (the O5-90 series, O5-91 to O5-95), which include the ISO 9000 series plus special military purchase requirements, will be used to audit suppliers in contractual situations.

In 1972 the British Standards Institution (BSI) published BS 4891, *A Guide to Quality Assurance*, which set out recommendations to organizations for quality and its management. This was followed in 1974 by BS 5179 (a three-part standard), *A Guide to the Operation and Evaluation of Quality Assurance Systems*, which was withdrawn in 1981 having been superseded in 1979 by the first issue of BS 5750.

During the mid-1970s there was a proliferation of quality system standards produced by a variety of second- and third-party organizations. In 1977 the Warner Report[5] stressed the need for a national standard for quality management systems, to reduce the number of assessments suppliers were being subjected to by their customers. It pointed to the shortcomings and fragmented nature of the British system of standards, and recommended that British standards be produced to provide a single base document for quality systems. In 1979 the BSI issued BS 5750, *Quality Systems*.

In 1987 the ISO 9000 series of international standards on quality systems were published by the International Organization for Standardization (ISO). These standards, while reflecting various national approaches and international requirements, are based largely on the 1979 version of BS 5750 and the eight or so years of UK user experience, mainly in manufacturing industry. Their text has been approved as suitable for publication as a British standard without deviation: BS 5750, Parts 0 to 3.[6] The ISO 9000 series have now been adopted by CEN (the European Committee for Standardization) and CENELEC (the European Committee for Electrotechnical Standardization) as the EN 29000 series, thus harmonizing the approach to quality systems among the European Community.

Government initiatives

In July 1982 a White Paper, *Standards, Quality and International Competitiveness*,[7] suggested that to maintain standards, certification bodies should be accredited by a central agency. The National Accreditation Council for Certification Bodies (NACCB) is a national statutory body which was established in June 1985 with the task of assessing the independence, integrity and technical competence of leading certification bodies applying for government accreditation in four areas: approval of quality systems, product conformity, product approval and approval of personnel engaged in quality verification. Accreditation, which is awarded in the UK by the Secretary of State for Trade and Industry, allows a certification body to demonstrate its competence. Some eighteen of the thirty or so certification bodies currently operating in the UK have been approved and listed in a directory[8] produced by NACCB. Companies assessed by an accredited certification body can use the symbol of a gold crown (signifying government) and gold tick (signifying approval) if the certification applied for falls within the scope of accreditation of the certification body.

The Department of Trade and Industry (DTI) through its National Quality Campaign (initiated as a result of the 1982 White Paper) and Managing into the 1990s programme, actively encourages British industry to consider more seriously its approach to quality management, and one of the methods advocated was registration to the BS 5750 series of standards. The DTI issues a central register of quality assured companies.[9] (The register lists the firms whose quality system has been approved by major users or independent third-party assessment bodies – this means the investigation is made by an independent organization, unrelated to buyer or seller. It also describes the assessment standard used – BS 5750/ISO 9000 or its equivalent – and details of the certification body.) The 1991 edition contains some 15,000 entries.

Acceptance of the ISO 9000 series of standards

Major industrial purchasers, particularly in the motor industry, have their own standards and procedures for assessing their suppliers' systems (e.g. the Ford Q-101 Worldwide Quality System Standard).[10] Because they tend to be specific, these standards are often more demanding in certain areas than the ISO 9000 series. But some organizations which meet the Ford equivalent requirements would not necessarily meet those of the ISO 9000 series, and vice versa.

The ISO 9000 series have not been accepted and used universally across the UK motor industry. However, it is interesting to note that in 1990 the Society of Motor Manufacturers and Traders' booklet *Quality Systems and the Motor Industry*[11] contained a quality policy statement, which

recommends that member and non-member companies recognise and take account of approvals to BS 5750/ISO 9000/EN 29000 Quality Systems Standards as a minimum when contracting work out and buying in supplies. It is strongly recommended that all UK automotive industry companies obtain approvals as applicable to this standard through accredited third party certification.

Registration to ISO 9001, 9002 or 9003 is a useful foundation leading to the development of a quality system to meet the independent system requirements of customers. A number of major purchasers use this registration as the 'first pass' over a supplier's quality system. They take the ISO 9000 series as the base, and assess only those aspects of the system which they regard as important (e.g. those not covered in the international standard – purchasers often require suppliers to have features additional to the ISO 9000 series within the system – or those covered in insufficient detail for the purchaser). On the other hand, many customers are not prepared to accept a supplier's registration and carry out a full assessment of its quality system. For example:

- Dale and Plunkett,[12] reporting on a study carried out in twelve fabricators, found that most were subjected to about six audits a year.
- Singer, Churchill and Dale,[13] in a study of the impact of quality assurance on thirteen suppliers to the nuclear industry, found that most companies are audited four or more times each year.
- Galt and Dale,[14] in a study of the supplier development programmes of a cross-section of ten UK-based organizations, found that five relied totally on their own evaluation of suppliers, three considered it to be a good starting point and only two accepted third-party recognition as being adequate for their evaluation purposes. 'It was clear that most of the firms considered their own quality standards to be above those required for the ISO 9000 series registration.'
- Boaden, Dale and Polding,[15] reporting on a recent study of TQM in the UK construction industry, make the point: 'One of the main arguments put forward for the ISO 9000 series of standards is that it will help to reduce second party assessments, the responses indicate that this has not happened in the construction industry; clearly a disappointment.'

The ISO 9000 series of standards: an overview

Introduction

In simple terms, the objective of the ISO 9000 series is to give purchasers an assurance that the quality of the products and/or services provided by a supplier meets their requirements.

The series sets out a definitive list of those features and characteristics it is considered should be present in an organization's management control system through documented policies, manuals and procedures, which help to ensure that quality is built into a process and achieved. The aim is systematic quality assurance and control. It is the broad principles of control, in general terms, which are defined in the standards, and not the specific methods by which control can be achieved. This allows the standard to be interpreted and applied in a wide range of situations and environments, and allows each organization to develop its own system and then test it against the standard.

The BS 5750 series was developed by the engineering sector of industry, and consequently many of the terms and definitions are engineering-based. They need to be interpreted in the light of the specific needs of individual organizations, which has led to problems in some sectors of manufacturing industry and in the majority of non-manufacturing organizations. Owen,[16] writing from the chemical industry, is critical of the series for being too orientated to the engineering industry, and Oliver[17] expresses the view that it 'uses language that the construction industry does not use and, by and large, does not understand'. Despite such difficulties, it has been applied in a wide variety of manufacturing situations and registration is being received in an increasing number of non-manufacturing environments: banking, legal, consumer, transport, hotel and catering, recruitment, marketing services and education.

The series of standards can be used in three ways:

- to provide guidance to organizations to assist them in developing their quality systems;
- as a purchasing standard (when specified in contracts);
- as an assessment standard to be used by both second- and third-party organizations.

Functions of the standards and their various parts

The ISO 9000 series consists of five individual standards, divided into four parts. The standards have two main functions. The first is an introduction to the series; it identifies the aspects to be covered by an organization's quality system and gives guidance in quality management and the application of the standards.

The second function is to define those features and characteristics of the system considered essential for the purpose of quality assurance in contractual situations, for three main types of organizational responsibility: design/development, production, installation and servicing; production and installation; and final inspection and test.

The four parts of the standard are:

1 ISO 9000 *Guide to Selection and Use* and ISO 9004: *Guide to Quality Management and Quality System Elements*. These are intended only as guidelines and cannot be used as reference standards to assess the adequacy of a quality system. The two standards are more reader-friendly than ISO 9001, 9002 and 9003: organizations embarking on the development of a quality system to meet the requirements of any of these three standards, or even of that of a major purchaser, should find the two guidance documents of considerable help.

ISO 9000 is a guide to the use of other standards in the series, and a thorough understanding of its content is essential if the series of standards is to be interpreted and used correctly.

ISO 9004 is a guide to good quality-management practice, and in this it provides more detail than ISO 9001, 9002 and 9003. It also refers to a number of quality aspects (e.g. quality risks, costs, product liability) that are not covered in as much detail in the three standards. Considerable emphasis is placed throughout on the satisfaction of customer needs and requirements.

2 ISO 9001: *Specification for Design/Development, Production, Installation and Servicing*. This standard covers circumstances in which an organization is responsible for conceptual design and development work, and/or where it may be required to cover post-delivery activities such as commissioning and servicing.

3 ISO 9002: *Specification for Production and Installation*. This standard covers circumstances where an organization is responsible for assuring the product and/or service quality during the course of production or installation only.

4 ISO 9003: *Specification for Final Inspection and Test*. This standard is used when conformance to specified requirements can be assured solely at final inspection and test.

In addition to these there is BS 5750, Part 4: *Guide to the use of BS 5750: Parts 1, 2 and 3*. (Parts 1, 2 and 3 are identical to ISO 9001, 9002 and 9003 respectively.) This is a guidance document and is useful to organizations in understanding the requirements of the three standards. It is structured in line with Part 1 and should be read in conjunction with that part of the BS 5750 series with which compliance is sought.

Principal clauses in ISO 9001

This section provides an overview of the principal clauses in ISO 9001 together with key factors in relation to the quality system. It will provide senior managers with a *concise outline* of a quality system and what is required in setting it up. In avoiding detail, we must not understate the responsibility of senior executives in the establishment, maintenance and development of such a system: their total commitment to and leadership of the process of registration to ISO 9001, 9002 or 9003 is vital, and it is only they who can deliver the resources and co-operation of appropriate personnel and provide the necessary direction.

Management responsibilities
- Corporate quality policy development, statement, deployment, implementation, communication and understanding.
- Organization, structure, responsibility and authority.
- Management representative for quality.
- Management review of the system.

Quality system
- Documentation and implementation of procedures and instructions.
- Quality manual.
- Quality plans, work instructions, inspection instructions, etc.

Contract review
- Definition of customer (internal and external) needs and requirements.
- Contract and tender compatibility.
- Capability.
- Product belief and configuration.
- Information monitoring and feedback.

Design control
- Design and development planning.
- Identify and allocate resources.
- Definition and control of design inputs, outputs and interfaces.
- Design verification.
- Review, approve, record and control design changes.

Document control
- Formal control and review of all documents, procedures, specifications, data and standards, etc.

Purchasing
- Assessment and monitoring of suppliers/subcontractors.
- Formal written definition of requirements and specification.

Purchaser-supplied material
- Verification, storage and maintenance of 'free issue' or purchaser-supplied material.

Product identification and traceability
- Unique and positive identification of material, parts and work-in-progress during all processes.
- Demonstrated traceability and its recording.

Process control
- Identify and plan the processes.
- Work instructions.
- Monitor key characteristics and features during production.
- Process qualification.
- Processes undertaken under controlled conditions.
- Criteria for workmanship.
- Control of special processes.

Inspection and testing
- Inspection and testing of goods received.
- In-process inspection and testing.
- Final inspection and testing.
- Inspection and test records.

Inspection, measuring and test equipment
- Control, calibration and maintenance.
- Documentation and calibration records.
- Traceability to reference standards.
- Handling and storage.

Inspection and test status
- Identification of inspection and test status throughout all processes.
- Confirmation that tests and inspections have been carried out.
- Authority for release of conforming product.

Control of non-conforming product
- Identification and control to prevent unauthorized use.
- Review and decide on appropriate remedial action.
- Reinspection.

Corrective action
- Procedures and reporting.
- Investigation and analysis of causes.
- Elimination of causes and abnormalities.
- Preventive action.
- Corrective action control.
- Assignment of responsibilities.
- Changes to procedures, working instructions, etc.

Handling, storage, packaging and delivery
- Methods which prevent product damage and/or deterioration.

- Maintenance of product integrity.
- Use of secure areas and rooms to prevent damage and/or deterioration.
- Receipt and delivery of items into and out of storage.
- Procedures to ensure that the product is packed to prevent damage throughout the entire production-to-delivery cycle.

Quality records
- Adequate records to demonstrate achievement of product quality and effective operation of the system.
- Retention time for records.
- Storage, retrievability, legibility and identification.

Internal quality audit
- Audit plan and verification.
- Procedures to ensure that the documented system is being followed.
- Compliance and effectiveness.
- Reporting of results to personnel.
- Corrective action to bring activities and the quality system into agreement with the standard.

Training
- Assessment and identification of needs.
- Written job responsibilities and specification.
- Planned and structured training programme.
- Training records.

After-sales servicing
- Contractual specification.
- Procedures for performing and verifying that needs and requirements are met.

Statistical techniques
- Process capability determination and acceptability.
- Product characteristic verification.

The set of requirements outlined in ISO 9001 can be supplemented for specific industries or products by quality assurance schedules or quality system supplements, which provide more detail.

Implementation guidelines for the ISO 9000 series of standards

At this point it is useful to list Long, Dale and Younger's[18] guidelines (as developed by the present authors), based on their research into the application and use of the ISO 9000 series in small and medium-sized enterprises; these may also be applied to larger organizations.

1   The development of a quality system to meet the requirements of ISO 9001, 9002 or 9003 should be managed as a project, with key steps, milestones and timescales being identified.

2   An organization should be clear on the reasons for seeking registration. Implementation for the wrong reasons will prevent the company from receiving the full benefits. In addition, implementing and maintaining the standard may prove a burden, in terms of costs and extra paperwork, with no compensating benefits. Registration must therefore not be sought just to satisfy major customers' contractual requirements or for marketing purposes. Indeed when most competitors are registered there is little marketing advantage; in many cases it is now an order-qualifying criterion.

3   There is a need to create a conducive environment for the development of a quality system which meets the requirements of the ISO 9000 series. This can be achieved by the formulation of organizational quality policy and quality objectives. Management must ensure that all employees implement and understand the quality policy and are given quality improvement objectives.

4   Prior to a programme of ISO 9000 series implementation a qualified quality auditor must audit the existing system against the appropriate part of the standard, to determine the company's quality status, enable management to assess the amount of work required and to plan for systematic implementation (without this knowledge the project planning process would be impossible). It is important to allow a realistic time for this so that it is done properly; otherwise far more time will be spent debugging the system later. It is essential to involve the appointed management representative during the audit.

5   Establish a steering committee, chaired by the CEO and comprising all department heads. Their participation is essential to gain cross-functional support for the project and to help ensure the smooth development and implementation of the system. In small companies with little or no second-tier management the CEO's wholehearted commitment and involvement are critical.

6   At all levels within the company training is required on the importance of product and service quality, in general, and the reasons for the quality system and its benefits, in particular. This will help to instil in employees the right attitude towards the ISO 9000 criteria and will encourage total participation. Accurate procedures, including operating and works instructions, are required, and must be practical, workable and easily implemented. Wherever possible, they should document what employees are currently doing: introduce changes only

where the standard renders it necessary. It goes without saying that the personnel who draft the procedures must be familiar with the ISO 9000 series requirements and with the areas they are covering.

7 The ISO 9000 series requirements should be regarded as the minimum. The aim should be to have a quality system which surpasses those requirements. A system which does no more than meet them proves only that controls, procedures and disciplines are in place; there is neither basis nor connected reliable data to monitor the process of quality improvement.

Quality system assessment and registration

The organization having written the necessary procedures and instructions, and developed its quality system to meet the requirements of the part of ISO 9000 for which registration is sought, the following lists the key issues in the route to registration. (It should be noted that there is some variation in the structure of the assessment carried out by the various certification bodies.)

1 Train and educate staff in the workings and operation of the system and test the procedures that have been developed. Education and training are key determinants in making sure that people follow procedures, complete the appropriate documentation, take corrective action seriously and provide timely and accurate information. Some companies supplement training plans by recognizing personal involvement: for example, performance rewards such as mugs, writing blocks, pens, etc.
2 Arrange for a pre-assessment of the system to be carried out by a suitably qualified person.
3 Consult the list of accredited certification bodies and carry out a supplier audit of them. It is important to establish the scope of the certification body's approval powers and its fee structure.
4 Apply to the chosen body; in response it will send an information pack. Upon completion of the necessary forms, the certification body will provide a quotation and details of fees. After agreeing a contract, the appropriate documentation (including the quality manual) is then sent to the certification body to check compliance against the standard. The body will want to see proof that the quality system has been in effective operation for six months.
5 If the documentation addresses the standard adequately some certification bodies proceed to the on-site assessment for a preliminary review. At this stage, the company is able to make appropriate system modifications and

establish corrective action to take account of the assessors' initial findings and comments.

6 The formal assessment involves an in-depth appraisal of the organization's procedures for compliance with the appropriate part of the standard. This is carried out by a small team of independent assessors appointed by the certification body and under the supervision of a registered lead assessor. The assessors should be familiar with the organization's field of activity. If the assessors discover a deviation from the requirements or identify any non-compliance with the documented procedures, a discrepancy report is raised.

7 At the end of the assessment, non-conformances are reviewed and the assessors report on their recommendations; this includes a verbal report to management by the lead assessor. The recommendation can be unqualified registration, qualified registration and non-registration. Any non-compliances with the appropriate part of the standard must be rectified before approval is given.

8 Once registered the certification bodies have a system of routine surveillance. Frequency varies but is generally twice a year. Visits may be unannounced.

9 Registration usually covers a fixed period of three years, subject to the regular surveillance visits, after which a quality system reassessment is made; the reassessment interval tends to vary with the certification body.

From their research into the implementation of the ISO 9000 series Long, Dale and Younger[19] have identified four factors that determine the time taken by organizations to implement the standard.

1 The status of the quality system prior to seeking ISO 9001, ISO 9002 and ISO 9003 approval. This status is determined by the presence or otherwise of activities which are in accordance with the standard and their existence in a documented form. When few activities are in place and/or activities are not documented then more time is required first to document and then to develop the system to meet the appropriate requirements.

2 The complexity of the company in terms of work locations, products manufactured, and the type and number of production processes and operating instructions. With increasing complexity then more procedures and work instructions are required to be documented.

3 The priority given by management to implementing the standard and the time they are prepared to set aside for the activity from their normal day-to-day work responsibility affects the progress of implementation. This is especially the case when there are no full-time personnel responsible for quality assurance.

4 The existence of a conducive environment is required for the

implementation and development of the standard. Resistance to change, lack of understanding about product and service quality and poor attitude among employees toward quality improvement are major obstacles in implementing the standard.

Benefits and limitations of the ISO 9000 series of standards

Since its introduction over ten years ago, the ISO 9000 quality system series has been widely accepted in the UK.

A number of benefits are claimed for the system, including:

- a reduction in customer complaints and non-conforming products, services and costs;
- a reduction in the number of audits and assessments, leading to a saving in resources needed for such activities;
- improved control, discipline, procedures, documentation and customer satisfaction;
- increased quality awareness, in particular, from those departments and people who traditionally did not see quality as their major concern;
- a better working environment.

For details see assorted BSI literature, Dale and Oakland,[20] SMMT,[21] Long, Dale and Younger,[22] Atkin,[23] Bulled,[24] Collyer,[25] Ford[26] and Hele.[27]

On the other hand, a number of difficulties and problems have been reported and discussed:

- whether to apply for ISO 9001 or 9002 registration, and whether it should be sought for the whole company or just one unit/division/site;
- interpretations of various sections of the standard;
- a lack of direction in relation to SPC;
- time taken in writing procedures;
- terminology used;
- weaknesses in some of the requirements.

Details are given by, Dale and Oakland,[28] Owen,[29] Oliver,[30] Long, Dale and Younger,[31] Sayle,[32] Owen[33] and Whittington,[34] and the letters pages of various issues of *Quality News* – the journal of the Institute of Quality Assurance.

The subject of the ISO 9000 series, when raised at conferences and symposiums, almost always leads to heated debate. Analysis of such discussions reveals that there are two small, diametrically opposed groups: firm believers in the system and those who are antagonistic towards it. The majority take the centre ground. They have no strong views one way or the other and, in the main, their organizations are registered because of customers' contractual requirements. They report that some of the benefits outlined above have been received and it is considered an aid to marketing. Many managers outside the quality function see the ISO 9000 series as a bureaucratic system and take the view that they should get the certificate and then do it all over again three years later.

What follows is an overview of the benefits and limitations of the ISO 9000 series, based on conference discussions, comments made by delegates on Ford three-day SPC training courses for suppliers held by UMIST, discussions with executives and consultants in the course of UMIST TQM research, and comments made by executives on early drafts of this appendix.

A quality system is a fundamental part of an organization's approach to TQM

The guidance provided in the twenty clauses of ISO 9001, and the independent assessment surveillance, are certainly aids in developing and maintaining the procedures, controls and discipline required in TQM. The system should help to bring more people in the organization in contact with quality and thus raise quality awareness. The ISO 9000 series does, however, tend to encourage the separation of a business into areas that complete the recording of requirements and those which do not. Finance, management information systems and human resources are little affected, except for training requirements. It is TQM that stimulates the business by creating the understanding that all its component parts have customers.

The UMIST TQM research experience indicates that in most companies it is not easy to involve every function and person in taking responsibility for their own quality assurance and making quality improvements in their processes (see Lascelles and Dale).[35] The ISO 9000 series can assist in making this happen.

Contractual requirements

Many customers require their suppliers to be registered to the ISO 9000 series, or before placing them on bid lists. Once a company is registered, it is more than likely to ask its suppliers, distributors and providers of service to do the same. In many sectors of industry and government procurement agencies, therefore, it is necessary from a marketing viewpoint, and without it a company will simply not get orders.

Suppliers have a habit of doing what their customers want, and there is no doubt that many organizations have secured registration simply to satisfy the demands of their major customers. This may not produce the required improvement ethos naturally, and any gains made will be short-lived if registration is perceived as a contractual requirement rather than as a foundation for ongoing improvement.

Some organizations also use it to demonstrate to customers (actual and potential) that they are committed to quality and have achieved what they often call 'the right level of quality'.

Once registration has been achieved, no organization can afford to lose it.

Registration is a starting point

Registration to the relevant part of the ISO 9000 series should be treated as the minimum requirement and the objective should be to develop and improve the system. An organization does not achieve superior-performing status merely by registration. The winners will be those with a dedicated commitment to never-ending improvement.

Registration leads to consistency, not improvement

There is little doubt that the preparation of systems, procedures, working instructions, etc., to meet the requirements of the ISO 9000 series will have a beneficial effect on a company's performance in terms of improved process yields, reduced levels of non-conformance, improved management control, etc. However, the underlying mechanisms of the ISO 9000 series are such that they will tend towards a steady-state performance. The series is designed to produce *consistency* in actions, products and services, which does not rule out high levels of non-conformance. Consistency, once achieved, can result in complacency.

Only with strong leadership and a written commitment to improvement in the systems review sections (this is *not* the norm) will an improvement cycle be triggered. Some organizations have done this by building on and widening their six-monthly quality systems management review meetings (which deal with issues such as quality audit and corrective action; production rejections, concessions and corrective actions; waste levels; supplier performance/concessions; customer complaints; and market trends and requirements) into monthly steering meetings for quality improvement.

Does not prevent defects

While recognizing that the requirements of the ISO 9000 series 'are aimed primarily at preventing non-conformity at all stages from design through to servicing', registration does *not* imply that non-conformities will not occur. The standard is not prescriptive as to the means of prevention: detection methods that rely heavily on inspection techniques, human or mechanical, appear to satisfy the standard in many aspects. This may be an acknowledgement of the fact that there are many processes where, given the state-of-the-art technology, it is not possible to achieve 'zero defects'.

The standard does provide that corrective action procedures should be established, documented and maintained to prevent recurrence of non-conforming product and that the system is maintained and developed through the internal audit and management review, but we are unconvinced that improvement is an explicit criterion by which ongoing certification is monitored, or indeed a basis for reassessment and registration. In general, the ISO 9000 series tends to measure the effectiveness of documentation, paperwork and procedures (this assessment is often termed a paperchase). But there is clear distinction between registration and capability, and senior management must recognize this. Product and/or service quality is determined by the individual organization, its people and processes and not by a quality system standard.

Proof of this difference is provided by a recent investigation carried out by Judy Mone[36] of the initial samples submitted by some 300 suppliers to the Leyland Daf assembly plant (it is a contractual requirement of Leyland Daf that all its suppliers are registered to the ISO 9000 series or its equivalent). She found that over 30 per cent of initial samples did not conform to requirements.

Failure to tackle the root cause of problems

The ISO 9000 series has a limited impact on the total improvement operation of an organization simply because it does not get at the root cause of problems: most problems are 'resolved' at branch level and the organization as a whole may not even be aware that a problem existed. No company-wide correction/prevention measures are adopted.

By way of comparison, the Ford motor-company requires its suppliers to demonstrate ongoing improvements in their quality systems and processes, and these improvements are assessed by supplier quality assistance personnel. There are no published data about inter- and intra-industry comparisons, nor is there any evidence that companies registered to the ISO 9000 series exhibit a better quality performance, and have a more positive approach to continuous and company-wide quality improvement, than those who are not registered.

Registration can engender too high expectations

Many organizations and executives have inflated views of the ISO 9000 series, often picked up from those selling advisory services. This can lead to high expectations of what the standard can achieve which, in the long term, may do it a disservice. The following are typical comments:

> Quality recognition of the ISO 9000 series from a national accredited certification body is prized nationwide because it is known to be difficult to achieve the high standards required by their impartial testing procedures.

> ... it will give the car-buying public a guarantee of complete satisfaction or their money back. What it aims to achieve is the world's coveted benchmark of quality: BS.5750 ... it is a standard that is recognized as being truly superb and is a move that no other rival car-maker can afford to ignore.

How can it be coveted and difficult to achieve when many thousands of companies in the UK have already met this requirement?

> Company X is the first in its industrial sector to obtain the prestigious ISO 9001 registration – a tremendous achievement ... very proud to be registered ... the most significant event in the company's history ... breaking new ground for quality ...

To the informed, these platitudes are saying no more than that the organization has taken the first step towards TQM.

Executive summary

- Quality assurance is *not* the province of the quality assurance department. Rather, it should be integrated into all processes and functions and every person should take personal responsibility for the quality assurance of his or her own processes.

- A quality system is a key building block for an organization's TQM activities.
- Customer pressure for proof from their suppliers that effective quality systems and procedures were in place led to the development of quality system standards.
- Quality system standards have their origins in military standards.
- The ISO 9000 series of standards harmonizes the approach to quality systems. The series consists of five individual standards divided into four parts.
- The ISO 9000 series sets out a definitive list of features and characteristics which should be present in an organization's quality system through documented policies, manuals and procedures and which help to ensure that quality is built into its processes.
- A number of organizations are not prepared to accept ISO 9000 series registration and wish to carry out their own assessments of the supplier's quality system. This view is expected to soften in future years.
- The process of registration to ISO 9001, 9002 or 9003 will lead an organization to improve control, discipline, procedures and documentation. This will result in some reduction in customer complaints, scrap and re-work, and lead to improved yields. However, once such registration has been achieved the mechanisms of the system are such that it will result in a steady-state performance which may or may not relate to a high level of non-conformance.
- Quality system registration to ISO 9001, 9002 or 9003 often results in a sense of complacency.
- Possession of quality system registration may demonstrate an organization's ability to produce and deliver conforming products – but does not guarantee it.
- CEOs should not have unduly high expectations of the benefits arising from ISO 9001, 9002 or 9003 registration.

Notes

1 BS 5750 (1987) Part 0, Section 0.1, *Principle, Concepts and Applications – Guide to Selection and Use*; (ISO 9000; 1987, *Quality Management and Quality Assurance Standards – Guidelines for Selection and Use*); Part 0, Section 0.2, *Principle, Concepts and Applications – Guide to Quality Management and Quality System Elements*, (ISO 9004, 1987, *Quality Management and Quality Systems Elements – Guidelines*); Part 1, *Specification for Design/Development, Production, Installation and Servicing*; (ISO 9001, 1987, *Quality Systems – Model for Quality Assurance in Design/Development, Production, Installation and Servicing*); Part 2, *Specification for Production and Installation*; (ISO 9002, 1987, *Model for Quality Assurance in Production and Installation*); Part 3, *Specification for*

Final Inspection and Test; (ISO 9003, 1987, *Quality Systems – Model for Quality Assurance in Final Inspection and Test*), British Standards Institution, London.

2 Dale, B. G. and Oakland, J. S. (1991) *Quality Improvement Through Standards*, Stanley Thornes, Cheltenham.

3 ISO 8402 (1986) (BS 4778: Part 1, 1987) *Quality Vocabulary*, International Organization for Standardization, Geneva.

4 BS 4891 (1972) *A Guide to Quality Assurance*, British Standards Institution, London.

5 Warner, F. (1977) *Standards and Specifications in the Engineering Industries*, National Economic Development Office, London.

6 BS 5750/ISO 9000 – see note 1, above.

7 Her Majesty's Stationery Office (1982) *Standards, Quality and International Competitiveness*, Government White Paper, Cmnd 8621, HMSO, London.

8 National Accreditation Council for Certification Bodies (1991) *Directory of Accredited Certification Bodies*, NACCB, London.

9 Department of Trade and Industry (1991) *DTI QA Register: The United Kingdom Register of Quality Assessed Companies*, vol. 2: Company Information, HMSO, London.

10 Ford Motor Company (1990) *Worldwide Quality System Standard Q-101*, Ford, Plymouth, Michigan.

11 Society of Motor Manufacturers and Traders (1990) *Quality Systems and the Motor Industry*, SMMT, London.

12 Dale, B. G. and Plunkett, J. J. (1984) 'A study of audits, inspection and quality costs in the pressure vessel fabrication sector of the process plant industry', *Proceedings of the Institution of Mechanical Engineers*, vol. 198, no. B2, pp. 45–54.

13 Singer, A. J., Churchill, G. F. and Dale, B. G. (1988) 'Supplier quality assurance systems; a study in the nuclear industry', *Proceedings of the Institution of Mechanical Engineers*, vol. 202, no. B4, pp. 205–12.

14 Galt, J. D. A. and Dale, B. G. (1991) 'Supplier development: a British case study', *International Journal of Purchasing and Materials Management*, Winter, pp. 16–22.

15 Boaden, R. J., Dale, B. G. and Polding, E. (1991) 'A state-of-the-art survey of total quality management in the construction industry', Research Report to the European Construction Institute, Loughborough.

16 Owen, F. (1988) 'Why quality assurance and its implementation in a chemical manufacturing company', *Chemistry and Industry*, August, pp. 491–4.

17 Oliver, B. (1991) 'Further thoughts on ISO 9000', *Quality News*, vol. 17, no. 3, pp. 122–3.

18 Long, A. A., Dale, B. G. and Younger, A. (1991) 'A study of BS.5750 aspirations in small companies', *Quality and Reliability Engineering International*, vol. 7, no. 1, pp. 27–33.

19 Ibid.
20 Dale and Oakland, *Quality Improvement*.
21 SMMT, *Quality Systems*.
22 Long, Dale and Younger, 'A study of BS.5750'.
23 Atkin, G. (1987) 'BS.5750 – practical benefits in the factory', *Works Management*, November, pp. 38–42.
24 Bulled, J. W. (1987) 'BS.5750 – quality management, systems and assessment', *General Engineer*, November, pp. 271–80.
25 Collyer, R. (1987) 'BS.5750 and its application', *Polymer Paint Colour Journal*, vol. 177, pp. 318–20.
26 Ford, E. (1988) 'Quality assured fabrication', *The Production Engineer*, October, pp. 36–8.
27 Hele, J. (1988) 'BS.5750/ISO 9000 and the metals processor', *Metallurgia*, March, pp. 128–34.
28 Dale and Oakland, *Quality Improvement*.
29 Owen, 'Why quality assurance'.
30 Oliver, 'Further thoughts'.
31 Long, Dale and Younger, 'A study of BS.5750'.
32 Sayle, A. J. (1987) 'ISO 9000 – progression or regression', *Quality News*, vol. 14, no. 2, pp. 50–3.
33 Owen, M. (1987) 'Ford, SPC and BS.5750', *Quality News*, vol. 12, no. 12, p. 323.
34 Whittington, D. (1989) 'Some attitudes to BS.5750: a study', *International Journal of Quality and Reliability Management*, vol. 6, no. 3, pp. 54–8.
35 Lascelles, D. M. and Dale, B. G. (1992) *Total Quality Improvement*, IFS Publications, Bedford.
36 Mone, J., Hibbert, B. and Dale, B. G. (1991) 'Initial samples and quality improvement: a study', *Proceedings of the Sixth National Conference on Production Research*, pp. 459–63.

Appendix B

Quality-Management Tools and Techniques: An Overview

Introduction

To support and develop continuous quality improvement, it is necessary to use a selection of quality-management tools and techniques: some simple, others more complex. Senior managers have a key role to play in ensuring the effective use of these tools and techniques. They must:

1 Be aware of their existence.
2 Having identified or been advised which of the tools and techniques are

appropriate to the organization's quality-improvement strategy, ideally have received education and training in their use. This need not be in great depth, a good overview may suffice, but it should provide senior managers with an indication of how the tools and techniques work, their purpose, the type of application to which they are best suited, and how they should be used.

3 Delegate responsibility for promoting the use of the tools to a subordinate. However, senior managers should maintain a participative role and show an active interest in the use of the tools and the results. Ideally the subordinate(s) should be someone who will use the tools (e.g. product and process engineers in designing experiments, SPC for production managers). Some CEOs delegate this task to the training or quality manager, who has then to persuade others to use them.

4 As with any other form of investment, endorse the expenditure required in terms of:
   (a) management time;
   (b) education and training;
   (c) development of people;
   (d) carrying out designed experiments;
   (e) applying mistake-proofing devices;
   (f) any additional equipment associated with quicker set-up operations;
   (g) the purchase of computer aids (hardware and software) associated with adoption of the more statistical/mathematical techniques;
   (h) implementing any countermeasure or corrective action recommended by the workforce.

Senior managers should be aware that a hidden expense is incurred in operating teams, particularly cross-functional ones. Participants are often expected to carry out their routine duties in addition to team activities. Consequently, either the team or the individuals' routine work suffers, sometimes both.

5 Accept that such expenditure is ongoing, not just one-off. It will be an investment in an appreciating asset and have greater returns than many earlier investment decisions, which may have depreciated over time.

6 Endorse the principle that the organization's key asset is its people, recognize the latent skills of the workforce and help foster, develop and utilize people's abilities and skills through a planned programme of education and training. The relevance of the training and its timing are critical factors in its effectiveness.

7 Ensure that the tools and techniques are being used effectively to facilitate improvement. They should be integrated into the way the business works rather than being used and viewed as bolt-on techniques.

8 Recognize that the process of continuous quality improvement is exactly that: never ending. The use of quality-management tools and techniques will facilitate and speed up this process and the gains.

The general contents of the quality-management 'toolbox' include:

- checklists, bar charts, tally charts, histograms and graphs;
- flow charts;
- Pareto analysis;
- cause and effect diagrams;
- scatterplots and regression analysis, including correlation;
- statistical process control (SPC);
- failure mode and effects analysis (FMEA);
- quality costing;
- design of experiments;
- quality function deployment (QFD);
- the seven 'new' quality control tools: relations diagrams, affinity diagrams, systematic diagrams, matrix diagrams, matrix data-analysis, process decision programme charts, and arrow diagrams;
- departmental purpose analysis (DPA);
- mistake-proofing (*poka-yoke*);
- additional statistical and mathematical techniques as appropriate.

This list is by no means exhaustive. Teamwork such as quality circles, employee involvement groups and the like, can also be considered part of the toolbox (teamwork is examined in chapter 7). However, the list gives the most popular, perhaps the best known, and those used in a wide variety of situations.

The various tools and techniques play different roles in quality improvement (e.g. data collection and presentation, understanding the problem, planning, setting priorities, finding causes, identifying relationships, structuring ideas, performance measurement, capability assessment, monitoring and maintaining control). Users must always be aware of the main uses of the particular tool or technique they are considering applying.

This appendix provides a brief summary of the tools and techniques listed above (other than quality costing, SPC and FMEA – see chapter 2 and appendices C and D respectively). Examples of the techniques are given from a series of business situations and different industries, enabling senior managers to visualize how they work in practice, and the potential areas of application in their organizations. Where appropriate, further reading is suggested for those who wish to extend their knowledge of a particular tool or technique.

Checklists, checksheets, bar charts, tally charts, histograms and graphs

Checklists (sometimes called inspection or validation checklists) are used as prompts and aids to personnel. They highlight the key features of a process, equipment, system and/or product needing attention, and ensure that the procedures for an operation, housekeeping, inspection, maintenance, etc. have been followed. A checklist for shift daily set-up is shown in figure B.1. Checklists are also used in audits of both product and systems. At the Leyland Daf assembly plant, a computer-aided quality assurance checklist system has been designed to provide an immediate and accurate measure of production non-conformities during vehicle assembly and test. An example of the dynamometer test checklist is given in figure B.2.

Checksheets are used as simple recording techniques for logging events such as non-conformities (including where they appear on the non-conforming item; when used in this way they are sometimes referred to as 'measles' charts or concentration diagrams), breakdowns of machinery and/or associated equipment, or anything else untoward in a process; they are prepared in advance of recording data. In table or diagram format they are extremely useful as a data collection device and record to supplement the attribute control charts (discussed in appendix C). The data from the checksheets provide the factual basis for subsequent analysis and corrective action. Figures B.3 and B.4 provide two examples from the many different kinds.

A highly visual form of checksheet is used by Nissan (UK). Line operators, from a work zone, place a ball in a slot on a board when a non-conformity is discovered on the production line; each slot corresponds to a particular non-conformity.

Tally charts are a descriptive presentation of data and help to identify patterns in it. They may be used as checksheets with attribute data (pass/fail, present/absent) but are more commonly used with measured or variable data (e.g. temperature, weight, length) to establish the pattern of variation displayed, prior to the assessment of capability and computation of process capability indices (e.g. Cp and Cpk – see appendix C). Tally charts are regarded as simple or crude frequency-distribution curves.

Statisticians tend to construct histograms rather than tally charts, but for analysis purposes they are much the same. A histogram takes measured data from the tally sheet and displays its distribution using the class intervals or value as a base – it resembles a bar chart with the bars representing the frequency of data. The histogram helps to visualize the distribution of data, and several forms should be recognized: normal, skewed, bimodal, isolated island, etc. There are a number of theoretical models that provide patterns and working tools for various shapes of distribution. The shape most often encountered is called normal or Gaussian.

Check list for shift daily set-up + cross check (and tool change checks + cross check)

Line No:- HVM   Operation:- AAH

Feature/detail to check	Morning shift record actual results/size	Cross check X	Tool changes 1st X	Tool changes 2nd X	2nd Shift check	Cross check X	Tool changes 1st X	Tool changes 2nd X	3rd Shift check	Cross check X	Tool changes 1st X	Tool changes 2nd X
Condition of master sample												
Condition of probes/fixture												
SPC/columns setting ok												
Gauging equip't set correct												
Gauges etc. in calibration												
Skirt dia.												
Top land dia.												
Groove root dia. GRV. 1												
GRV. 2												
GRV. 1												
Groove width GRV. 1												
GRV. 2												
GRV. 1												
Groove position GRV. 1												
GRV. 2												
GRV. 1												
Grv. run & form GRV. 1												
GRV. 2												
GRV. 1												
Grv. surface finish GRV. 1												
GRV. 2												
GRV. 1												
Grv. wave & chatter GRV. 1												
GRV. 2												
GRV. 1												
Groove root radii GRV. 1												
GRV. 2												
GRV. 1												
Groove parallel to crown												

Day:-

Date:-

Grv. drill hole position				
Grv. drill hole break thru				
Grv. drill hole dia.				
All finished chamfers				
Weight				
Daily pass-off + cross check and each tool change/set-up + cross check to be signed by the process controller responsible.				

Time	D3	D1	C3	C2	C1	B'edge	B	O/E	C2 rad	1	2	3	4	5	6

Figure B.1 Daily set-up checklist
Courtesy of A. E. Piston Products Ltd.

Quality Assurance Checklist — DYNAMOMETER TEST

Item No.	FEATURE TO BE CHECKED	Pass ✓	Fail X	Check V=visual F=funct.
	ZONE IDENTITY: POST DYNAMOMETER			
686	Check rear light clusters full function			V
600	Check clutch master cylinder & connections for leaks (C44 only)			V
687	Check lower front grille assembly (DAF 1900 only) – alignment, security, function/no fouls and undamaged			V/F
660	Check H.T.M. operation – (tilt cab) – if applicable			F
661	Check manual tilt operation (tilt cab) – if applicable			F
662	Check cab roof & rain channels for damage/defects			V
663	Check H.T.M. system for oil leaks – if applicable			V
664	Check cooling system for water leaks			V
665	Check fuel system for fuel leaks			V
666	Check power steering system for oil leaks			V
667	Check all engine fittings/connections for leaks			V/F
670	Check for omission of plugs on underside of cabs & wings			V
671	Check throttle mechanism for lubrication			V
672	Check splitter pipes are run correctly – no fouls			V
673	Check wiring for side flashers located in securing clips			V
674	Check clutch slave cylinder & connections for leaks and dust cap fitted over bleed nipple			V
675	Check gearbox & fittings for oil leaks			V
676	Check rear axle(s) for oil leaks			V
677	Check hydraulic brake system for leaks			V
678	Check steering box/connections for oil leaks			V
679	Check H.T.M. operation (if applicable) and gear lever does not foul when lowering cab			F
680	Check manual tilt operation (if applicable) and gear lever does not foul when lowering cab			F
681	Check cab tilt lock mechanism & fully lubricated			F/V
794	Check front panel support stay – function/no damage (C44 only)			F/V
682	Check coolant level (see through header tank) & alignment of tank			V
600	Check clutch master cylinder & connections for leaks (all except C44)			V
683	Check clutch fluid reservoir level – no contamination & cap to body integrity			F/V
684	Check hydraulic brake reservoir level – no contamination & cap to body integrity			F/V
685	Check air restriction indicator – secure/inner sleeve not visible			V
	INSP. SIGN:			

Figure B.2 Dynamometer checklist
Courtesy of Leyland Daf.

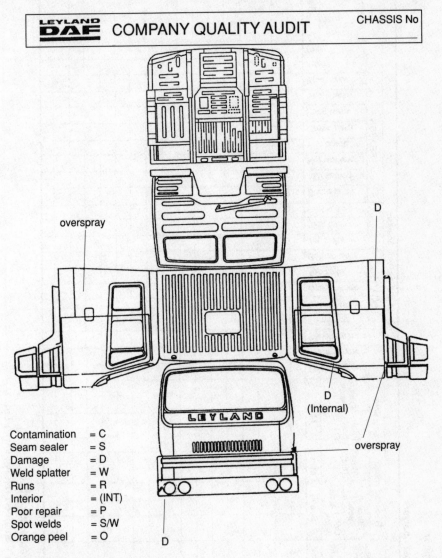

Figure B.3 Vehicle checksheet
Courtesy of Leyland Daf.

Corrugator log lost time analysis

Reduced speed and lost time analysis

Corrugator Instruction No.	Log				Reduced speed			Lost time		LOCATION											REASON										Shift A B C D Day
	Gross time per C.I.	Change-overs			Running speed		Time (hrs)	Total per C.I.	Occur-rence	Operating end	Rotary shear	Slitter/creaser	Trim chute	Board guides	Bottom knife	Top knife	Bottom belts	Top belts	Side two	End two	Board jam	ADI setting	Not working	Wet board	Cross warp	Long warp	Scorched	Short crew	Mech	Elect	Remarks
		1st plan	Chop	Overtime	Opti-mum	Actual																									
	Time				Speed		Mins.	Mins.	Mins.																						

Figure B.4 Corrugator checksheet
Courtesy of Bowater Containers (Heavy Duty) Ltd.

pH	Frequency	Total
Tally chart Effluent analysis – pH		
4.75 – 5.25		0
5.25 – 5.75		0
5.75 – 6.25		0
6.25 – 6.75	II	2
6.75 – 7.25	IIII	4
7.25 – 7.75	IIII IIII I	11
7.75 – 8.25	IIII IIII II	12
8.25 – 8.75	IIII IIII	10
8.75 – 9.25	IIII	4
9.25 – 9.75	I	1
9.75 – 10.25		0
10.25 – 10.75		0

Figure B.5 Tally chart
Courtesy of Grace Dearborn.

Figure B.5 shows a tally chart based on a statistical analysis of an effluent plant, and figure B.6 is a histogram constructed from the data collected on the tally chart.

Bar charts are simple pictorial representations which facilitate the understanding of numerical data. They are often used for presentation of the results of a Pareto analysis. (A Pareto diagram is a specialized form of bar char.) Figure B.7 is a bar chart depicting the weekly and cumulative pouch processing errors at Girobank.

Graphs, be they presentational (i.e. to convey data in some pictorial manner) or mathematical (i.e. from which data may be interpolated or extrapolated), are used to facilitate understanding and analysis of the collected data, investigate relationships between factors, attract attention and make the data memorable. A wide choice of graphical methods is available (i.e. line graphs, pie charts, Gantt charts, radar charts, band charts) for different types of application. Figures B.8 and B.9 are examples of a line graph and a pie chart respectively.

Flow charts

Process mapping (sometimes called blueprinting or process modelling), in either a structured or unstructured format, is a prerequisite to an

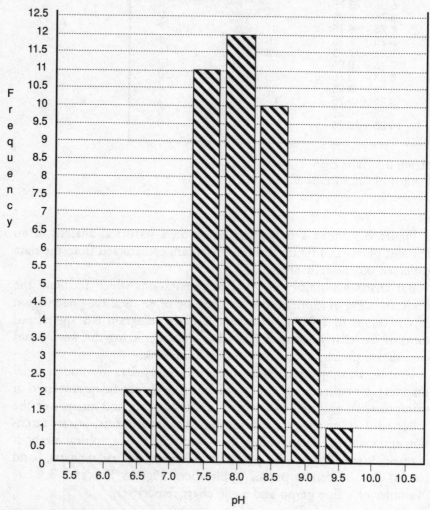

Figure B.6 Histogram
Courtesy of Grace Dearborn.

Cheque processing services (CPS)/nights.   Pouch processing errors.   Cash vehicle elimination (CVE).

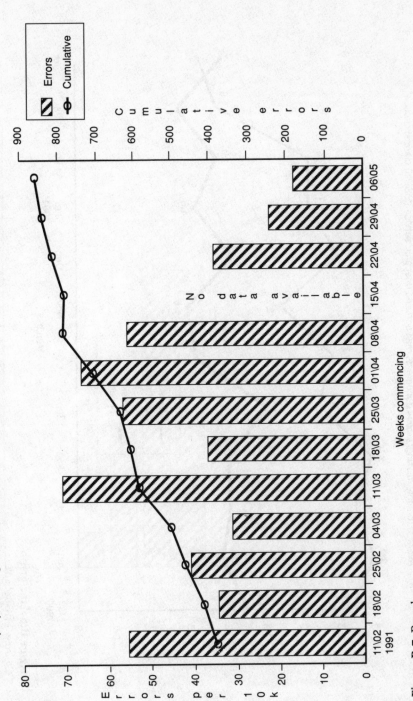

Figure B.7 Bar chart
Courtesy of Girobank.

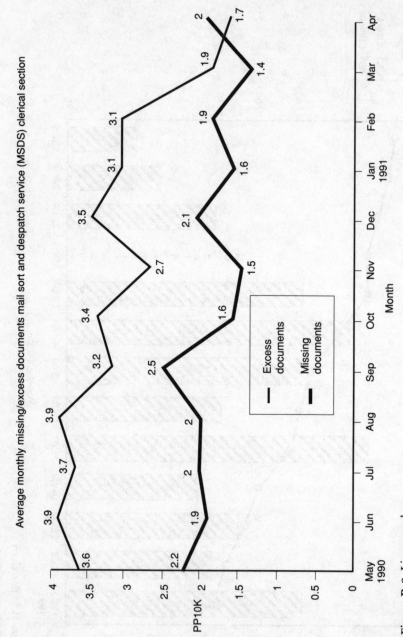

Figure B.8 Line graph
Courtesy of Girobank.

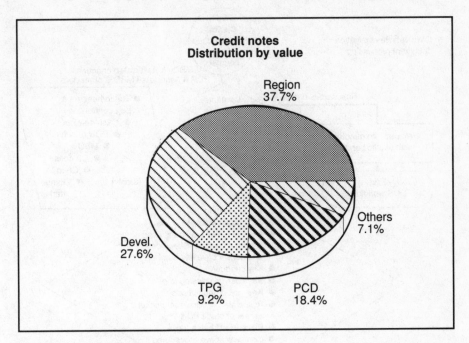

Figure B.9 Pie chart
Courtesy of Grace Dearborn.

in-depth understanding of the process, before the application of tools and techniques such as FMEA, SPC and quality costing. A flow chart is employed to provide a diagrammatic picture, by means of a set of symbols, showing all the steps in a particular process or sequence of events.

Traditionally, these charts have employed conventional symbols to define activities such as operation, inspection, delay or temporary storage, permanent storage and transportation, and are much used by operations and methods and industrial engineering personnel (see Currie[1] for details).

Used in a manufacturing context, a chart may show the complete process, from goods received through storage, manufacture and assembly to despatch of final product, or simply some part of it in detail. What is important is that each stage is included to focus attention on aspects of the process or subset where problems have occurred or may occur, to enable corrective action to be taken or countermeasure put in place.

There are a number of variants of the classical process flow chart, including those tailored to an individual company's use with different

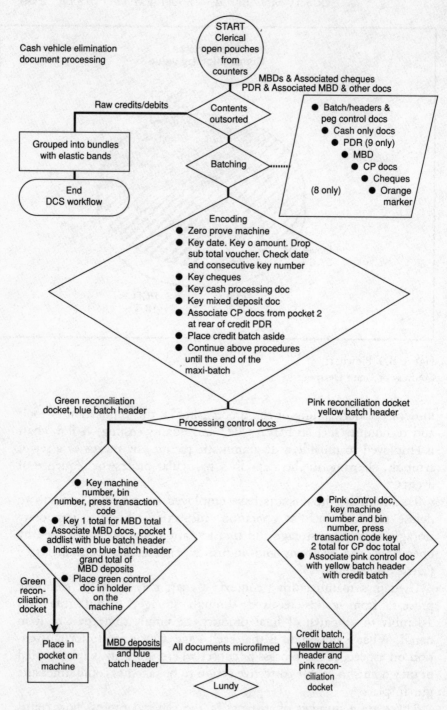

Figure B.10 Flow chart
Courtesy of Girobank.

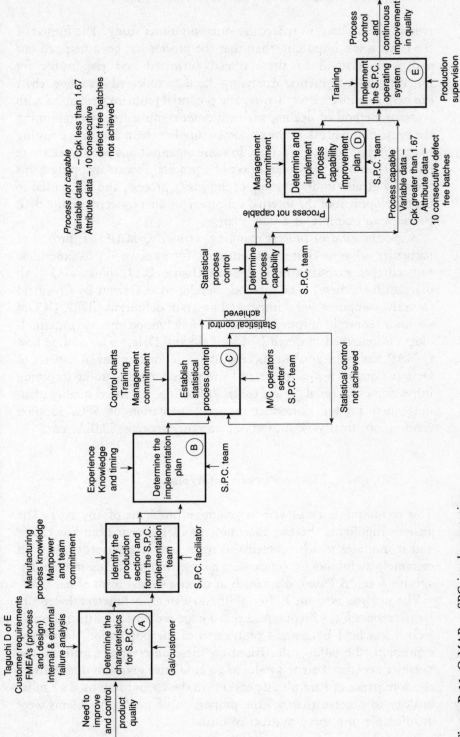

Figure B.11 Q-MAP – SPC implementation

symbols being used to reflect the situation under study. The format of the chart is less important than that the process has been mapped out and is understood by those directly involved and responsible for initiating improvements. Analysing the data collected on a flow chart can help to uncover irregularities and potential problem points. It is also a useful method of dealing with customer complaints, by establishing the cause of the break in the customer/supplier chain and thus pointing to appropriate corrective action. In some organizations people are aware only of their own particular aspect of a process. Process mapping helps toward a greater understanding of the whole process, and is essential to the development of the internal customer/supplier concept. Figure B.10 provides an example of a flow chart.

A specific kind of process mapping, termed Q-MAP, has proved of particular value to Garrett Automotive, for instance, its Skelmersdale turbocharger manufacturing division (figure B.11 shows a Q-MAP diagram used there). The method, developed at Garrett by Crossfield from the computer-aided integrated program definition (IDEF) (ICOM – input, control, output, mechanism – definition method) methodology, is described in detail by Crossfield and Dale,[2] who outline how Q-MAP has been applied successfully in modelling major aspects of Garrett's quality assurance systems and procedures, including incoming inspection of material, gauge control/planning, advanced quality planning, new product introduction, implementation of SPC, supplier certification, final view inspection, warranty analysis, FMEA, etc.

Pareto analysis

This technique is employed to prioritize problems of any type. The analysis highlights the fact that most problems stem from few causes and it indicates which problems to solve and in what order. It is an extremely useful tool for condensing a large volume of data into a manageable form. A Pareto diagram is in effect a special form of bar chart.

The analysis is named after Wilfredo Pareto, a nineteenth-century Italian economist, who observed that a large proportion of the country's wealth was held by a small proportion of the population; hence the expression, the 80/20 rule. Based on these observations, early in the twentieth century Lorenz produced a cumulative graph to demonstrate the dominance of Pareto's 20 per cent. In the 1950s Juran used a similar analogy to observe that a large proportion of quality problems were attributable to a small number of causes.

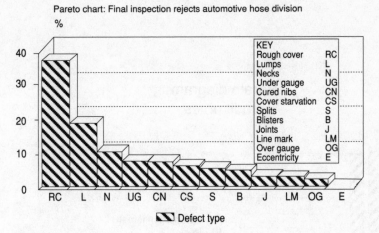

Pareto chart: Final inspection rejects automotive hose division

KEY
Rough cover — RC
Lumps — L
Necks — N
Under gauge — UG
Cured nibs — CN
Cover starvation — CS
Splits — S
Blisters — B
Joints — J
Line mark — LM
Over gauge — OG
Eccentricity — E

Defect type

Figure B.12 Pareto diagram: inspection rejects
Courtesy of BTR Hose.

The technique involves ranking the collected data, usually via a checksheet, with the most common problem at the top and the least at the bottom. The contribution of each problem to the grand total is expressed as a percentage, and cumulative percentages are used in compounding the effect of these problems. Ranking is usually in terms of occurrence and/or cost. The results are often presented in two ways: ranked data as a bar chart and cumulative percentages as a graph. Figure B.12 shows an example based on the final inspection rejects at BTR Hose, and figure B.13 is an analysis of 1,200 credit notes, with a value in excess of £600,000, at Grace Dearbon Ltd.

Pareto analysis is a very simple technique, but extremely useful in focusing attention on the major contributor(s) to a quality problem in order to generate ideas and suggestions for its reduction if not elimination. It is not a once-and-for-all analysis; used regularly and consistently, the presentational part of the technique demonstrates clearly the step-by-step improvements made over a period.

Cause and effect diagrams

These were developed by the late Kaoru Ishikawa,[3] as one of his advocated seven basic tools of quality control, commonly referred to in Japan as Q7. Cause and effect diagrams are often called Ishikawa diagrams, and sometimes fishbone diagrams because of their skeletal

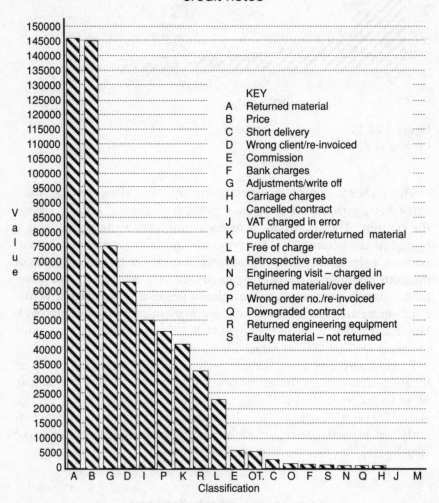

Figure B.13 Pareto diagram: credit notes
Courtesy of Grace Dearborn.

appearance. The effect (a specific problem or a quality characteristic/ condition) forms the head, and possible causes and sub-causes the bone structure, of the fish. The diagrams illustrate in a clear manner the possible relationships between some identified effect and the causes influencing it. They also help to uncover the root causes of a problem and generate improvement ideas.

They are typically used by a quality circle or other team as part of a brainstorming exercise to extract ideas and opinions as to the possible major cause(s) of the problem, and then recommendations to resolve or counteract it.

It is important to define the problem or abnormality clearly, in as much detail as possible, to enable possible causes to be identified. This can be quite difficult, and the team leader must define a manageable problem (if it is too large it may need subdividing into a number of sub-problems) and ensure that the team's efforts and contributions are maximized constructively. There are three types of diagrams.

1 *5M cause and effect diagram* The main 'bone' structure or branches would typically comprise machinery, manpower, method, material and maintenance. Teams often omit maintenance, and hence use a 4M diagram, while others may add a sixth M (Mother Nature) to form a 6M diagram.

 In non-manufacturing areas the four Ps (policies, procedures, people and plant) are sometimes more appropriate.

 As with any type of cause and effect diagram, the exact format is less important than the process of bringing about appropriate countermeasures for the identified and agreed major cause(s) of the problem.

2 *Process cause and effect diagram* The team members should be familiar with the process under consideration. It is therefore usual to map it out using a process flow chart and seek to identify causes for the problem at each stage of the process. If the process flow is so large as to be unmanageable, the sub-processes or process steps should be separately identified. Each stage of the process is then brainstormed and ideas developed.

3 *Dispersion analysis cause and effect diagram* This diagram is commonly used after a 4M/5M/6M diagram has been completed. The major causes identified by the group are treated as separate branches and expanded upon by the team.

Figure B.14 shows a 6M cause and effect diagram produced by process supervisors on the causes of waste. Figure B.15 shows the main reasons for the issue of credit notes. This cause and effect diagram and the Pareto diagram given in figure B.13 were produced by a quality-

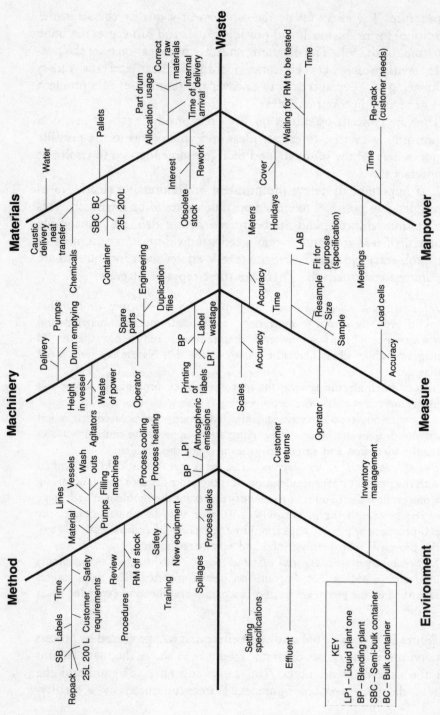

Figure B.14 Cause and effect diagram.
Courtesy of Grace Dearborn.

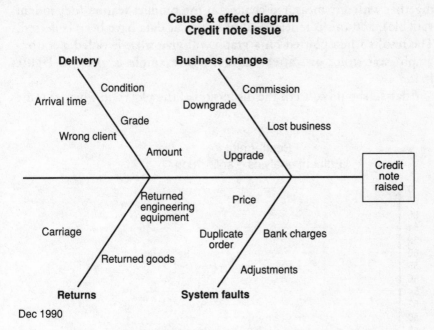

Cause & effect diagram
Credit note issue

Delivery

Condition

Arrival time

Grade

Wrong client

Amount

Business changes

Commission

Downgrade

Lost business

Upgrade

Credit
note
raised

Returned
engineering
equipment

Price

Carriage

Duplicate
order

Bank charges

Returned goods

Adjustments

Returns

System faults

Dec 1990

Figure B.15 Cause and effect analysis
Courtesy of Grace Dearborn.

improvement team comprising sales office supervisor, credit control manager, credit note process clerk and a business analyst.

It is interesting to note that the conventional diagrams originated by Ishikawa have been developed and refined by Ryuji Fukuda[4] at Sumitomo Electric, and termed cause and effect diagrams with addition of cards (CEDAC) – the cards being used to reflect the team's continually updated facts and ideas. This type of diagram is currently in use at a number of organizations.

Scatterplots and regression analysis (including correlation)

Scatterplots are used when examining the possible relationship or association between two variables or factors, and indicate the relationship as a pattern. For example, one variable may be a process parameter (e.g. temperature, pressure, screw speed), and the other some measurable characteristic or feature of the product (e.g. length, weight, thickness). As the process parameter (independent variable), is changed it is noted together with any measured change in the product feature (dependent variable), and this is repeated until sufficient data have been collected. The results when plotted on a graph will give what is called a scatter-graph, scatterplot or scatter diagram. An example is given in Figure B.16.

Analysis should concern the dispersion of the plots and whether some

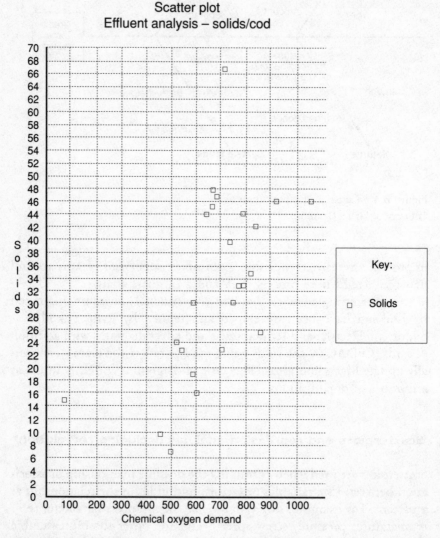

Figure B.16 Scatterplot
Courtesy of Grace Dearborn.

linear, or known non-linear, relationship exists between the two variables. In this way the scatterplot is a valuable tool for diagnosis and problem-solving. Regression analysis would subsequently be used not only to establish lines of best fit, but also to provide the basis for making estimates or predictions of, say, the product variable for a given value of the process parameter. In this way, it is possible to reduce the amount of data measured, collected, plotted and analysed.

How valid or reliable such estimates are is largely a function of the degree of correlation between the two variables (if indeed only two variables are under consideration), and whether the estimates are interpolated (i.e. from within the range of collected data) or extrapolated (i.e. outside that range).

Where there are more than two variables, multivariate regression analysis should be used, but a good background of statistical knowledge is required to undertake this analysis.

Design of experiments

These techniques involve the identification and control of those parameters or variables which have a potential influence on the output of a process, choosing two or more levels of these variables and then running the process at those levels. The concept of optimizing product design, process design and process operation by experimental devices has been in existence for many decades.

One approach, often called the classical approach, would be to change one variable or factor at a time while keeping all others constant. The experiments are run until some optimum level is found for the single factor. Then keeping this fact or at that level, variations are made to another factor to find *its* optimum – the other factors being kept constant – and so on. This approach is widely criticized, however, not least for the fact that no information is or would be provided about any interactions that may occur between the factors being tested. In addition, it is not easy to hold the factors constant from experiment to experiment, and this itself creates variation.

An alternative approach is to consider all combinations of the factors, (the factorial approach). This may be feasible for a small number of factors but even with, say six factors at two levels, the minimum number of experiments or runs would be 2^6, i.e. 64. Despite the fact that main effects and interactions could both be measured, the cost of running such a large number of experiments could be prohibitive. This problem may be overcome by the use of fractional factorial designs, often presented in the form of orthogonal arrays. For example, seven factors at two levels, i.e. 128 experiments in the full factorial approach, could be covered using an L8 orthogonal array, i.e. eight cells or experiments. However, although economies in the design of the experiment are achieved, there is an inevitable loss of information, usually that of some possible interactions between factors. Despite this drawback, most practitioners appear to favour this latter approach. The key steps in designing and running such an experiment are:

Step 1 Identify the main parameters/factors (e.g. temperature, the percentage of constituents making up a product or mix of material) and interactions. A cause and effect diagram may aid this. This step should be undertaken by people familiar with the process under investigation, using engineering know-how, combined perhaps with 'gut feeling'.

Step 2 Establish the levels at which each parameter/factor is to be tested.

Step 3 Steps 1 and 2 will identify the orthogonal array to be used (there are a number of popular arrays with perhaps seven covering most applications and these should be considered the 'cookbook'). In the orthogonal array (see figure B.17) decide the data to be placed in each column in relation to the factors being tested, monitoring interactions and detecting noise. It is usual to place those control factors which are more difficult to change in the first and second columns on the left of the array. The rows and columns of the orthogonal array form the experimental plan.

Step 4 Organize the experiment and carry it out. This often involves considerable organization in tracking the products involved in the experiment.

Step 5 Analyse and interpret the results, looking for relevant interactions.

Step 6 Carry out a confirmation run at the optimum settings to validate the conclusions.

Design of experiments dates back to the work of Sir R. A. Fisher in the 1920s and historically required a great deal of statistical knowledge and understanding, which most users found somewhat intimidating. Much effort has been devoted to simplifying the task. In the late 1970s the work of Genichi Taguchi on experimental design made what is regarded by many as a major breakthrough in its application, (see Taguchi[5] for details of his method). The Taguchi method differs from the classical methods in a number of areas, which will not be discussed here.

Taguchi is a statistician and electrical engineer who was involved in rebuilding the Japanese telephone system, and has been applying

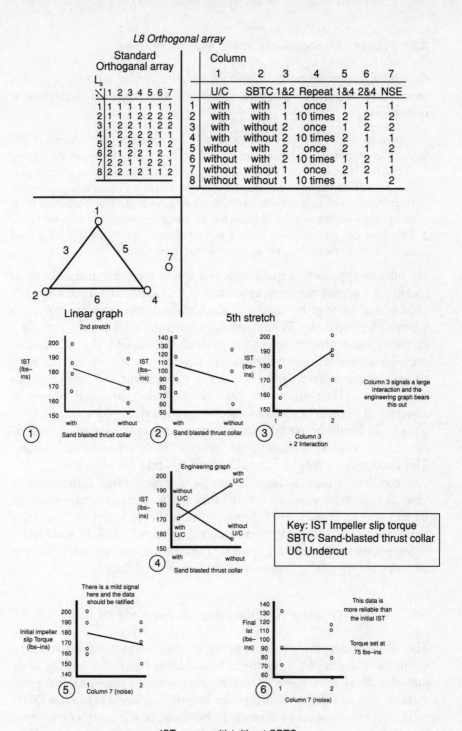

Figure B.17 Taguchi design of experiments

Source: Crossfield, R. J. and Dale, B. G. (1991) 'Applying Taguchi methods to the design improvement process of turbochargers', *Quality Engineering*, vol. 3, no. 4, pp. 501–16.

design of experiments in the Japanese electronics industry for over twenty-five years. He promotes three distinct stages of designing-in quality:

1 System design – the basic configuration of the system is developed.
2 Parameter design – the numerical values for the system variables (product/process parameters, called factors) are chosen so that the system performs well, no matter what disturbances or noises it encounters. There are three types of design factors: control, signal and null. The emphasis is on using low-cost materials and processes in the production of the system.
3 Tolerance design – if the system is not satisfactory, tolerance design is used to improve performance by tightening the tolerances.

His off-line approach to quality control is well accepted in the West, in particular with the engineering fraternity, but inevitably there are many criticisms of some of his statistical methods and, rather surprisingly, the advocated philosophy. What the critics seem to forget is that Taguchi's methods have proved successful in both Japan and the West, and organizations adopting his methods have succeeded in making continuous improvement; it is this which is important, not the methods used. There is little doubt that his work has led to increased interest in a variety of approaches and methodologies relating to design of experiments. It should be noted that a number of people have made significant improvements with the other approaches to experimental design. The maxim to be applied should be: if it works for you, use it.

Some details from a Taguchi design of experiments carried out at Garrett Automotive, which investigated a proposed engineering change to remove the thread relief diameter from the end of a turbocharger shaft, are given in figure B.17; for more details see Crossfield and Dale.[6]

Suggested reading, in addition to Taguchi himself, includes Lochnar and Matar,[7] Bendell, Disney and Pridmore[8] and Barker.[9]

Quality function deployment (QFD)

The QFD methodology (sometimes termed customer-driven engineering) was developed in Japan at Mitsubishi's Kobe shipyard. It arose out of a need to achieve simultaneously a competitive advantage in quality, cost and delivery. All the leading companies in Japan use QFD.

The technique seeks to identify those features of a product or service that satisfy the real needs and requirements of customers (market- or customer-required quality). This analysis also takes into account discussions with the people actually using the product, to obtain data on such issues as:

- what they feel about existing products;
- what bothers them;
- the features new products should have; and
- what is required to satisfy their needs, expectations, thinking and ideas.

It is usual to express the customers' needs in their own words, and then translate them into technical language. Superior-performing companies are using QFD to identify product and service features (including additional features) customers will find attractive. In this way quality characteristics, features, and/or technical advantages can be established to differentiate products from competitors'. These features are then translated into design requirements, and deployed through each phase in the manufacturing cycle to ensure that what is delivered to customers truly reflects their needs.

QFD is a key tool to help build quality into the upstream processes and in the early stage of new product development. This helps to avoid problems in the downstream production and delivery processes, and shortens new-product/service development time. It promotes proactive rather than reactive development.

Marketing executives should note that the market analysis matrix (see figure B.19, for example) used in QFD provides a formal mechanism and structure for the data collected by marketing departments for customer needs, competitive benchmarking, new product ideas, market survey data, etc.)

QFD employs a step-by-step approach, from customer needs and expectations through product planning and development, process planning and production planning, to manufactured products.

In simple terms, QFD comprises:

- Translate customer objectives and 'wants' into product or service design 'hows' (i.e. product planning and design). Comparative analysis is made of competitive products and/or services; this is termed 'why'. Any conflicts between the 'wants' and 'hows' are prioritized and a logical trade-off is made. Every 'how' is costed and target values set – 'how much'.
- Design requirements are then deployed to the next phase in the manufacturing cycle (i.e. product development and detailed design); again, any conflicts are prioritized and trade-offs agreed and made.
- The analysis is continued throughout the complete process from manufacture to delivery and even after-sales (i.e. process planning and production planning). In this way technology, restraints and reliability and quality assurance control points are identified.

1. Product planning

Product	Turbocharger
Model	T-X

Product requirements

Correlation
- ● Strong possibility
- ◇ Positive
- X Negative
- XX Strong negative

Relationships
- ● Strong – 6
- O Medium – 3
- △ Weak – 1

Customer needs — Importance
- 1 – Minimal
- 2 – Minor
- 3 – Desirable
- 4 – Necessary
- 5 – Mandatory

Customer satisfaction

Satisfaction
- 1 – Poor
- 2 – Fair
- 3 – Average
- 4 – Good
- 5 – Excellent

Relationship matrix

Customer need	Importance rating	Turbine performance	Compressor performance	Product durability	Lube system integrity	Vibration resistance	Actuator durability	C.H.R.A. balance	Regulator calibration	Operating noise	Bearing system durability	No coking conditions	Mounting system integrity
Adequate amount	3	●	●	●			●		●		O		O
Fast response	5	O	O	●			●		O		O		△
Smooth response	4	●	O	●							O		O
Low end response	4	●	●	●			●		●		O		△
Low fuel usage	4	●	●						O				△
Air / exhaust	3				●	●							●
Oil / water	4				O	O						O	
Safe product	5			●	●	●	●						O
No break downs	5	△	O	●		●		O	●	O	●	●	O
No turbo noise	4	O	O			O					●		●
No exh emissions	5					●	●		●				●

Customer satisfaction — Products compared

Customer need	T (7)	A (2)	B (4)	C (6)	Disadvantage
Adequate amount	3	3	3	3	
Fast response	4	4	4	3	
Smooth response	4	4	5	3	Y
Low end response	3	3	3	3	
Low fuel usage	3	3	3	3	
Air / exhaust	4	4	4	3	
Oil / water	2	1	2	4	Y
Safe product	3	3	3	4	
No break downs	3	4	2	4	Y
No turbo noise	2	4	3	5	Y
No exh emissions	4	4	4	4	

Customer needs groupings: **Reliable product** → **Good performance** (Good power: Adequate amount, Fast response, Smooth response, Low end response, Low fuel usage; No leaks: Air / exhaust, Oil / water), Safe product, No break downs, No turbo noise, No exh emissions

Product requirement specifications

Technical product evaluations — Rating scale	
1 – Poor	
2 – Fair	
3 – Average	
4 – Good	
5 – Excellent	

Products — Performance ratings for product requirements

Products													Est. cost
A-2	3	3	3	4	3	5	1	5	5	3	3	4	360
B-4	5	3	4	4	3	2	3	2	5	4		3	285
C-6	3	4	3	5	4	4	4	4	4		3	4	345
T-7	3	4	3	4	2	3	5	3	1	4	3	4	330
T-X (Improved)	5	5	4	4	5	4	5	4	1	5	4	4	270

Quality history

														Weights
Field repairs – quantity / 1000	1.5	1.5	5.0	1.4	0.9	3.4			2.5	5.0	4.0	2.7		
Warranty cost – cost / unit sold	.22	.17	.35	.24	.02	.60			.32	.45	.27	.18		
Customer rejects – qty / 1000									2.5					
Internal quality costs / unit sold							.10	.05	.50					

Evaluation summary

														Weights
Product req't importance (1, 3, 5)	5	5	5	3	5	1	5	1	1	3	1	1.5		60%
Competitive disadvantage – after improvement actions			Y	Y	Y	Y			Y					
Quality problems (1, 3, 5)	3	3	3	3	5	1	5	5	5	5	5	3		20%
Technical difficulty (1, 3, 5)	3	3	3	3	5	1	3	5	5	5	5	1		20%
Overall product req't importance	4	5	4	5	5	4	3	4	3	4	3	4		

Relative rank	
1 – Low	
2 – Medium	
3 – High	

Proprietary

Figure B.18 Quality function deployment – 'house of quality'
Courtesy of Garrett Automotive.

The analysis is progressive and can be stopped at any point. However, Japanese experience is that the greatest benefit is derived when all phases of the process are completed. A multidisciplinary team is used and the usefulness of the process flow chart again cannot be overstated. A number of the seven new quality control tools are also used to assist with the QFD process. Figure B.18 shows an example of the 'house of quality' developed by the use of QFD at Allied Signal.[10]

CEOs wishing to develop their knowledge of QFD are recommended to read Akao[11] and Eureka and Ryan.[12]

The seven new quality-control tools

The so-called seven new tools of quality control (most of which have already been used in applications other than TQM) were developed by the Japanese to collect and analyse non-qualitative and verbal data, particularly from sales and marketing, and design and development activities. In Japanese companies they are typically used by quality circles in sales and design areas and in QFD. A full description of tools is beyond the scope of this appendix. They are, however, covered in detail by Mizuno,[13] Ozeki and Asaka[14] and Barker.[15]

In brief, the tools are:

1 *Relations diagram* Used to identify and clarify complex cause and effect relationships in order to find the causes of and solutions to a problem, and to determine the key factors in a preventive activity. They are also employed to identify the key issues leading to a desired result. A relations diagram is a freer, broader version of a cause and effect diagram.

2 *Affinity diagram* Used to categorize verbal data about previous unexplored issues, problems and themes which are fuzzy and difficult to understand. The systematic analysis is facilitated by a diagram which uses the affinity between opinions and partial data to help understand the problem. The classification of factors can be expressed in cause and effect diagram format.

3 *Systematic diagram* Used to search systematically for the most appropriate and effective means of planning to accomplish a task or solving a problem; events are represented in the form of a tree diagram. This tool is used when the causes that influence the problem are known, but a plan and method for resolving the problem have not been developed.

4 *Matrix diagram* Used to clarify the relationship between results and causes or between objectives and methods, and to indicate their relative importance. These factors are arranged in rows and columns on a chart, with the intersections identifying the problem and its concentration. Symbols are

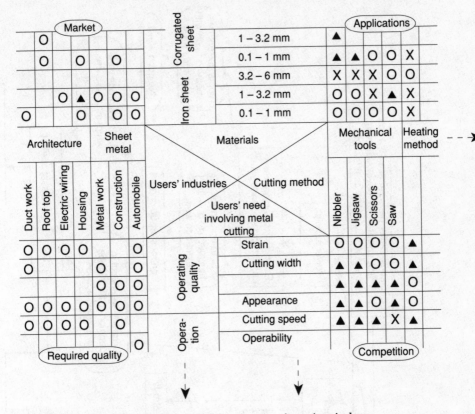

Figure B.19 Market analysis matrix for the metal-cutting industry
Courtesy of the Daihen Corporation.

used to depict the presence and strength of a relationship between sets of data. There are a number of types of matrix diagram.

5 *Matrix data analysis* Used to arrange the data presented in a matrix diagram in a clear manner. Various symbols are employed to indicate the strength of a relationship between variables. A series of planning matrices are used in QFD. An example of a matrix used for market analysis is shown in figure B.19.

6 *Process decision program chart (PDPC)* Used to select the best processes to obtain the desired outcome from a problem statement by evaluating all possible events and conceivable outcomes. Figure B.20 shows how the PDPC method was used to resolve a bottleneck engineering problem. It can be seen that countermeasures and actions for potential problems are detailed.

7 *Arrow diagram* Used to establish the most suitable daily plan for a series of activities in a project, and to monitor its progress efficiently. The sequence of the steps involved and their relation to one another are indicated by an arrow.

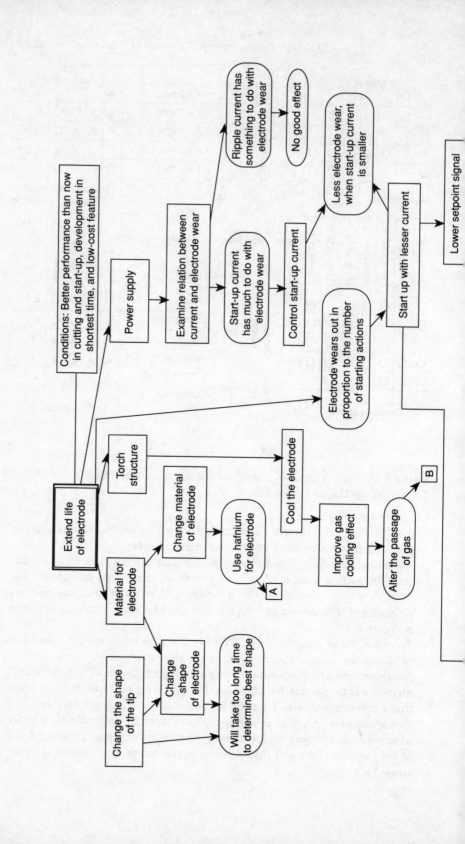

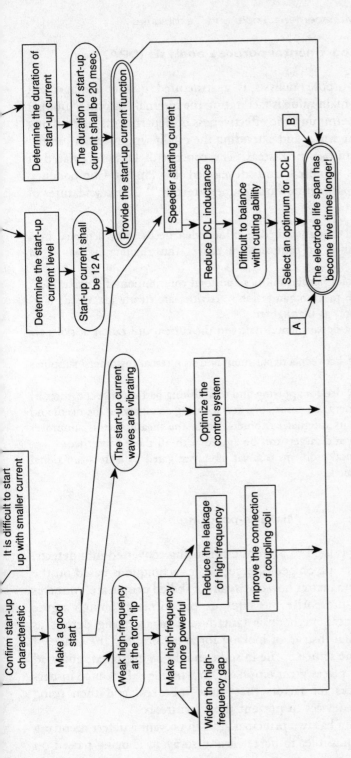

Figure B.20 An example of a bottleneck engineering problem solved by the PDPC method. Courtesy of the Daihen Corporation.

Departmental purpose analysis (DPA)

Departmental purpose analysis is a structured quality-management tool. Perhaps its main value is facilitating the internal customer/supplier relationship, determining the effectiveness of departments, identifying non-value-adding work, and extending the quality-improvement initiatives to non-manufacturing areas. The concept of DPA originated at IBM[16] and was adopted and developed by Philips Components, Blackburn as departmental improvement review.[17] The key features of DPA are:

- A departmental task analysis determines what needs to be achieved by a department to meet the company's objectives, thus aligning the two sets of objectives.
- The purpose, roles, responsibilities and total contribution of a department to adding value to an organization's activities are clearly identified; non-value-adding work is highlighted.
- The workload of departmental staff and the current utilization of skills are ascertained.
- The relationship between a department and its internal customers/ suppliers is defined.
- The basis is provided for applying and establishing performance measures by which a department can ensure that it is focusing on satisfying the needs and expectations of its internal customers. From the measurements, improvement objectives and targets can be agreed with all those concerned.
- Inter-departmental problems that can be investigated by a cross-functional team are identified.

Mistake-proofing

Mistake-proofing is used to prevent errors being converted into defects. Developed by the late Shigeo Shingo,[18] the technique is based on the assumption that no matter how observant or skilled people are, mistakes will occur unless preventive measures are put in place. Shingo argues that using statistical methods is tantamount to accepting defects as inevitable, and that instead of looking for and correcting the causes of defective work, the source of the mistake should be inspected, analysed and rectified. He places great emphasis on what he calls source inspection, which checks for factors that cause mistakes, and then using mistake-proofing devices to prevent their recurrence.

Mistake-proofing has two principal aims to prevent a defect occurring or, if this is not possible, to detect it and so avoid it being passed on to the next stage. The system is applied at three points in the process:

1 preventing the start of a process in the event of an error;
2 preventing a non-conforming product from leaving a process;
3 preventing a non-conforming part being passed to the next process.

Mistake-proofing employs the ingenuity and skills not only of the engineers, who may develop and fit the devices, but also of the operators who have first identified the cause of the mistake and then participated in the corrective action measures. In Japanese companies quality circles are active in developing and using mistake-proofing devices. These may be simple mechanical counters which ensure that the correct number of parts are fed into a machine, or cut-offs, limit or float switches which provide some regulatory control of the process or operation. The assumption is made that, if something can be fed in wrongly, it will be unless some preventive measure is taken. This is the essence of mistake-proofing. It is usual to integrate the mistake-proofing device

Operation: Welding exhaust pipe to silencer.
Requirements: The silencer must be fitted with the manufacturer's embossed name on the
same side of every assembly.

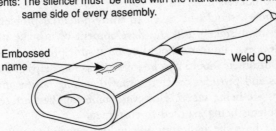

Concern: The silencer is elliptical in section and can be loaded on to the welding jig
with the embossed name either way up.
Poka-yoke: A proximity switch is fitted in the circuit of the welder which must be activated
by contacting the rolled seam (only on one side of the silencer) before the
welding operation may commence.

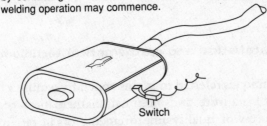

Figure B.21 Mistake-proofing example
Courtesy of Nissan Manufacturing (UK) Ltd.

and signal with an audible or visual warning to indicate that something has gone wrong.

An example is given in figure B.21.

Based on their research into mistake-proofing in a European motor industry supplier, Dale and Lightburn[19] offer the following guidelines to organizations approaching the development of mistake-proofing.

- Mistake proof at the earliest possible opportunity, certainly at the development stage and before any pre-production activities are undertaken.
- Involve manufacturing and quality department personnel in the Research and Development activity and ensure that there is a forum for the discussion of manufacturing and design problems and their interfaces; cross-function teams, and concurrent and simultaneous engineering should facilitate this.
- The design and process FMEA, analysis of customer reject returns, warranty claims, field failure reports, in-house scrap and rework, and inspection data should help to pinpoint potential problems that could be resolved by mistake proofing.
- It is much easier to mistake proof new products than develop devices for existing products.
- A team approach should be taken to study potential problems and likely causes of mistakes, and the development of mistake proofing ideas and devices. The team should be multi-disciplined and involve operators. Customers should also be involved as this helps to build up relationships and provides concrete proof that long lasting improvement actions are being taken. However, some suppliers are sensitive to their problems being exposed to customers.
- There should be some basic training in the principles, techniques, applications, and use of mistake proofing as well as other activities like problem solving and team building.
- To broaden the experience to mistake proofing techniques, and applications, information should be shared with other companies using the concept.

Other statistical and mathematical techniques

Some of the techniques referred to in this appendix require a fairly basic understanding of statistics and minimal mathematical prowess. To advance the process of quality improvement, organizations need to consider the use of some of the more advanced statistical techniques.

Advanced statistical techniques include time series analysis, significance testing (parametric and non-parametric) and analysis of variance. Operational research techniques such as simulation should also be considered.

Mathematical models form the basis for much of the statistical and operational research techniques, and although computers and appropriate software can reduce considerably the computational requirements, to gain the benefits of such aids an understanding of their outputs is required.

Executive summary

- To support and develop a process of continuous improvement an organization needs to use a selection of quality-management tools and techniques.
- It is wise to start with the more simple tools and techniques such as the seven quality control tools (cause and effect diagrams, histograms, checksheets, Pareto diagrams, control charts, scatterplots and graphs).
- It is important that the tools and techniques currently employed are used effectively before attempts are made to introduce others.
- A planned approach for the application of tools and techniques is necessary.
- Do not single out one tool or technique for special attention.
- The techniques should be used in combination.
- Recognize that quality-management tools and techniques play different roles: data collection, and presentation, planning, establishing priorities, determining causes of problems, identifying relationships, capability assessment and monitoring, and maintaining control, etc. It is important that management are fully aware of the main purpose and use of the tools and techniques they are considering applying in the organization.
- The CEO and senior managers have a key role to play in the effective use of quality-management tools and techniques. They should, for example:
  - develop their knowledge of the tools and, when appropriate, use them in their day-to-day activities and decision-making;
  - delegate responsibility for their promotion to suitable individuals;
  - maintain an active interest in their use;
  - endorse expenditure arising from the education and training required in and the improvement activities resulting from their use.

Notes

1 Currie, R. M. (1989) *Work Study*, Pitman, London.
2 Crossfield, R. T. and Dale, B. G. (1990) 'Mapping quality assurance

systems: a methodology', *Quality and Reliability Engineering International*, vol. 6, no. 3, pp. 167–78.

3 Ishikawa, K. (1976) *Guide to Quality Control*, Asian Productivity Organization, Tokyo.

4 Fukuda, R. (1990) *CEDAC: A Tool for Continuous Systematic Improvement*, Productivity Press, Cambridge, Mass.

5 Taguchi, G. (1986) *Introduction to Quality Engineering*, Asian Productivity Organization, Tokyo.

6 Crossfield, R. T. and Dale, B. G. (1991) 'Applying Taguchi methods to the design improvement process of turbochargers', *Quality Engineering*, vol. 3, no. 4, pp. 501–16.

7 Lochnar, R. H. and Matar, J. E. (1990) *Designing for Quality: An Introduction to the Best of Taguchi and Western Methods of Statistical Experimental Design*, Chapman and Hall, London.

8 Bendell, A., Disney, J. and Pridmore, W. A. (1989) *Taguchi Methods: Applications in World Industries*, IFS Publications, Bedfordshire.

9 Barker, B. (1985) *Quality by Experimental Design*, ASQC Press, Milwaukee.

10 Allied-Signal Inc. (1989) *Quality Function Deployment – A Guide for Implementation*, Allied-Signal Inc., Michigan.

11 Akao, Y. (1990) *Quality Function Deployment: Integrating Customer Requirements into Product Design*, Productivity Press, Cambridge, Mass.

12 Eureka, W. E. and Ryan, W. E. (1988) *The Customer-Driven Company: Managerial Perspectives on QFD*, ASI Press, Michigan.

13 Mizuno, S. (1988), *Management for Quality Improvement; The Seven New Q.C. Tools*, Productivity Press, Cambridge, Mass.

14 Ozeki, K. and Asaka, T. (1990) *Handbook of Quality Tools*, Productivity Press, Cambridge, Mass.

15 Barker, R. L. (1989) 'The seven new Q.C. tools', *Proceedings of the First Conference on Tools and Techniques for TQM*, IFS Conferences, Bedford, pp. 95–120.

16 Lewis, L. (1984) *Quality Improvement Handbook*, IBM, Hampshire.

17 Payne, B. J. (1990) 'The quality improvement process in service industries', in B. G. Dale and J. J. Plunkett, (eds), *Managing Quality*, Philip Allan, Hertfordshire.

18 Shingo, S. (1986) *Zero Quality Control: Source Inspection and the Poka Yoke System*, Productivity Press, Cambridge, Mass.

19 Dale, B. G. and Lightburn, K. (1992) 'Continuous quality improvement: why some organisations lack commitment' *International Journal of Production Economics*, vol. 27, no. 1, 57–67.

Appendix C

Statistical Process Control

This appendix outlines the concept and underlying principles of statistical process control (SPC), and examines how an organization should set about the introduction and development of the technique. Senior management's role in the effective use of SPC is highlighted.

What is SPC?

SPC is generally accepted to mean control (management) of the process through the use of statistics or statistical methods. Perhaps because of this generalized definition, or people's poor understanding of SPC, misconceptions have arisen about its applicability and usefulness.

There are three main uses of SPC:

- to assess the performance of a process;
- to provide guidance on how the process may be improved;
- to provide feedback information to assist with management decision-making.

SPC can be used in most manufacturing areas, industrial or processing, and in non-manufacturing situations including service and commerce (see Owen[1] and Oakland and Followell[2] for details). There are many types of control charts, not just those most frequently quoted in texts (e.g. the average ($\overline{X}$) and range (R) charts for variables (measurable) data and the attribute charts for non-conforming items or non-conformities – np, p, c and u charts) There are variations of, derivatives from and alternatives to np, p, c and u charts but this appendix will be restricted primarily to the underlying principles and interpretation of control charts rather than a prescriptive catalogue of all available charts.

It is important to note that whenever the term 'engineering' is used, it should be regarded in its most general sense (i.e. that of understanding the skill and expertise involved in a process).

SPC is about control, capability and improvement, but only if used correctly and in a working environment conducive to the pursuit of continuous quality improvement, with the full involvement of every company employee. It is the responsibility of the CEO and other senior managers to create these conditions, and they must be the prime motivators and provide the necessary support to all those engaged in SPC.

It should be recognized at the outset that on its own SPC will not solve problems, the control charts record only the 'voice' of the process and SPC may, at a basic level, simply confirm the presence of a problem. Other quality-management tools and techniques are available (see appendix B) which support and facilitate quality improvement and, in many instances, they may have to be used prior to and concurrently with the application of SPC to facilitate analysis and improvement.

History and development of SPC

There is little new in the techniques of SPC. In America, in the 1920s, Dr Walter Shewhart, in applying statistics to quality, developed control charts.[3] At around the same time, Dudding was conducting similar work in the United Kingdom. The differences between American and British control charts will be referred to later.

When first evolved, the control chart used data that provided a good overall picture of the process, and had control limits set out from the process average. These limits reflected the inherent variation of the process. Consequently, a process with more variation, comparatively speaking, than another will have wider limits (i.e. the greater the variation the wider the limits). But as this variation was established from an accurate review or study, the limits were deemed to reflect the actual capability of the process. The charts so constructed were called charts for controlling the process within its known capability. As the word 'capability' has in the last decade been taken to mean something slightly different, the charts tend now to be called performance-based charts (i.e. to control the process within its known performance).

When this idea was put to potential users, they asked: But what if the control limits are outside the specification limits? This resulted in the development of a chart where the control limits were set inside the specification limits by a margin that is, again, a function of the inherent variation in the process: processes with greater variation will have limits set further inside the specification limits than those with less variation. To reflect this these charts were called modified control charts, or charts to control the process to specification limits. These charts tend now to be called tolerance-based charts. A further derivation of this type of chart is one where alternative modified limits are used.

If an organization's quality objective is to produce parts or services to specification, the so-called tolerance-based chart may prove useful – signals may be given to alert operational personnel of the likelihood of producing out-of-specification products. If the chart facilitates this objective, the quality objective has been achieved. But in terms of improvement, what is the next step to be taken? The usual response is no response and, consequently, little improvement in organizational performance is likely to take place.

Using the performance-based charts with limits that reflect the inherent variation of the process, and having some statistical estimate of this variation, the objective is to establish its source(s), perhaps using experimental design tools and techniques, and strive to reduce it on a never-ending improvement basis. Thus, control limits should reduce over time, reflecting the reduction in process variation and so demonstrating a commitment to quality improvement.

In SPC terms, this is where Western companies should be now, striving to reduce variation by using control charts to monitor their processes, and the data generated from the charts aggressively to pursue never-ending improvement. If an organization is not at this stage, management need to evaluate their use of SPC critically and see what is going wrong.

Some basic statistics – averages and measures of dispersion

Averages, of which there are many in statistics, are a measure of location. The principal ones are mean (arithmetic), median and mode.

The arithmetic mean is determined by adding all the values together and dividing by the number of values. It can be distorted by extreme values and it may not correspond to any one particular value in the set of data. The median is the value which splits the data in half. Fifty per cent of the values are equal to or less than the median and fifty per cent are equal to or greater than it. The mode is often interpreted as that part of the measurement scale where values occur most frequently.

These averages, or measures of central tendency, give an indication of where most of the values tend to cluster. In the context of SPC, the arithmetic mean attracts most attention, be it the mean of a sample, of a series of samples or of a series of sample means. This average is a measure of accuracy and it gives an indication of how well a target or some nominal value is being achieved.

In most data, there will be some dispersion, or spread of values, around the average, say the mean. This dispersion may be quite small or it may be large, so some measure of it is required. Several measures could be used, the most common being the range and the standard deviation. The former is easy to calculate, the latter rather more difficult.

The range is the difference between the smallest and the largest values within the data being analysed (there may be circumstances where this simple approach can be troublesome, but provided common sense is used, it can be regarded as an acceptable definition).

The standard deviation is a measure of by how much, on average, each value differs from the mean. The formula(e) associated with this statistic can be intimidating but many pocket calculators are now programmed to make the calculation.

There is a relationship between the range and the standard deviation, which is used in many of the calculations in SPC. (The relationship is mentioned later in the appendix.) It is sufficient to accept that the range and/or the standard deviation give an indication of the variability of the data; they are measures of precision.

In summary, an average gives an indication of accuracy and a measure of dispersion is an indication of precision.

Process variation

All processes will exhibit variation, which may be large or immeasurably small. Their output will therefore exhibit variation in some degree. Depending upon its magnitude, variation may be a source of annoyance to the customer, whether the end user or the next process.

A number of management decisions are based on interpreting variations in figures, whether they be sales, production or financial, and misinterpretation could lead to incorrect decisions being made. Therefore, it is important that senior management develop their knowledge of variation and its cause.

One of the objectives of SPC is to ascertain as accurately as possible the extent of the variation present in the process, and whether it is due to:

- some unassignable cause, i.e. simply the vagaries of random sampling (this is often called common cause or random variation);
- some assignable or real cause, i.e. attributable to some aspect of the process which may have changed, e.g. tool wear or raw materials. This is often called special cause variation.

Control charts will help to identify process variation. Special causes should be identified and rectified and, hopefully, with improved process design their occurrence will in the long term be minimized. In the short term their presence should be highlighted and a reaction programme established to deal with them. It is imperative in the management and control of processes to record not only the occurrence of such causes, but also any remedial action taken. This provides a valuable source of information in the form of a process log, to avoid repetition of previous mistakes and help develop improved processes. When such causes are absent (due to their rectification or non-presence), the process is said to be in control, that is, only common cause variation is present.

To make best possible estimate of the inherent variation of a process, there must be evidence of stability or predictability of the process. A control chart (as in figure C.1, for example) will help achieve this.

The limits of the level of variation acceptable to the customer are often defined by the specification, or tolerance, which may be laid down by the customer or, on its behalf, by the designer. It is imperative that the designer be aware of the process variation to enable the reproducability of parts, products and services to meet physical and functional requirements. Customers are demanding increasingly less variation by reducing the tolerance band, which requires greater uniformity around the nominal or target value. Some simply declare the nominal value of the specification to potential suppliers, and orders are placed with the organization which can assure the minimum variation. These approaches are commensurate with the ideas of Taguchi's[4] quadratic loss function, which, in general terms, suggests that the greater a product deviates from the target value the greater is the 'loss to society'.

It is apparent from this line of thinking that in terms of loss to society there is little difference between a part which is just inside or on the specification limit (upper or lower) and one which is just outside. The nearer to the nominal or target value, the smaller the loss to society. This concept of course depends on the interpretation of loss to society, but it is increasingly apparent that greater demands are being made for parts, products and services to be consistent at around the perceived nominal value.

SPC, if properly used, will give an indication of the magnitude of this variation; it will not give the source(s). Management efforts and technical and engineering activities should be directed at establishing the likely source(s) and, more important, reducing the variation on a never-ending basis. Of course, such efforts should take costs into account and achieve a balance between them and the costs of *not* meeting customers' requirements.

Variable and attribute data

Variable (or measured) data

These data would be the result of using some form of measuring system (e.g. vernier or pressure gauge, thermometer, odometer). The accuracy and precision of the measurements recorded are a function not only of the measuring system but also of those using it. It follows, therefore, that it is essential to ensure the accuracy of the measuring system to minimize the potential errors in the data.

Measurements may refer to product characteristics (e.g. length, diameter, weight, arrival times) or to process parameters (e.g. temperature, screw speed, pressure, shot weight). Control over process variables gives earlier feedback and leads to better diagnosis of the causes for variation than measurement of product characteristics. Typically, the measurements may be labelled:

$$x_1, \; x_2, \; x_3 \ldots , \; x_{n-1}, \; x_n$$

where n is the sample size or number of measurements collected;

the (arithmetic) mean, $\bar{x} = \dfrac{1}{n} \sum_{i=1} x_i$

The range, $R = x_{largest} - x_{smallest}$

and the standard deviation, $S = \sqrt{\dfrac{\Sigma (x_i - \bar{x})^2}{n-1}}$

Attribute (or countable) data

Such data would be the result of an assessment using go/no-go gauges (as a proxy for measured data) or pass/fail criteria (e.g. conforming/non-conforming). It is important to minimize subjectivity when using the pass/fail type of assessment, and to assist those employed in this activity the boundaries of acceptance and rejection must be clearly defined; reference standards or illustrations may help in this regard, agreed with the customer where possible. It is also necessary to differentiate between non-conformities and non-conforming items or units. A non-conformity may be a blemish or presence of some non-preferred feature (e.g. a scratch on surface finish). The product could still be usable but the occurrence would/may be a source of annoyance to the customer. The objective is to minimize or eliminate the source of these problems. A non-conforming item or unit is one that fails to meet the assessment criteria for one or more reasons; in other words, it may have one or several non-conformities.

To illustrate the difference: a letter, for signature, may have a misspelt word in it and if noticed by the 'inspector' would be corrected – a non-conformity. However, a letter with a number of errors may be rejected by the 'inspector', who may ask for retyping – a non-conforming letter.

With attribute data, again the average (i.e. the number or proportion of non-conforming items or the number or proportion of non-conformities) is the main source of interest. The sample or subgroup size is also needed.

Control chart design

It is obvious that the larger the sample size or the greater the amount of data available, the more confident the inferences that can be made about the population or batch parameters from the sample statistics which have been calculated (e.g. the mean and the standard deviation). (Remember that these statistics and any derived indices (e.g. those relating to capability) are only estimates.) However, taking large samples from a process, in particular when dealing with variable data, is costly, time consuming and can be disruptive to production. Compromises must be made, therefore, so small samples should be taken as frequently as is practical and economical. It should be remembered that samples are snapshots at one point in time. The more frequently they are taken the quicker the response to any signalled changes in the process.

A general rule, widely used, is to take samples of five, every hour, when dealing with variable data. This is not a rigid rule, however, and common sense must prevail when establishing the sampling procedure. Some processes do not lend themselves to samples of five (e.g. a die with four impressions). Others may exhibit greater or less variation over time, and samples may have to be taken more or less frequently than every hour. It is not unusual to see control charts being used where the sample size is one, with samples being taken twice or even once per day. The sampling procedure adopted must reflect a clear understanding of the process behaviour.

With attribute data, the sample or subgroup size must be much larger ($n > 25$) to ensure that the statistical theory supporting the design of the control chart is valid. Indeed, the subgroup size may be very large, particularly when checking or testing batches or in appraising paperwork procedures. This may appear somewhat paradoxical when related to the comments made earlier about the sample sizes used with variable data, but to counter this it is suggested that attribute data are more readily available (often through management information systems). Many organizations may collect data relating to scrap, credit notes, mistakes made, reject rates, etc., but may not analyse it in control chart format.

Control chart design must both reflect a clear understanding or engineering/technical knowledge of the process and be such that those administering the chart (i.e. collecting the data and calculating and plotting data points) can do so with ease and confidence, not only in what they are doing but what the chart is saying to them.

Whatever type of control chart is chosen, a reaction programme has to be established to enable those filling in the chart to record any action taken on the process. It is also important to maintain a process log. Executives should note that the control chart is a formal communication from the operator to them about the state of the process; it can be regarded as their window on the organization's operating processes.

Types of control charts

There are many many types of chart:

- pre-control;
- multi-vari;
- traffic lights (green, amber and red portions signifying the necessary responses);
- individual values (X_i) and moving range (R);
- moving average ($\overline{X}$) and moving range (R);
- average ($\overline{X}$) and range (R);
- average ($\overline{X}$) and standard deviation (S);
- median ($\tilde{X}$) and range (R);
- cumulative sum (CUSUM);
- number of non-conforming items (np);
- proportion (or percentage) of non-conforming items (p);
- number of non-conformities (c);
- proportion of non-conformities (u).

The choice can be intimidating to the potential user. It is important, however, that the selection of the appropriate charting technique fulfils the quality-improvement objectives of the organization, to satisfy the needs and requirements of the customer.

It is worth noting that there are slight differences between some of the American and British control charts which reflect the degree of risk of incorrect signals (the action limits are slightly wider on some British charts). A further complication is that it is not unusual to have both warning and action limits on British charts, whereas American ones tend to have only the latter. (This should not detract from the underlying philosophy of quality improvement.)

The main practical problem with warning limits is that they tend to pollute and confound the control chart, confusing the operator in relation to identifying and reacting to out-of-control conditions, and/or they can lead to over-control. On the other hand, it is often claimed that they can help to pick up potential out-of-control conditions, particularly in relatively stable processes.

Construction of control charts

To illustrate the statistical concepts of SPC and underlying philosophy of continuous improvement of quality, the discussion of variable charts and attribute control charts is limited to average ($\overline{X}$) and range (R), and number of non-conforming items (np).

$\overline{X}$ and R chart

As was mentioned earlier, to set up the control chart the sample size and frequency must be determined and sufficient data (about twenty samples of size n) accurately reflecting the normal performance of the process collected. Sample means ($\overline{X}$) and range (R) are calculated and these data points are plotted on the appropriately scaled chart.

Reference values are then calculated:

- grand average (or process average), $\overline{\overline{X}}$, which is the mean of the sample means: this gives an indication of the accuracy (when compared to the target or nominal value) or setting of the process;
- mean range, $\overline{R}$, which is the average of the sample ranges. This gives an indication of the variability (precision or lack of it) of the process. The mean range is a measure of within-sample variation only. This will be referred to later when discussing capability.

These two reference values are drawn on the appropriate sections of the chart, and it is around these values that the boundaries of what may be called statistically acceptable limits (i.e. control limits) are drawn.

Given that the control limits reflect what is likely to occur most of the time (99.73 per cent) with a stable process, they are set at plus and minus three standard errors around the grand average. To overcome the complication of standard errors, the mean range is multiplied by a constant derived from statistical tables.

Control limits on average charts are set at:

Upper: $\quad \text{UCL}_{\overline{X}} = \overline{\overline{X}} + A_2\overline{R}$

Lower: $\quad \text{LCL}_{\overline{X}} = \overline{\overline{X}} - A_2\overline{R}$

(A_2 is a constant derived from statistical tables and is dependent upon the sample size.)

And on the range chart:

Upper: $\quad \text{UCL}_R : D_4\overline{R}$

Lower: $\quad \text{LCL}_R : D_3\overline{R}$

(D_3 and D_4 are constants derived from statistical tables and are dependent upon the sample size.)

The chart, with these initial control limits, may initially look as shown in figure C.1.

With small sample sizes there tends to be no lower limit on the range chart. If any of the study data points indicate out-of-control conditions, and if permanent remedial action has taken place to eliminate the abnormality, it is permissible to take out those data from the calculation of the initial limits. The limits are used not only to answer the question, Was the process under statistical control during the study period?, but also for ongoing control.

The control chart should tell operators when to leave the process alone, and/or when some action is required. Features appearing on the chart which may signal out-of-order conditions are:

- any point outside the limits;
- any unusual patterns or trends within the limits;
- any run of points (approximately seven or more) in a particular direction upwards or downwards;
- any run of points (approximately seven or more) all on one side of the average ($\bar{\bar{X}}$ or $\bar{R}$);
- approximately two-thirds of the data points should lie within the middle third of the chart.

The presence of an out-of-control point is an indication that the process is not behaving as expected. Having identified the cause of the variation corrective action should be taken (see figure C.2).

It was said when discussing variation that these causes often signal operational changes (i.e. tooling, raw material, shift, operator). It is the responsibility of operational personnel to get and keep the process under control. That does not mean that they can prevent special causes from occurring, but requires them to identify and rectify them to bring the process back under control. However, it can sometimes prove difficult to establish the cause of the out-of-control condition. The support of team members (the process operator being part of the team) will be helpful in this respect. Occasionally the cause cannot be identified because statistically a false alarm has been given by the chart. The probability of this is very small but should at least be acknowledged. A team in each working zone, comprising operating, maintenance, technical/engineering and quality personnel, can prove invaluable in eliminating special and common causes of variation.

It should be noted that, with a run of seven or more points either

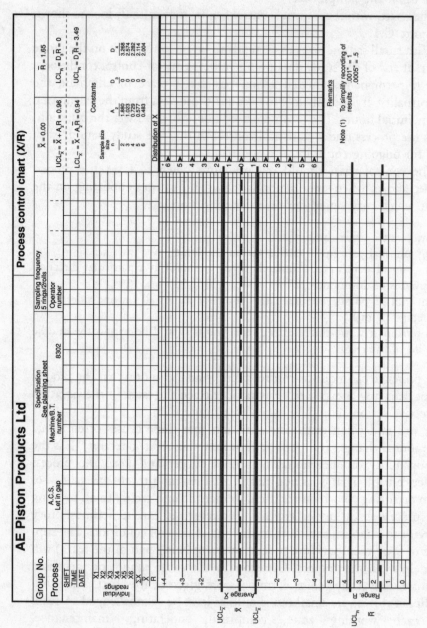

Figure C.1 Control chart: basic format
Courtesy of A. E. Piston Products Ltd.

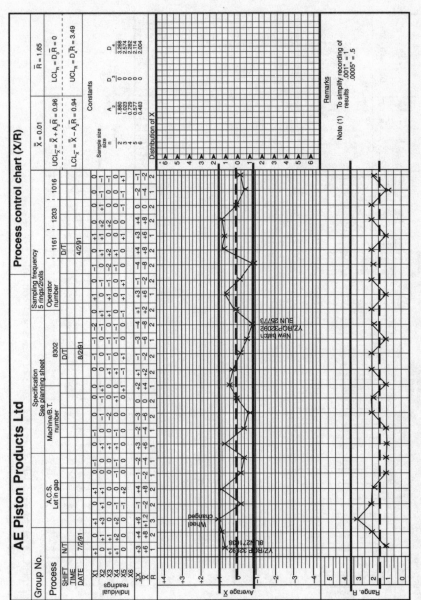

Figure C.2 A process which is not in a state of statistical control
Courtesy of A. E. Piston Products Ltd.

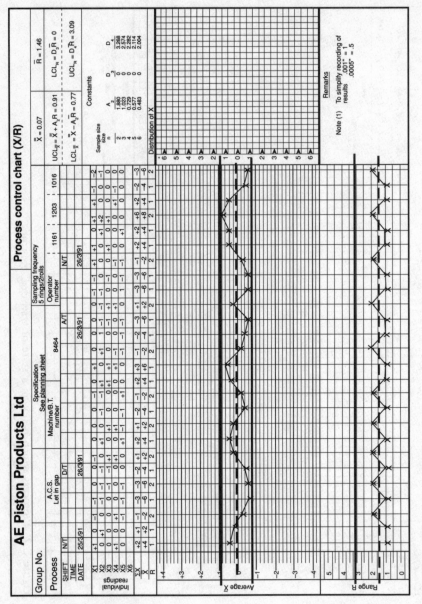

Figure C.3 A process which is in a state of statistical control
Courtesy of A. E. Piston Products Ltd.

downwards or all below $\bar{R}$ on the range, the chart is suggesting that the variation (within sample) is not as high as expected, perhaps a process improvement.

Where the chart indicates no out-of-control conditions (special causes) the process is said to be in statistical control (i.e. only common cause variation is present). The process is stable and therefore predictable (see figure C.3). However, this shows only how the process has normally performed in the recent past; it does *not* mean that everything is fine; it could be that a stable process has poor capability (i.e. out-of-specification parts are being produced).

In such a situation, the inspection activity must continue, although the data analysis may permit clearer estimates of what percentage of work should be quarantined for scrap, rework and reinspection. Senior management, together with engineering and technical personnel, are responsible for seeking out (using, for example, design of experiments) the likely sources of the excessive variation, and implementing countermeasures to reduce the abnormalities.

The quality objective should be to get the process in control, and for it to be fully capable, using SPC as a preventive activity. This situation may be reached and then the need to continue to use SPC in this way may be questioned. SPC might eventually be used primarily as an audit or for some problem-solving activity, as in many Japanese companies, where it is generally used only to prove process capability and where problems arise.

Attribute chart – number of non-conforming items (np)

As mentioned earlier, the sample or subgroup sizes tend to be larger ($n \geqslant 25$) with attribute data than with variable data. With an np chart the sample size is kept constant. The data points are plotted on the appropriately scaled chart, as outlined previously.

The process average, $n\bar{p}$ is then calculated to be the average number of non-conforming items per sample (constant size) over the study period. This average is sometimes referred to as the chronic state of the process. This value is shown on the chart and the statistical control limits will be set around it.

Upper: $UCL_{np} = n\bar{p} + 3 \sqrt{n\bar{p} \left(1 - \dfrac{n\bar{p}}{n}\right)}$

Lower: $LCL_{np} = np - 3 \sqrt{n\bar{p}\left(1 - \dfrac{n\bar{p}}{n}\right)}$

where n is the sample size.

The calculation of the lower limit will often reveal a negative value, so no lower limit will be used.

The limits are then drawn on the chart to assess for statistical control. The chart is interpreted for out-of-control conditions in a manner similar to that described above for variable (measured) data. If a remedied special cause is evidenced by the study data, it is quite permissable to discount that sample data from the calculation of np and the control limits.

Signals similar to those for variable data are given for out-of-control (special causes) conditions. A run of seven or more points in a downward direction or all below np would suggest that the state of the process is not as bad as originally thought, i.e. a process improvement may be indicated. This would also be the case if a point appeared below the lower control limit (if present). Obviously, the very presence of non-conforming items means that the process is not 100 per cent capable, but a percentage measure can be calculated to provide an indication of process capability.

In terms of process improvement, activities should be generated to reduce the process average ($n\bar{p}$). To facilitate this, it is important that in addition to recording and plotting the data points on the chart, additional data recording should be made of the reason(s) the item(s) was/were classified as non-conforming. To bring about improvement, the causes of rejected work must be known, and then be prioritized for remedial action or countermeasures.

Construction and interpretation of control charts: dos and don'ts

The following dos and don'ts, taken from Dale and Shaw,[5] may help organizations to avoid some of the difficulties and traps encountered in the construction and interpretation of control charts.

Do

- Ensure that the data used to construct the initial control limits are a true reflection of process performance.
- Use data which are already available to assess the feasibility of using SPC in a particular situation, determine the type of control chart to be used and set up initial control limits. However, don't lose sight of the dangers of using historical data; examine the data closely and the means by which they were collected.

- If there is some uncertainty about what can or cannot be measured, use attribute data as a short-term expedient, then progress to the use of variable data.
- Ensure that control charts are kept simple.
- Move the data collection upstream from product characteristics to process parameters.
- Stand back from the data portrayed on the control chart and question what message they are giving. This will help to ensure that some of the fundamentals of control charting have not been ignored.
- Use SPC teams in each department to assist in the construction of control charts.
- Examine the distribution of sample means from a process.

Don't

- Lose sight of the statistical theory on which control charts are based or the underlying logic of SPC.
- Be afraid to experiment with the control chart format, sample size, sampling frequency, and characteristics and parameters measured.
- Ignore potential relationships between product characteristics and process parameters.
- Be tempted to measure and control too many characteristics and parameters.
- Forget that the process can exhibit within-sample and between-sample variation.
- Worry about abandoning control charts based on ill-conceived sampling procedures and making the decision to start afresh.

Process capability

Because it is easier to understand, the capability of processes using attribute data is considered first.

With the np chart, it is usual to express the average number of acceptable items per sample as a percentage to quantify capability, i.e.:

$$\left(1 - \frac{n\bar{p}}{n}\right) \times 100\%$$

With the p chart, it is simply the average proportion of acceptable items expressed as a percentage, i.e. $(1 - \bar{p}) \times 100\%$.

With charts for non-conformities, c and u, it is somewhat meaningless to talk about capability; it is preferable to quantify the average non-conformities per sample or average proportion of non-conformities per item into a measure of defects per 100 units (DHU).

- c̄ is average number of non-conformities per constant sample size: translate this into non-conformities per 100 items;
- ū is average proportion of non-conformities per item; multiply this figure by 100 to get DHU.

It should be noted that some organizations translate defects per unit (DPU) into parts per million (PPM), and from this obtain an equivalence in terms of Cp and Cpk (these capability indices are generally reserved for measured data).

With measured data, the use of indices such as Cp and Cpk has been increasing during the past decade. The Cpk index is found as the result of comparing the perceived spread (± three standard deviations) of the process with the specification width or tolerance band.

$$Cp = \frac{\text{Total specified tolerance}}{6 \text{ standard deviations}}$$

It is not unusual to have customers specify to their suppliers' minimum requirements for Cp, for example $Cp \geqslant 1.33$ or $Cp \geqslant 2.00$. What this means in effect is that all parts should lie comfortably inside the specification limits. $Cp = 1.33$ implies that the tolerance band equals eight standard deviations, i.e. $8/6 = 1.33$; $Cp = 2.00$ implies that the tolerance band equals twelve standard deviations, i.e. $12/6 = 2.00$. It therefore follows that:

1 the specification limits have to be wide – commensurate with excellent physical and functional requirements of the product – or
2 the process variation as determined by the standard deviation has to be small; or
3 conditions 1 and 2 both apply.

As the Cp index compares 'spread of the process' with the tolerance band, it is concerned primarily with precision – it takes no account of the accuracy or setting of the process. For this reason CP is often defined as process potential, i.e. what the process is potentially capable of achieving.

The Cpk indices, however, take into account both accuracy and precision by incorporating in the calculations, $\overline{\overline{X}}$, i.e. the process (or grand) average. There may be two formulae (USL and LSL are upper and lower specification limits, respectively):

$$Cpk = \frac{USL - \overline{\overline{X}}}{3 \text{ standard deviations}}$$

$$Cpk = \frac{\overline{\overline{X}} - LSL}{3 \text{ standard deviations}}$$

It is customary to quote the smaller of the two values, giving the more critical part of the measurement's distribution. Similar minimum requirements are often prescribed for Cpk as are mentioned above for Cp.

Because Cpk indices assess both accuracy and precision, they are often defined as process capability measures. That is, the Cpk gives an estimate of how the process actually performs, i.e. its capability, whereas the Cp gives an estimate of its potential, i.e. what it could do if the setting were on the nominal or target value of the specification. In calculating both Cp and Cpk it is necessary to know or estimate the process standard deviation ($\hat{\sigma}$). This is often estimated using the formula $\hat{\sigma} = \overline{R}/d_2$ (where d_2 is a constant derived from statistical tables), exploiting the relationship between the range and the standard deviation which was mentioned earlier.

With reference to this the following points should be noted:

- $\overline{R}$ is the average within sample variation. Present in the process may be considerable between-sample variation which should be included in $\hat{\sigma}$. If this is not investigated $\hat{\sigma}$ could be underestimated, hence any Cp or Cpk index will be overestimated.
- The indices implicitly assume that the data (measurements), when drawn out as a histogram or frequency distribution curve, give a reasonable approximation to the informal (or Gaussian) distribution curve. While many processes will offer data that comply with this, there are exceptions and some modifications in the calculations may be necessary.

These comments on capability relate to data collected over the long term (many days or shifts) from a stable, in-control and predictable process. Short-term capability often needs to be investigated, particularly for new products or processes (it may be required as part of a supplier verification programme, i.e. initial sampling requirements or first article inspection). The time scale is then dramatically reduced to cover only a few hours' run of the process.

It is recommended that data are collected in almost the same manner as for initial control chart study, but the frequency of sampling increased to obtain as many samples (of size n) as possible (perhaps twenty) to give a good picture of the process. Data are plotted on the control chart with appropriate limits, but the following indices are calculated:

- P_p is preliminary process potential;
- P_{pk} is preliminary process capability.

The formula is exactly as for Cp and Cpk but the minimum requirements may be higher, e.g. $P_p \geqslant 1.67$, i.e. 1.67 implies that the tolerance band is ten standard deviations: $10/6 = 1.67$.

It should not be forgotten that all capability indices are estimates derived from estimates of the process variation ($\hat{\sigma}$). The reliability of or confidence in the estimate of the process standard deviation is a function of:

- amount of data collected;
- manner in which the data were collected;
- capability of the measuring system, i.e. its accuracy and precision;
- skill of the people using the measuring system;
- people's knowledge and understanding of statistics.

Introduction of SPC

In introducing and managing SPC, an organization needs some guidelines so that the application can develop along the lines which are likely to result in positive progress. There is no sure-fire guarantee of success, but the key factors listed below are derived from the available experience and evidence acquired from the motor industry.

1 Senior management awareness and their commitment to the use of SPC are essential.
2 Establish a steering committee whose responsibilities include:
  (a) planning the programme of implementation;
  (b) organizing a training programme;
  (c) developing diagnostic and improvement actions;
  (d) providing and managing resources and establishing an improvement infrastructure;
  (e) creating a suitable work environment for SPC in which everyone can work together for the benefit of all.
3 Appoint/develop a statistical facilitator, who should be an expert in process improvement methods and whose basic functions include:
  (a) introducing and facilitating process improvements, including teamwork;
  (b) advising thereon as and when required;
  (c) assisting with developing strategies to advance TQM and the process of quality improvement;
  (d) carrying out training on SPC and related technology;
  (e) assisting with aspects relating to the charting and analysis of data;
  (f) ensuring management awareness;

(g) participating in quality assurance and improvement meetings, workshops and user groups and liaising with the relevant steering committees;

(h) keeping everybody informed of progress and developments.

4 Provide adequate training.

5 Start with a pilot scheme. It is important that the implementation of SPC is not rushed; it should be a gradual process. Once SPC has been demonstrated in the pilot area its success can be used to sell it to other sections and units.

6 Expand the programme and maintain the gains.

These factors are not all-embracing and other issues will need to be resolved as SPC develops. Further details of these factors are given by Owen,[6] Dale and Shaw[7] and Ford Motor Company.[8]

Many organizations face problems in implementing, using and developing SPC – mainly self-inflicted. Organizations tend to move too quickly through the implementation programme; SPC programmes are long term and must be accepted as such by senior management. Dale, Shaw and Owen[9] indicate that from their research work in the use of SPC in the automotive supply industry, the range of difficulties encountered can be summarized as:

- Senior management do not take their obligations for SPC and continuous quality improvement seriously.
- The role of the facilitator is devalued and insufficient thought given to the role the facilitator plays in SPC and the person who actually fills the position.
- Personnel not directly responsible for control of a process are collecting and charting process data.
- Control charts are being displayed away from the process.
- There is a lack of action on the data presented on control charts.
- There is some uncertainty of how to apply SPC to a particular process and confusion in deciding which charting technique to use.
- There is a lack of confidence to experiment with the use of SPC. For example, a number of organisations believe that they cannot use SPC due to short production runs, the wide variety of parts and sizes produced on their machines, and their processes do not lend themselves to SPC.

If executives are aware of these difficulties prior to the introduction of SPC they have a much better chance of overcoming them through appropriate action.

Executive summary

- SPC is a management tool to assist with the reduction of process variability as a means of improving product and service consistency. Like any other quality-management tools and techniques, it needs the right organizational culture for it to work.
- SPC is applicable to all processes, not just those concerned with manufacturing.
- SPC will be effective over the longer term only if it is treated as one aspect of TQM.
- Successful and properly applied SPC has been known to evolve into effective TQM.
- The SPC programme needs to be planned.
- All members of senior management should have a good understanding of SPC, be committed to its philosophy and application and use it as a common language to facilitate process improvement.
- The following are the types of questions which should be addressed by the CEO and senior management to minimize problems and maximize their chances of longer-term success with SPC.
  - Why are we introducing SPC and what do we expect to achieve from its use?
  - Have we a strategy for SPC?
  - How does SPC fit into our overall strategy and policy on TQM?
  - Do we and our middle and first-line managers fully understand SPC and how it might be used in our day-to-day activities?
  - Have all employees been briefed on why we are using SPC and made aware of its potential for improving the processes under their control?
  - Do we take an active interest in SPC by looking at control charts on a regular basis and asking questions of the people charting the data?
  - Are we sufficiently aware that control charts are an additional communication medium at operational level.
  - Do we need a steering committee for SPC and, if so, what is to be its role?
  - Are there sufficient people in the organization with the right level of SPC expertise to act as champions?
  - Will the facilitator be full or part time and to whom will he or she report?
  - Do we have a planned programme of education and training for SPC?
  - Is too much effort being spent on SPC training and not enough on actual problem-solving?
  - Is there a tendency to overcomplicate the training on SPC?
  - Is there too great a time lag between being trained in SPC and actually using the techniques?
  - Are people intimidated and frightened by SPC? Have we fallen into the trap of failing to understand the logic behind SPC?

o Is there a mechanism in place for reacting to out-of-control conditions, eliminating special causes, and reducing common causes of variation?

Notes

1 Owen, M. (1989) *SPC and Continuous Improvement*, IFS Publications, Bedford.
2 Oakland, J. S. and Followell, R. F. (1990) *Statistical Process Control*, Heinemann, London.
3 Shewhart, W. A. (1931) *Economic Control of Manufactured Product*, Van Nostrand, New York.
4 Taguchi, G. (1986) *Introduction to Quality Engineering*, Asian Productivity Organization, Tokyo.
5 Dale, B. G. and Shaw, P. (1990) 'Some problems encountered in the construction and interpretation of control charts', *Quality and Reliability Engineering International*, vol. 6, no. 1, pp. 7–12.
6 Owen, *SPC*.
7 Dale, B. G. and Shaw, P. (1988) 'Statistical process control: the lessons to be learnt', *International Journal of Vehicle Design*, vol. 9, no. 3, pp. 276–86.
8 Ford Motor Company (1985) *Statistical Process Control Course Notes*, Statistical Methods Council, Ford, Brentwood, Essex.
9 Dale, B. G., Shaw, P. and Owen, M. (1990) 'SPC in the motor industry: an examination of implementation and use', *International Journal of Vehicle Design*, vol. 11, no. 2, pp. 115–31.

Appendix D

Failure Mode and Effects Analysis

What is FMEA?

Preparation of FMEA

Uses of FMEA

FMEA Training

The Value of FMEA as a Quality-Management Technique

Difficulties

Executive Summary

A number of major purchasers are now looking to their suppliers to use potential failure mode and effects analysis (FMEA) as part of a process of advanced quality planning. This appendix provides an overview of the concept, and how FMEA should be employed by an organization as a planning tool to assist with building quality into its products and processes.

What is FMEA?

Potential FMEA was developed in the aerospace and defence industries. It is a systematic and analytical quality-planning tool for identifying, at product, service and process design stages, what might go wrong either during the manufacture of a product or during its use by the end customer. Its effective use should lead to a reduction in:

- defects during the production of initial samples and in volume production;
- customer complaints;
- failures in the field; and
- warranty claims.

There are two main categories of FMEA: design FMEA and process FMEA. The former addresses the issues of what could go wrong with the product as a consequence of a weakness in the design, and it also assists in the identification or confirmation of critical characteristics. The latter concentrates on the reasons for potential failure during manufacture and in service as a consequence of a non-compliance to specification and/or design intent.

The procedure involved in the development of a FMEA is iterative. In brief, it:

1 starts by focusing on the function of the product and/or process;
2 identifies potential failure modes;
3 assesses the effects of each potential failure;
4 examines the causes of potential failure;
5 reviews current controls;
6 determines a risk priority number (RPN);
7 recommends the corrective action to be taken to help eliminate potential concerns;
8 monitors the corrective action taken and countermeasures put in place.

The RPN comprises an assessment of occurrence, detection and severity of ranking.

The occurrence is the likelihood of a specific cause which will result in the identified failure mode; based on perceived or estimated (in the case of process capability) probability, it is ranked on a scale of 1 to 10. The detection criterion relates in the case of design FMEA to the likelihood of the design verification programme pinpointing a potential failure mode before it reaches the customer; a ranking of 1 to 10 is used. In process FMEA, it relates to the existing control plan. The severity of effect, on a scale of 1 to 10, indicates the likelihood of the customer noticing any difference to the functionality of the product or service.

The resulting RPN should always be checked against past experience of similar products and situations. The requisite information and actions are recorded in a standard format; an example of a process FMEA is shown in figure D.1.

After the RPN has been determined the potential failure modes should be tackled, in descending order of RPN, for improvement action to reduce/eliminate the risk of failure occurring.

It is worth noting that the British standards (e.g. BS 5760)[1] differentiate between FMEA and FMECA (failure mode effect and criticality analysis), where the latter prioritizes the potential failure modes. The difference is really not important, as most practitioners using the

Garrett Automotive Group

Failure Mode and E

Process (1) _Turbo Assr 452038/9–1_
Product name/part no(2) _Turbo TB2544_
MD/process responsibility(3) _Manuf Dept GAL_
Other MD(s)/involved (4) _Garrett SA_
Outside suppliers affected? Yes(5) _No_

SQA or manuf en
Product enginee
Application engin
Sched job no (9)
FMEA data orig (

(11) Part name(s) Part no vendor(s)	(12) Process operation reference function	(13) Potential failure mode	(14) Potential effect(s) of failure	(15) Potenti cause(s) failure
Turbine hsg. arm & valve assy. bushing	Fit bush and arm valve assy. to turbine hsg	Bush out of position	Low boost	Assay variation
		Arm jams in bush	Valve sticks, high, low boost	Mis-align of arm an bush
Valve assy. crank assy.	Weld crank assy	Weld fails	Low boost	Eccentric weld, inco weld paramete
Crank assy.	Weld crank assy	Low end float	Valve sticks, high, low boost, arm seizure	Worn feel strip, feel strip not u
		Incorrect crank angle	Difficult calibration, poor performance	Incorrect v set up, se variation
		Incorrect orientation	Induced stress on centre housing oil connections	Assembly variation
THWA, CHRA, clamp, bolt, seal ring	Assemble THWA to CHRA and compressor seal ring	Loose bolts	Audible gas leak, oil pull over, rub induced noise	Low torqu assembly incorrectly
Compressor hsg. elbow fitting	Compressor hsg sub assy	Fitting comes loose	High boost	Low torqu assy tool incorrectly

continu

Sign below

art/J Aldridge ____ ext ____
Movir ____ ext ____
I 711 ____ ext ____
r 90 ____ rev 'B' Jun 90

Existing conditions					(21) Recommended action(s) and status	(22) Responsible for action and date	(24) Resulting			
(16) Current or seen controls	(17) Occurrence	(18) Severity	(19) Detection	(20) RPN risk priority no.			(23) Action(s) taken and date	Occurrence	Severity	Detection
ush position auge, perator auge check 1 10	7	7	9	441	Carry out capability study on first assy build Report No 90/22 Indicated process improvement still required by manufacturing	Manufacturing and quality assurance	Report No 90/022 (452039-1) CPK= -0 46 Cp=0 11 100% gauging to be used until process capable	7	7	9
perator eck for free ovement	2	7	3	42						
itial set up, et lab ectional test, perator sual, weld ntrol settings	7	7	9	441	Re-assess RPN following ISIR and capability study	Manufacturing and quality assurance	Report No 90/032 (452039-1) Cpk=0 37 Cp=1 14 End float gauge introduced GG2249 100% check reqd	7	7	9
perator gilance, hysical check r end float nd valve unction by perator	2	7	9	126	Carry out capability study on ISIR batch Report No 90/022 further study improvement	Manufacturing and quality assurance		2	7	8
perator hecks initial arts on set p. QA audit heck	3	7	8	168	Carry out capability study on ISIR batch Report No 90/022 Cpk = 0 12 Cp = 03 further study reqd	Manufacturing and quality assurance	Report No 90/032 (450239-1) Cpk=1 47 Cp=1 56			
irst off by QA. iitial set up. IA audit	6	6	3	108	Carry out capability study on cmm	Manufacturing and quality assurance				
00 per cent heck. QA udit, torque ool calibration y quality ssurance	2	7	7	98	Carry out capability study on cmm	Manufacturing and quality assurance				
Method of ssembly, 100 er cent visual ver check by uality ssurance	2	7	2	28						

ure **D.1** Process failure mode and effects analysis: manufacturing
rtesy of Garrett Automotive.

iterative approach outlined above prioritize through the magnitude of the RPN.

From design FMEA, the potential causes of failure should be studied and actions taken before designs and drawings are finalized. Likewise, with process FMEA, actions must be put into place before the process is set up. Used properly, FMEA prevents potential failures occurring in the manufacturing, production and/or delivery processes or in the end product in use, and will ensure that processes and products are more robust and reliable. It is a powerful technique and there is little doubt that a number of the product recall campaigns which are well publicized each year could have been avoided by its effective use. However, it is important that the technique is seen not just as a catalogue of potential failures but as a tool for pursuing quality improvement.

The concept, procedures and logic involved with FMEA are not new; every forward-thinking design, planning and production engineer and technical specialist informally carries out various aspects of FMEA, as do most of us in our daily routines. However, this mental analysis is rarely committed to paper in a format which can be evaluated by others and discussed as the basis for a corrective action plan. What FMEA does is to provide a planned, systematic method of capturing and documenting this knowledge; it forces people to use a disciplined approach and is a vehicle for obtaining collective knowledge and experience through a team process.

Studies indicate that the first time a service organization is aware that something has gone wrong with its service is when customers complain. Clearly, a simplified version of FMEA would be of benefit in non-manufacturing situations. A pilot study carried out and facilitated by Catie Gresling by UMIST staff (Gosling, Rowe and Dale)[2] within the Data Capture Services of the Headquarters Operations Directorate at Girobank has confirmed that it is beneficial in paper-processing activities. An FMEA was used in a project with the One Trip Pouch Group, a newly established team dealing with documents from post office counters, which are first received in pouches. A process flow chart (see figure B.10, appendix B) illustrates the complex nature of the internal customer/supplier relationships. This flow chart assisted in identifying a number of sub-processes where individual FMEAs would be appropriate.

A process FMEA was carried out at the early stages of processing, where pouches are opened and sorted. Some of the details of the FMEA are shown in figure D.2. This process involves multi-handling of the various types of documents covering different transactions. The exercise

(10) Process name	(11) Process function	(12) Potential failure mode	(13) Potential effect(s) of failure	(14) Potential causes of failure	Existing conditions (15) Current or foreseen controls	Detec	Occur	Sever	(19) RPN	(20) Recommended action(s) and status	(21) Responsible for action and date	Resulting (22) Actions taken and date	Detec	Occur	Sever	RPN
Batching units	To batch credit & debit docs. in groups of 100 at Sesam machine	Docs. batched in groups >100	Terminal will accept 100 docs. per batch. Maxibatch overflow.... rebatching excess docs. in reconcil area	Operator does not recognise 100 in batch. Operator has misread marker for 100 docs.	Tape marker on pigeon hole at Sesam machine DPO's judgement Sampling from the appraisal point	1	3	5	15	Check total on PDR and make up to batches of 100. Incorporate a stationery counting machine at the batching stage	A. Pittaway, C. Gosling	Trial of doc. counting machine				
		<100	Miscalculate volume of work forecast													
		Staples attached to documents	Jam microfilm camera. Document could be missed if stapled to doc. Document could jam Lundy terminal	Postmasters sent staple with document Operator did not identify staple	Flickcheck by operator, feeling for staples	7	3	7	147	More scrutiny by the operator. Investigate feasability of staple. Detection and removal device to be fixed into Sesam. Inform postmaster of his error.	A. Pittaway, C. Gosling	Trial of metal detector				
		Paperclips attached to docs	Could jam the microfilm camera. Could damage the membrane coverslip on the ISN printer	Lack of scrutiny by the operator	Flickcheck by the operator	1	3	7	21	AS ABOVE						

Figure D.2 Process failure mode and effects analysis: clerical
Courtesy of Girobank.

concentrated on 'raw credits and debits', which are batched into groups of 100. Sub-process FMEAs were also carried out at the microfilming stages and for the transport of batches in the group.

The study has illustrated the benefits of using process FMEA as a structured format through which the progress of improvement can be documented in a cohesive manner and assessed at a glance. It also emphasized the importance of the corrective action section of the analysis.

The FMEA technique is described in BS 5760.[3] Major purchasing organizations, such as Ford Motor Company[4] and Jaguar Cars,[5] have published their guidelines on FMEA, as has the Society of Motor Manufacturers and Traders.[6] It also features as a subject in textbooks on quality and reliability management.[7]

Dale and Shaw,[8] as part of their research work on the quality improvement process, conducted a questionnaire survey on the use of FMEA by seventy-eight Ford Motor Company suppliers, all of whom had received total quality excellence (TQE) and SPC training through Ford's Northern Regional Training Centre based at UMIST. The remainder of this appendix is based on the main findings of this research.

Preparation of FMEA

It is encouraging that the majority of organizations surveyed by Dale and Shaw have developed a strategy for the use of FMEA. Exactly 50 per cent of the respondents had carried out an FMEA for each component supplied to Ford. Some carry out FMEA only on new products, others produce FMEA for product families, material categories, main assemblies and process routes rather than for each component, i.e. generic FMEA. Those organizations producing a process FMEA for various process routes tend to be manufacturers of raw material. In these cases, the process FMEA is updated to include any additional requirements specific to a new product. For example, with the manufacture of glass, models fall into defined parameters such as size, shape and printed/non-printed. New models are processed down a specific process route depending on the relevant characteristics.

To prepare an FMEA, a good working knowledge of the manufacturing process and/or design is required. It is clear that a small number of organizations believe they do not have the knowledge to apply the technique. Some buy the process technology from different suppliers and bolt it together. The users often do not understand the technology used in the process, which makes FMEA more difficult to apply. An initiative which needs be pursued in such situations is for the customer organization to prepare an FMEA in conjunction with the equipment supplier.

When preparing a process FMEA, it is helpful to be able to consult the design FMEA. The majority of organizations said that the two FMEAs are not available at the same time. A number do not have design authority and commented that their customers were not prepared to make the design FMEA available to them. Although Ford is not prepared to release FMEAs, its FMEA booklet[9] does promote design and manufacturing team discussions to improve the process engineers' understanding of the design intent and any design concerns. However, in some cases (e.g. strip manufacture) it is not necessary for the design and process FMEAs to be available at the same time.

There are few organizations where the design and process FMEAs are prepared by the design and planning engineer on their own; if the FMEA is to become a meaningful working document input must come from a variety of functions, using a team approach. The three main people involved in the preparation of a design FMEA, in conjunction with a design engineer, are the quality engineer, production engineer, and process engineer. The four main people involved in preparing a process FMEA, in conjunction with a planning engineer, are the quality engineer, production engineer, first-line supervision, and process engineer.

The individuals chosen to be members of the team should have the relevant experience, be well motivated and have the time to carry out the full range of tasks involved with FMEA. It is also important for each team to co-opt as additional members anyone deemed to have specific and specialist knowledge.

Field experience indicates that the preparation of an FMEA and its analysis take longer to complete with a large team than with a smaller one. This needs to be considered in establishing an FMEA team.

In some 75 per cent of respondent organizations, members of the senior management team had participated in the preparation of FMEA, and line operators in around 25 per cent. A number of organizations commented that senior managers and operators had not participated as team members directly, but had contributed via discussions with team members.

Examination of the data relating to the preparation of design and process FMEAs reveals a number of encouraging signs.

1 FMEA appears rarely to be carried out in isolation by either a

design or planning engineer. Others were involved in FMEA preparation either through teamwork or by the design and planning engineer circulating it and asking for comments. Either method facilitates cross-fertilization of ideas, but the danger with the latter method is that people need to be chased to respond; there is also some reluctance to comment in detail on a document prepared by others.

Respondents were asked to rate, on a scale from 1 (not at all) to 5 (very much) the extent to which teamwork is used in FMEA preparation. The mean score was 3.2, indicating an above average rating. Teamwork is an essential feature of TQM, and its facilitation through FMEA preparation will be beneficial to the process of continuous quality improvement. The team must contain the right mix of people to provide the expertise, but the size of the team needs to be restricted to the smallest number possible; otherwise decision-making becomes protracted. It is also important that teamwork does not dilute accountability, and overall responsibility for FMEA must be assigned to some individual.

2   Teamwork is not something at which Western organizations excel; it is not a natural working method (see chapter 7). The activities of individuals can be easily identified and their performance rewarded. It is more difficult to recognize and reward a person who is a good team member, and group accomplishments. People also tend to look on teamwork as a sideline activity, something they do in addition to their normal day-to-day responsibilities. It is encouraging that the majority of organizations are using teamwork in the preparation of FMEA. In the longer term this should help to foster and advance their process of quality improvement.

3   Customers and suppliers are involved in the preparation of design and process FMEAs.

4   Those responsible for production preparation are involved in design FMEA and manufacturing supervisors in process FMEA.

5   The majority of organizations use previous data in preparation of a current FMEA, including previous FMEAs, warranty claims, field service reports and non-conformance information.

Respondents were asked to rate, on a scale from 1 (not at all) to 5 (very much) to what extent engineers feel that FMEAs are an important part of their job. The mean score was 3.0, indicating an average rating. FMEAs are laborious and time consuming and engineers often view them as unexciting. In relation to the time constraints, the majority of organizations took the view that FMEA did impose an additional workload on staff – in many cases up to 20 per cent. This increased workload tends to occur when FMEAs are being prepared for the first time. After reaching this stage the activity will be related just to new products and updates and modifications to existing ones. The rigorous application of FMEA at the right time with appropriate attention to the causes of high risks will, in the longer term, result in a reduction of staff workload by virtue of the preventive nature of the technique. In the majority of organizations computer software is not used to prepare and compile FMEAs. Its use to assist with updating FMEA documentation should also help to reduce the workload. Research is needed, however, to assess the merits of the various software aids available.

The main individuals with overall responsibility for design FMEA are the chief engineer, design engineer and technical director. In the case of process FMEA, it is the quality, production engineering and technical managers. It is clear that many quality managers are having to take overall responsibility for process FMEA; the responsibility should be that of the production engineering and preparation department.

A variety of techniques, in a number of different combinations, are used to assist in FMEA preparation, cause and effect analysis, process flow charts and SPC being the most common. SPC and FMEA are complementary techniques: FMEA helps to identify process parameters and product characteristics which should be monitored using SPC, and process improvement from SPC should be fed back to update the FMEA. Capability data from SPC are used to establish rankings for the RPN.

The following are ways in which the preparation of FMEA may be strengthened.

- In major Japanese companies, the engineers responsible for production preparation are resident in the design office, to ensure that the design engineers produce designs which are easy to manufacture and that potential areas for non-conformance are identified in the design stage and then eliminated. In the production preparation stage the design engineers are resident in the production preparation office to see that the design intent is put in place during production.
- The expertise of suppliers should be used more fully when FMEAs are being prepared, and organizations need to develop a procedure for involving them. The major Japanese companies are adept at using their suppliers in developing their product, calling them guest designers.
- The knowledge of maintenance personnel, setters and operators should be used to a greater extent than at present in preparation of process FMEA.
- Channels for feed-forward and feedback of information between customer and supplier need to be developed.

Uses of FMEA

Respondents were asked to select and rank the three main reasons for using FMEA. The most common was that it was a mandatory requirement of Ford. (The next stage should be for them to consider how they might fully utilize the technique to assist their improvement process.) The second- and third-ranked factors were to improve product quality and to improve customer satisfaction. Perhaps surprising was the low score attributed to concerns about the regulations governing product liability, reducing the number of product recalls and warranty claims. Improvements in product quality will lead directly to such a reduction. It is clear that organizations do not have a good understanding of this relationship.

In the vast majority of cases, respondents were preparing FMEAs at the right time, that is, as part of the initial design and development phase and in the production preparation and advanced quality planning phases; ideally before the purchase of tooling and equipment. It is encouraging that FMEAs are being used in design reviews. In a number of cases the process FMEA was triggered by an initial feasibility review carried out on all new parts and processes as part of the advanced quality planning process.

More than half the respondents had an established procedure for review/update of the FMEA, mostly at a set frequency, from once to four times a year. Others updated the analysis only as a follow-up to:

- a change in the part or process;
- major concerns/complaints/warranty claims;
- failures;
- initial sample rejection;
- process improvement action;
- a change to a design, drawing and/or tooling or any other type of engineering change;
- the introduction of new machinery;
- the addition of an operation.

The FMEA should always be treated as a living document and be continually updated; not filed away and forgotten. Some organizations claim they have difficulties updating the FMEA, due to the paperwork this entails.

Copies of the design FMEA are sent principally to the design, quality and process engineers; process FMEAs to the planning, quality and process engineers. In only a minority of organizations are the design and process FMEAs made available to customers and/or suppliers. It is clear from comments made by respondents that they consider FMEAs to contain detailed, confidential information and while they are shown to and discussed with customers and suppliers, copies are never issued. The product liability legislation has no doubt hardened this line of thinking. However, as mentioned earlier, concern about the regulations governing product liability was not a main reason for companies using FMEA.

FMEA training

Just over half the responding organizations had provided formal training to personnel participating in FMEA preparation. Of those that had not, a number commented that staff learnt to prepare FMEAs after reading the Ford and Jaguar manuals. In the main, any training carried out was by company personnel and external consultants; in a number of organizations, Ford supplier quality engineering personnel explained, taught and supervised the introduction of FMEA.

The majority of organizations conduct FMEA training on an *ad hoc* basis, as and when required; in only a minority is it part of a structured training programme.

The three main groups of personnel to receive FMEA training are quality staff, production engineering staff and middle management. It is surprising that few organizations provided FMEA training for their design personnel. The duration of the FMEA training provided is not extensive; the most popular period being either a day or half a day.

There is considerable dissatisfaction with the currently available FMEA training. A number of organizations made comments along the lines of 'There appear to be few, if any, good outside training courses on FMEA which are available.'

As with SPC, Ford is the major purchasing organization encouraging its suppliers to use FMEA as part of advanced quality planning. Jaguar Cars appears to be the other major organization giving strong signals to its supplier base about the use of FMEA. Ford is clearly a major influence on the UK supplier base developing and maintaining a process of quality improvement.

The value of FMEA as a quality-management technique

Respondents were asked to rate, on a scale from 1 (not at all useful) to 5 (very useful) the usefulness of FMEA as a quality-planning technique.

The mean rating was 3.9, indicating an above average usefulness. Less than 50 per cent of respondents said that by using FMEA they had been able to identify a major failure mode which otherwise would not have been identified.

Only a minority of respondents said they had been able to apply FMEA to non-manufacturing areas. The applications given by respondents covered the following procedures:

- warehousing and shipping;
- accounts;
- engineering;
- maintenance;
- maintaining a documented batch traceability and batch integrity system from receipt of raw materials through component manufacture, assembly and despatch to various customer locations;
- packing and stores;
- heat treatment;
- review of a quality audit technique resulting in the identification of a non-capable process.

It is encouraging, however, that a number of organizations indicated that they did intend to use FMEA in non-manufacturing areas as part of their activities to promote TQM. It is clear from comments made by respondents that they would like to use the technique more extensively. The comments suggest greater awareness than expected about the application of FMEA in non-manufacturing areas.

Difficulties

Respondents were asked to identify and rank the five main difficulties they had encountered in their use of FMEA. Twenty-four different difficulties were identified, as shown in table D.1. The four main difficulties shown tend to be management- and concept-orientated difficulties rather than technical difficulties in FMEA preparation. Suppliers appear to face less difficulties with the implementation and use of FMEA than they did with SPC. Perhaps this is because FMEA does not require as much basic statistical knowledge. On the other hand, organizations appear to be less knowledgeable about FMEA than they are about SPC. There are a number of reasons for this, including:

- SPC has received more publicity than FMEA;

Table D.1 The difficulties encountered in using FMEA

Difficulty	Score
Time constraints	123
Lack of understanding of the purpose of FMEA	107
Lack of training	88
Lack of management commitment	80
Deciding on the occurrence of failure	51
Obtaining consistent priority numbers	51
Deciding the severity of failure	45
Identifying failure modes	43
Determining the effects of failure	39
Deciding the likelihood of detecting the failure	38
'Just the latest fad' attitude	32
Deciding the causes of failure	31
Updating the FMEA	30
Lack of worked examples	29
Prioritizing corrective action	26
Paperwork generated	26
Conflict between personnel from different areas	23
Terminology used	17
Deciding the function of a part	15
Identifying the customer	6
Lack of resources to apply corrective actions	6
Availability of people	4
Deciding on effective recommended actions	2
Deciding whether the FMEA should be on an individual or product group basis	2

Note: The 78 respondents were asked to select and rank the five main difficulties they had encountered in the use of FMEA. The score was awarded by allocating 5, 4, 3, 2 or 1 points to the first, second, third, fourth and fifth factors respectively.

- there are more SPC training courses than for FMEA;
- major customers have focused on getting suppliers to use SPC;
- SPC is a technique with which everyone in the organization should be familiar, whereas with FMEA knowledge tends to be restricted to small groups of specialists.

The findings of Aldridge, Taylor and Dale[10] in relation to the difficulties encountered in the early attempts to use FMEA at Garrett

Automotive give an indication of the problem:

- The design FMEA was undertaken retrospectively and not early in product development.
- The design FMEA was completed by the product engineer with little or no input from other experienced personnel.
- Design verification programmes were poorly documented even though they were executed reasonably satisfactorily.
- The FMEA was not made available to the manufacturing engineer as an aid to compiling a process FMEA. This was often used as an excuse by them not to complete the process FMEA.
- Problem areas identified by FMEA were not adequately addressed or given low RPNs; it was perceived that this would worry the customer and perhaps jeopardise business.
- Recommended actions tended to be poorly identified or omitted even when a high RPN identified that they were required.
- There was a reluctance by the manufacturing engineers to take a leading role in the preparation and use of FMEA.

Executive summary

- FMEA is a key tool in an organization's advanced quality-planning process and many of the well-publicized product and service failures could have been avoided by its effective use.
- FMEA provides a planned systematic method of capturing and documenting knowledge and identifying critical characteristics.
- There are two main types of FMEA: design and process.
- The preparation of FMEA should be a team activity.
- Executives need to be aware that preparing an FMEA is a time-consuming activity and they should be sympathetic to this.
- Cause and effect analysis, SPC and process flow charts are commonly used to assist in preparation of an FMEA.
- FMEA should be seen as an essential part of people's jobs.
- An FMEA should be prepared as early as possible in the design and/or production preparation processes.
- The main difficulties in preparing FMEA are time constraints, lack of understanding of the technique, lack of training and lack of management commitment.
- FMEA is equally applicable to non-manufacturing areas and service situations.

In concluding this summary the dos and don'ts put forward by Aldridge, Taylor and Dale[11] as advice to help organizations avoid and overcome some of the difficulties encountered in the preparation and use of FMEA are quoted.

Do:

- Drive the implementation with senior management's backing.
- Ensure all personnel who are likely to be involved with FMEA are aware of the potential benefits arising from the procedure and the need for the identified corrective action to be implemented.
- Make FMEA meetings short (the suggestion is of one hour duration) but regular.

Don't:

- Start the FMEA process when the design has reached an almost fixed state; change will be that much harder to effect.
- Allow failure modes to be dismissed lightly with comments such as 'we have always done it like this' and 'that will cost considerable monies to change' without first considering the feasibility and cost of the change.
- Use the techniques as just 'window dressing' for the customer. There is little difference in the effort required in using it in this way to that of the correct manner.

Notes

1 BS 5760: Part 1 (1985) *Guide to Reliability and Maintainability Programme Management*, British Standards Institution, London.
2 Gosling, C., Rowe, S. and Dale, B. G. (1992) 'The use of quality management tools and techniques in financial services: an examination', Seventh OMA Conference, UMIST, June.
3 Part 1, Guide to Reliability.
4 Ford Motor Company (1988) *Potential Failure Mode and Effects Analysis: An Instruction Manual*, Ford, Brentwood, Essex.
5 Jaguar Cars (1986) *FMEA – A Guide to Analysis*, Jaguar Cars, Coventry.
6 Society of Motor Manufacturers and Traders (1989) *SMMT Guidelines to Failure Mode and Effects Analysis*, SMMT, London.
7 Groocock, J. M. (1986) *The Chain of Quality*, John Wiley, New York; O'Connor, P. D. T. (1985) *Practical Reliability Engineering*, John Wiley, Sussex.

8 Dale, B. G. and Shaw, P. (1990) 'Failure mode and effects analysis in the UK motor industry: a state-of-the-art study', *Quality and Reliability Engineering International*, vol. 6, no. 1, pp. 179–88.

9 Ford, *An Instruction Manual*.

10 Aldridge, J. R., Taylor, J. and Dale, B. G. (1991) 'The application of failure mode and effects analysis at Garrett Automotive Ltd', *International Journal of Quality and Reliability Management*, vol. 8, no. 3, pp. 44–56.

11 Ibid.

Index